To our dear friends
Ivy & Eric,

Albert & Eleanor
4-8-85

EXPLORING
THE WORLD
OF THE JEW

EXPLORING THE WORLD OF THE JEW

JOHN PHILLIPS

MOODY PRESS

CHICAGO

© 1981 by
THE MOODY BIBLE INSTITUTE
OF CHICAGO

Library of Congress Cataloging in Publication Data

Phillips, John, 1927
  Exploring the world of the Jew.

  Bibliography: p. 235
  1. Laws—History. 2. Judaism—History.
3. Israel—History. I. Title.
DS118.P48   909'.04924   81-16844
ISBN 0-8024-2411-2   AACR2

2 3 4 5 6 7 Printing/GB/Year 87 86 85 84 83 82

CONTENTS

FOREWORD

When John Phillips asked me if I would read the manuscript for this book, *Exploring the World of the Jew,* my first reaction was one of hesitation. Did I have the time necessary to read so voluminous a manuscript? But when I glanced at the table of contents my interest was aroused. That was the beginning of a most rewarding experience.

The book is well written. It is both interesting and informative. Although it reads in places like fiction, it is a statement of fact about the remarkable Jew. Quite naturally it begins at the beginning. Commencing with Abraham, the reader is led step by step through three major periods of Jewish history, an excellent survey of the thirty-nine books in the Old Testament, from Genesis to Malachi. This section is a "must" reading for every student of the Old Testament. If this book had been available in the early 1950s when I taught Old Testament History at the Philadelphia School of the Bible (now the Philadelphia College of the Bible), I would have assigned it as required reading.

The chapter "The Wandering Jew" gave me a greater appreciation for God's chosen people. It kindled within me a greater desire to pray for Jews and to seek to reach them with the gospel of Christ.

The author's section on the Talmud was an education. Here one sees the religious Jew, his departure from the Torah, and his creation of a complicated substitute that only led him farther away from Jehovah.

In our Lord's Olivet Discourse He predicted that there would arise "false Christs" (Matthew 24:5, 24). Mr. Phillips has provided an abundance of information showing how Christ's prediction was fulfilled. He traces with historical accuracy the false messiahs, beginning with Theudas ten years after the crucifixion of Jesus and continuing on to the nineteenth century. Here is good material for the teacher and preacher of prophecy.

But time marched on, and with its passing there came a new Judaism—the birth of the state of Israel when the flag of David was unfurled. From chapter 10 to the end of the book the reader will follow Israel's every move from May, 1948 to the present.

What is Israel's future? In the first fourteen chapters Mr. Phillips displays his knowledge of Jewish history and his ability to communicate that knowledge. He treats with equal skill the biblical teaching on Israel's future. Our author is an astute student of both history and prophecy.

Reading *Exploring the World of the Jew* was a refreshing experience.

LEHMAN STRAUSS

PREFACE

Frederick the Great of Prussia once challenged Count Nikolaus von Zinzendorf, a Moravian Christian at his infidel court, to defend the Bible. The Count replied in two words: *"The Jew!"* It was an astute reply. The world of the Bible is the world of the Jew, and the story of the Jew in history is one long confirmation of the accuracy of the Bible.

Almost every day the Jew and the state of Israel are thrust into the forefront of the news. The land of Israel is small, and the Jewish people are but a very small minority of the world's population, yet between them they seem to keep the whole world in a state of tension and unease.

What is so remarkable about the Jew? It is not merely that, as a race, he was old when Rome was young. It is not just that he has outlived every nation and empire that has persecuted him. It is not only his astonishing success in every field of endeavor to which he turns his hand, or his long sufferings through the ages in scores of lands. It is not merely that he has defied the laws of history and preserved his racial identity though scattered in a hundred countries for hundreds upon hundreds of years. All those things are remarkable, and all of them are explored in this book. But there is something more.

The Jew is God's timepiece, set up in the midst of the nations of mankind, to announce our hour and position in God's prophetic program for this earth. When the nation of Israel was reborn in 1948 a sobering chime was struck on that great clock.

The world of the Jew is an interesting and fascinating world. The Christian world in particular is indebted to the Jew. The Jews gave us our Bible, gave us our Savior, gave us the church. We owe it both to ourselves and to the Jewish people to know more about that amazing nation and people. Exploring the world of the Jew will give us a better understanding of the Bible and a keener awareness of where we stand today in relation to prophetic truth.

9

A word or two must be said about how this book came to be written and the manner in which its great themes have been handled.

Some years ago, Arthur Miller, at that time a sales representative for Moody Press, suggested that it would be a good thing if somebody would revise and update a book by L. Sale-Harrison entitled *The Remarkable Jew*. That book had been in my library for years, and I knew it well. On rereading it I decided that what was needed was an entirely new approach. Many areas of interest were not covered at all in Mr. Sale-Harrison's volume. For instance, few Christians know anything about the Talmud, how it came into being, what it contains, the influence it has had on Jewish life and thought, and how it has been an instrument for survival for the Jew down through the ages. *The Remarkable Jew* did not explore that side of the story at all. Then, too, so much has happened in the Jewish world since that book was written that to attempt to revise it would have called for whole new chapters. I came to the conclusion that what was needed was a fresh start.

I acknowledge my limitations. I am neither a professional historian nor theologian. But I have had a continuing interest in Israel and the Jewish people for many years. I was stationed in Haifa while in the British army during the last two years of the British Mandate over Palestine. I was an eyewitness to the end of an era— to some of the momentous events that ushered in a new age, one that heralds the coming of the Apocalypse.

I was there on stage, so to speak, and saw some of those "illegal" immigrant ships come into British territorial waters. A British destroyer would go out to intercept the vessel. Its captain would be arrested and its crew subdued. It would be brought into Haifa docks, where all business was suspended and the quays cleared. The Jewish refugees from the horror camps of Europe would be disembarked, passed through hastily-erected tents where they were sprayed with DDT to kill the lice, and then forced into the hold of a British cargo vessel. Now under the British flag, they would be transported to Cyprus, a British territory, to be interned pending some solution to the Palestine problem. My sympathies were with the Jews. I was thoroughly ashamed of British foreign policy at that time, young as I was.

In approaching this book a decision had to be made. The book could be written in sequence, following strict chronological order, or it could be written by subject, grouping material around a series of topics. I soon discovered that the sequential approach was impractical. The world of the Jew is too vast, the story is too long, there are so many bypaths beckoning to be explored.

It seemed that the practical approach was the topical. This has not been without its problems, the chief of which has been the necessity of going back occasionally over the same historical ground. Summaries have been added here and there to orient the reader as to how the various topics are related. A historical time chart, to give a frame of reference for the whole book, is in the Appendix. There I have sought to list the major events in world history from the time of Abraham to the present and to pinpoint in that time chart the major events of Jewish history. By referring to the chart the reader will be able to keep a sense of chronological sequence even though the material covered makes it necessary for us occasionally to retrace our steps.

I am grateful to those who reviewed the manuscript in its rough form and made comments and suggestions. I am particularly grateful to Steve and Sue Sussman, who looked at the book for me through Jewish eyes.

We have an interesting journey ahead of us. The Jewish race was old when Hannibal hurled his armies across the Alps in his march to Rome, when Alexander wept because there were no more worlds to conquer, and when Buddha was evolving his religious principles in the distant East.

Come then! Explore with me the remarkable world of the Jew.

JOHN PHILLIPS

1

THE OLD TESTAMENT JEW:
THE THEOCRACY

ABRAHAM AND THE PATRIARCHS

Several centuries before Hammurabi of Sumer began building his empire and writing down his legal code, a wealthy man of Ur began to have strange stirrings in his soul. How could it be right, all this bowing down to idols made of wood and stone, this senseless worship of the moon, this popular religion of the land of his birth?

Suddenly the God of his forefathers, the God of Enoch and Noah and Shem, broke in upon his soul. It was a momentous day for mankind, for the man whose eyes were opened that day was Abraham, the founder of the Hebrew racial family and one of the most important men God ever made.

About 2090 B.C. Abraham, heeding the call of God, packed his bags and marched out of Ur. He journeyed across the Fertile Crescent and found himself descending into the land of Canaan, the promised land. In that land he dwelt as a stranger and a sojourner all his life, patiently waiting for God to make good His promise that all that land would be given to him and to his seed (Genesis 12-25).

Abraham died, and so did Isaac his son, with the promise still slumbering in the womb of time. Jacob was born and lived to raise a dozen boys who one day would become the fathers of the twelve tribes of Israel. With Jacob, the fortunes of the elect family took a move forward. At first they moved in a wrong direction—or so it must have seemed, for the growing clans left the promised land and migrated into Egypt (Genesis 25-50).

THE HEBREWS ENSLAVED IN EGYPT

In Egypt the family became a nation and multiplied so spectacularly that the reigning pharaoh grew afraid. Suppose an enemy were to invade Egypt. Would not these Hebrew foreigners side with the foe? He deliberated how best to prevent his people's being overwhelmed by the rising Hebrew tide and decided that genocide was the answer. Toss all newborn Hebrew males to the crocodiles of the Nile, enslave the rest, and within a generation the Hebrew race would be extinct. That was the answer! The plan was tried, and it failed (Exodus 1).

Moses the lawgiver was born. He was saved from death by the faith of his parents and by the intervention of an Egyptian princess, probably the famous Hatshepsut.[1]

That royal lady defied her father's decree, adopted Moses, and brought him into the court and reared him as her son. She doubtless planned to confer upon him, if not the throne of Egypt, certainly some high position in the state. When he was fully grown, however, Moses declined the honors the princess had in mind and cast in his lot with the downtrodden Hebrew slaves. He went too far for his own safety when, indignant over the beating of a fellow Hebrew, he slew the Egyptian slavedriver.

Before he could be arraigned and charged with murder, Moses fled to Sinai, where he lived for the next forty years. He married the daughter of a nomadic Midianite chieftain, Jethro, and followed a quiet, contemplative life as a shepherd (Exodus 2).[2]

THE EMPIRE-BUILDING PHARAOH

Meanwhile great changes took place in Egypt. Pharaoh died, and the throne was seized by Hatshepsut. That determined woman was able to keep Thutmose III, the rightful heir, off the throne for years, filling his heart with a rage that beggars description. When once he did finally seize the throne he vented his rage on Hatshepsut's monuments and then proceeded to thoroughly thrash the surrounding nations, pushing Egypt's frontiers to the broad banks of the Euphrates.

MOSES VERSUS PHARAOH

The throne changed hands once more, and then Moses came back. He was no longer an Egyptian prince but the vice-regent of God (Exodus 3-13). There was an inevitable confrontation with the Egyptian throne. By this time Amenhotep IV was the pharaoh. Understandably, he was most reluctant to release his many millions of valuable slaves at the bare word of a shepherd from the wilderness, even though the shepherd did speak Egyptian with a flawless, cultured accent. There followed that amazing series of judgment miracles, which form so prominent a part of the historical narrative of Exodus and are appealed to repeatedly in the Psalms as evidence of God's goodness to Israel and of His power over the nations. Pharaoh vacillated back and forth as the judgments proceeded. Each was designed not only to produce the maximum discomfort and damage and awe, but also specifically to demonstrate the impotence and uselessness of Egypt's gods. When the lesser plagues failed to touch the pharaoh's conscience, God finally attacked the very lives of the Egyptians themselves. Moses was instructed to institute the Passover feast.

As the Hebrew people sheltered behind the shed blood of the Passover lamb, the judgment angel spread his wings over Egypt and slew every firstborn son throughout the land. That broke Pharaoh's resistance. He gave the order for the Hebrews to leave the land. Out they marched, rank by rank, laden down with spoils, a triumphant host. The first exile was over. The Israelites, now a mighty nation, were on the way to the promised land at last.

THE EXODUS

The children of Israel crossed the Red Sea as God parted it before them and commenced their journey to Canaan (Exodus 14-16). They were guided by the mysterious Shekinah glory cloud, the visible token of God's presence among them. It led them by an unexpected way, for instead of striking due east along the coastal road to Canaan, it turned southward toward Sinai. As yet the tribes were neither cohesive nor mature enough to fight the battles that awaited them in Canaan. God evidently decided, as G. Campbell Morgan so quaintly expressed it, that the longest way round was the shortest way home.[3]

Three days' journey over the pebbly ground, through weary wadies, and along the bare white limestone hills of the northern tableland brought the great host to Marah, the place of bitter water. Then came Elim with its wells, affording respite on the way. Further south the landscape changed, and the Hebrews found themselves marching through the wilderness of Sin, a dreary, flat, and desolate place. Its inhospitable and forbidding nature proved a great trial.

About a month's journey on the way, the supplies they had brought with them from Egypt began to fail, and, worn out with the hardness of the way, the Hebrews began to complain. Constant criticism of God and Moses, despite the unending flow of miracles that sustained them each step of the way, became the characteristic attitude of the whole company.

The host continued south until it reached Rephidim and the beginning of the Sinaitic range (Exodus 17). The landscape now took on the appearance of a jumble of mountains thrown together in wild confusion, peak rising above peak to a height of 9,000 feet. Here it was that Moses first smote the rock and brought forth the life-giving stream. Here, too, Amalek came with drawn swords to give Israel her first taste of war. Here also Jethro joined the host briefly, bringing with him Moses' wife and his sons, and leaving only after sensibly advising Moses to delegate some of his administrative responsibilities to others.

Three months had now passed, and the vast multitude reached that innermost mountain range after which the whole Sinai Peninsula is named. Running through it were many wadies, like so many roads, all seemingly leading to the grand, central sanctuary where God was about to give to Moses and Israel His law. The people had arrived at Horeb, or Sinai, the mount of God (Exodus 18-19).

THE GIVING OF THE LAW

They halted at Sinai for some considerable time. There, amidst awe-inspiring scenes of splendor and terror, the law was given, broken, and given again (Exodus 20-24). Moses received the Ten Commandments, graven on stone by the finger of God. There were given the hundreds of interpretative laws, which expanded the Decalogue into hundreds of detailed requirements. The foundations of Judaism were laid—the God-given religious system of the Hebrew people, all centering on the Tabernacle, the sacrifices, and the priesthood. The Levites were set apart as a tribe to minister in religious things. Aaron, the brother of Moses, was divinely appointed as Israel's high priest, and his family was set aside to have exclusive right to the priesthood. Israel was numbered and formally organized for war. There too, on the anniversary of their exodus from Egypt, they kept their first Passover feast as a memorial. And from Sinai Israel marched again to the sound of the silver trumpets and with faces pointed eagerly now toward the promised land.

The forward journey, however, proved to be even more forbidding than anything they had experienced before. Watchful enemies eyed their progress, the Edomites to the east and the Amorites ahead. The people tramped wearily across open plains of sand and gravel. The ground beneath their feet was hard and carpeted for miles with small, sharp, polished flint. It was a land of serpents and scorpions and drought. It is called "that great and terrible wilderness" (Deuteronomy 8:15). Yet God brought them safely through.

At last the tribes arrived at Kadesh-barnea, and there preparations were made for the conquest of Canaan. Twelve spies were sent ahead to assess the resources of the land and the possible resistance of the foe. The majority turned in a report of doom. The cities, they said, were great and fenced, "walled up to heaven," and there were giants in the land, the very sons of Anak themselves. Two of the spies, Joshua and Caleb, brought back a report full of faith and encouragement. Sure, they said, the enemy was strong, but God was stronger. The enemy was already defeated! The pessimism of the ten overruled the glorious optimism of the two. The tribes dug in their heels, refused to make another move, sighed after the "good old days" in Egypt, and declared that death in the wilderness was preferable to war with impregnable cities and invincible giants.

For that final outburst of unbelief, God sentenced the whole host to death. He would answer their prayer. All those twenty years old and upward should indeed perish in the wilderness. Only Joshua and Caleb should be exceptions (Numbers 1-14).

THE WILDERNESS WANDERINGS

The disconsolate tribes moved from place to place waiting while a whole generation died and a new generation grew up. Their progress around the wilderness was marked by a long trail of bleaching bones and sad funeral pyres. At length the sandglass of forty years ran out, and Moses brought the tribes back to Kadesh-barnea. Only five people were now left of the old generation—Moses, Aaron, and Miriam; and Joshua and Caleb who alone had hope of Canaan.

Miriam died. Aaron died. Moses alone remained. With what

feelings he must have ordered the host to march on! Now fresh trials were in store. The Edomites closed their frontiers to Israel, forcing the people to make a wide detour through the barren Arabah. They were attacked by Arad, a Canaanite king.

They continued on their way through the intensely hot and inhospitable Arabah desert where, for their constant complaining, the new generation was bitten by "fiery serpents." The great company arrived on the other side of Edom and fought and conquered Sihon, king of the Amorites. They continued north to Bashan until they had the Jabbok to the south of them and the Jordan to the west. There they fought and conquered Og, another of the giant kings of whom once they had been so very much afraid (Deuteronomy 1:4).

Flushed with victory, the tribes now viewed the mountains of Abarim. And there it was that Moses, the last of the old guard, handed leadership over to Joshua and fell asleep in the arms of God (Deuteronomy 34).

THE CONQUEST OF CANAAN

Moses had led the people out of Egypt; Joshua was to lead them into Canaan. Initial preparations were made, some of a religious nature and some military. Two spies were sent in to take a fresh look at what lay ahead. Then, having crossed the Jordan as miraculously as the old generation had crossed the Red Sea, the new generation of Israelites prepared to take possession of the promised land.

Their way was blocked by the immensely strong fortress of Jericho. But what are walled cities to a people in fellowship with the living God? Down Jericho went, and the victorious Israelites put the city to the sword, sparing only Rahab and her family because of her faith and her kindness to the spies.

There came a temporary setback at Ai because of unjudged sin in the Hebrew camp. When Ai fell the Canaanites woke up to the fact that the hour of doom was upon them. The wily Gibeonites made a cunning peace with Joshua, and that meant that the whole of southern Canaan was now open to Joshua's troops (Joshua 1-9).

Adoni-zedek, king of Jerusalem, patched together a hasty alliance with the frightened Canaanites of the area, but the coalition was no match for Joshua, who swept away his enemies like chaff before the wind. A second coalition in the north, led by Jabin, king of Hazor, likewise crumbled beneath Joshua's heavy blows, and that ended Canaanite organized resistance to the Hebrew tribes. After some seven years of war the whole country was in Hebrew hands (Joshua 10-12).

Joshua was an able general, but he lacked the vision and the breadth of perspective of Moses, and, for all his generalship, he made three fatal mistakes. He failed to secure the coastline of Canaan, leaving the Philistines and the Phoenicians deeply entrenched there. He failed to complete mopping up operations and left pockets of Canaanite resistance dotted up and down the country. Worst of all, he failed to wipe out the filthy and idolatrous fertility cults of the land. To "go awhoring after false gods" was far more than a poetic expression so far as the Canaanite religion was concerned. Joshua's failure to cut this cancer completely out of society was to have serious results for the Hebrew people. As a result of Joshua's mistakes the next four hundred years or so of Hebrew history were to be disastrous.

THE JUDGES

According to Acts 13:19, the period of the judges lasted for 450 years. During that period there was constant battle with the various Canaanite tribes, who had recovered from the thrashing Joshua had given them and hungered for revenge. Joshua died somewhere between ninety and a hundred years of age, and the central government fell apart. The frequent apostasies of Israel led to a series of servitudes to the surrounding pagan peoples. The cycle went round and round—sin followed by servitude, servitude followed by sorrow, sorrow followed by supplication, supplication followed by salvation; then the same round all over again.

There were seven major periods of servitude—to the Mesopotamians; to a coalition of Moabites, Ammonites, and Amalekites; to the Canaanites; to the Midianites; to the Ammonites; and to the Philistines. There were fourteen judges (if we count Abimelech the usurper, and if we carry the period through the days of Eli and Samuel). Of those Othniel, Ehud, Barak (with the help of Deborah), Gideon, Jephthah, and Samson occupy the bulk of the book of Judges (Judges 1-16). Samson was the most colorful of the judges, but his exploits seem to have been intermittent, and the twenty years of his erratic activities seem to overlap with the administrations of some of the other judges.

CHART OF THE DAYS OF THE JUDGES

The Enemy	Subjection	Deliverer	Peace
Mesopotamia	8 years	Othniel	40 years
Moabites Ammonites Amalekites	18 years	Ehud	80 years
Canaanites	20 years	Deborah Barak	40 years
Midianites	7 years	Gideon	40 years
		Abimelech Tola Jair	3 years 23 years 22 years
Ammonites	18 years	Jephthah	6 years
		Ibzan Elon Abdon	7 years 10 years 8 years
Philistines	40 years	Samson	(20) years
		Eli	40 years
		Samuel	20 years
	111 years		339 years

Years of Oppression	111 years
Years of Peace	339 years
Total (Acts 13:19)	450 years

The judges themselves were not judges or rulers in the accepted sense of the word. They were more in the nature of local deliverers, raised up by God to alleviate oppression in answer to the cry of Israel in her misery. The whole period of the judges was marked by moral and civil disorder, although at the same time there is evidence that here and there a high degree of personal piety and devotion to the Mosaic law did prevail, as in the case of Boaz (Ruth 2-4).

The last five chapters of Judges give us in appendix form the moral and spiritual degeneracy of the times. That the Levite who led the apostasy of chapter 18 was actually a grandson of Moses so horrified the Jews of a later age that they seem to have deliberately changed the name "Moses" to "Manasseh."[4] The events described in this appendix probably relate to the earlier period of the judges, but they are appended to the book as being characteristic of the entire period.

As the dreary centuries wore on, and as the Philistines became more and more the oppressors of Israel, it became the cry of some that the nation had no hope of survival so long as it remained a miscellaneous collection of tribes. They must unite. What was needed was a king. Both Samson and Samuel had led the people more than once to victory over the Philistines, but the disheartened people wanted something more earthly, more material, more tangible than a theocracy. They wanted a monarchy. They longed for a strong, centralized national government, headed by a warrior king. They wanted to be like the nations around them. The more Samuel, the prophet and judge, sought to wed them closer to Jehovah and His direct rule over them, the more clamorous they became. They wanted a king. At last, a broken-hearted Samuel let them have their way (1 Samuel 1-8).

NOTES

1. The dating of the Exodus has been hotly debated by scholars. Here we follow that adopted by Merril F. Unger in *Unger's Bible Dictionary* (Chicago: Moody, 1966), pp. 331-34. There is something very attractive about the thought that Hathshepsut was Moses' foster mother. She certainly was strong-willed enough to have defied the pharaoh's decree. The same dating is followed by John C. Whitcomb, Jr. ("Old Testament Kings and Prophets," chart [Winona Lake, Ind.: John C. Whitcomb, 1966]).
2. Jethro, Moses' father-in-law, is called *Reuel* ("the friend of El"). Alfred Edersheim thinks this implies he was a worshiper of the God of Abraham. The Midianites were descended from Abraham through his subsidiary wife Keturah. Jethro is also called *Jether* (Exodus 3:1; 4:18), which means "Excellency" and was probably his title as tribal chief priest. See Alfred Edersheim, *The Bible History: Old Testament*, 7 vols., reprint (Grand Rapids: Eerdmans, 1956), 2:42.
3. G. Campbell Morgan, *Searchlights from the Word* (New York: Revell, 1929), p. 28.
4. Judges 18:30.

2

THE OLD TESTAMENT JEW:
THE MONARCHY

Saul Becomes King

Israel's first venture into monarchy was a disappointment. It is evident both from the dying but prophetic words of Jacob (Genesis 49:8-12) addressed to Judah and from the laws in the Mosaic code regarding the divine responsibilities of kings (Deuteronomy 17:14-20) that God had always intended to give Israel a king. Israel's sin was in demanding a king from the wrong motives, in looking for that king in the wrong tribe, and in demanding a king before it was God's time to give them one.

A Benjamite by the name of Saul was chosen, a weak and ineffective monarch who accomplished little really worthwhile. He spent most of his life as king trying to murder David, his son-in-law, because he knew David was destined one day to take his place upon the throne (1 Samuel 9-31).

Saul was a man of impressive stature. He embodied the basic ideals Israel had at the time. The people were much more concerned with the martial qualities of the man they chose than with his moral qualities. Saul's character reflected Israel's basic national defect of combining professed zeal for Jehovah with a total disregard of any real heart-yieldedness to Him.

Saul's Failures

Saul's want of true spirituality eventually cost him both his throne and his life. His first great failure was at Gilgal (1 Samuel 13). A serious situation had developed—the Philistines were threatening the complete decimation of his army, and troops were deserting daily. The prophet Samuel had assured him that all would be well, only he *must* wait for God's time. Samuel would come at the end of a week and would offer the appropriate sacrifices. Then Saul's armies would triumph over the foe.

Saul waited a week but impatiently went ahead and offered the sacrifice himself when Samuel still, seemingly, delayed. No sooner had he finished than the prophet appeared. Saul had failed the test. He had intruded himself into the priest's office. For his self-will, impatience, and disobedience, his kingdom was to be given to another.

When Saul discovered that it was David, the young national hero, who was to be his rival for the throne, his jealousy knew no bounds. From then on he did little but pursue David, making at least twenty-four separate attempts on his life. Even Jonathan, Saul's son and heir, was maligned and nearly murdered by his father because of his outspoken love for David (1 Samuel 18-20).

Saul's reign ended in disaster. He could receive no answer to his prayers. So, having knocked in vain at heaven's door, he went down to Endor and knocked at the door of hell (1 Samuel 28). He consulted a witch in the hope that somehow she could conjure up Samuel from the dead. Samuel had told him that rebellion was "as the sin of witchcraft." And so it proved to be.

The battle that took place next day at Gilboa was one of utter defeat for Israel. Saul himself, wounded in the battle, threw himself on his sword and committed suicide. Jonathan and two of Saul's other sons perished as well.

THE TRAINING OF DAVID

David's time had almost come. He had held his hand, even though he had known for some twenty years that the kingdom was to be his. He had been secretly anointed by Samuel down on the Bethlehem farm. He had been shown to Israel as the Lord's true anointed when, as a teenager, he had slain singlehandedly the giant, Goliath of Gath. He had served at Saul's court, had been married to his younger daughter, and had carried out numerous expeditions against the Philistines at Saul's command, even though he must have known that it was Saul's hope that he would be killed in doing so.

When Saul's maniacal hatred had expressed itself finally in open attempts at murder, David had taken to the hills. The wilderness had been his home, and there he had gathered about him the outcasts of Israel. He had fashioned them into a tough, competent fighting force. From their ranks came those "mighty men" who later formed the backbone of his administration. Many were the adventures he had experienced, many the hair-breadth escapes. Many were the themes he wove into his psalms from the vicissitudes of those days.

DAVID BECOMES KING

For the next seven years there was desultory civil war between David and the house of Saul headed by Ishbosheth, one of Saul's sons, and Abner, Saul's general. At length Abner made peace with David only to be murdered by David's general, Joab, who saw him as a potential rival. Ishbosheth, too, was murdered, to the horror and disgust of David. But with the removal of his two principal adversaries, all opposition collapsed. The united tribes crowned David king at Hebron. David was thirty-seven years old (2 Samuel 1-5).

David was Israel's greatest and truly ideal king. He brought peace and prosperity to the land, put its archives in order, promoted the true faith, wrote half the Hebrew hymnbook, established a dynasty that was to continue to the coming of Christ, and set about collecting those enormous heaps of treasure that would later be used in building the Temple of God.

There were dark clouds in his sky as well as sunny days, and those overcast and ominous days were all brought on by his sins. For even if David was "a man after God's own heart," he was also a very great sinner. But David's remorse and repentance were as deep and sincere as his sin had been high-handed and blatant. That is quite evident from several of his psalms. He never failed to learn from the things that happened to him and never ceased to grow in the knowledge of God. His last act was to secure the succession for Solomon, a later son born to Bathsheba and God's revealed choice for the throne.

THE REIGN OF SOLOMON

David's work was carried on by Solomon in the early days of his reign. He was Israel's most magnificent king. He raised Israel to the status of a world power and built the Temple. During his reign wealth flowed into the kingdom like a golden tide. His wisdom was proverbial; people came from distant lands just to sit at his feet (2 Chronicles 1-9).

CHART OF KINGS OF ISRAEL AND JUDAH

JUDAH	Good or Bad	Years of Reign	I Kings	II Chronicles	ISRAEL	Good or Bad	Years of Reign	I Kings	II Chronicles
Rehoboam	Bad	17	12:1	10:1	Jeroboam I	Bad	22	12:19	10:2
Abijah	Bad	3	15:1	13:1					
Asa	Good	41	15:9	14:1	Nadab	Bad	2	15:25	
					Baasha	Bad	24	15:27	
					Elah	Bad	2	16:8	
					Zimri	Bad	(7 days)	16:9	
					Omri	Bad	12	16:17	
Jehoshaphat	Good	25	22:41	17:1	Ahab	Bad	22	16:29	18:1
					Ahaziah	Bad	2	22:40	
Jehoram	Bad	8	22:50	21:1	Jehoram	Bad	12	II Kings 3:1	22:7
Ahaziah	Bad	1	II Kings 8:24	22:1	Jehu	Bad	28	9:2	22:7
(Athaliah)			11:1	22:10	Jehoahaz	Bad	17	13:1	
Jehoash (Joash)	Good	40	11:4	23:1	Jehoash (Joash)	Bad	16	13:10	25:17
Amaziah	Good	29	14:1	25:1					

CHART OF KINGS OF ISRAEL AND JUDAH—CONT'D

JUDAH	Good or Bad	Years of Reign	II Kings	II Chronicles
Uzziah (Azariah)	Good	52	15:1	26:1
Jotham	Good	16	15:32	27:1
Ahaz	Bad	16	15:38	28:1
Hezekiah	Good	29	18:1	29:1
Manasseh	Bad	55	21:1	33:1
Amon	Bad	2	21:19	33:21
Josiah	Good	31	22:1	34:1
Jehoahaz	Bad	(3 months)	23:31	36:1
Jehoiakim	Bad	11	23:36	36:4
Jehoiachin	Bad	(3 months)	24:6	36:9
Zedekiah	Bad	11	24:17	36:11
BABYLONIAN CAPTIVITY			25:1	36:13

ISRAEL	Good or Bad	Years of Reign	II Kings	II Chronicles
Jeroboam II	Bad	41	14:16	
Zachariah	Bad	(6 months)	14:29	
Shallum	Bad	(1 month)	15:10	
Menahem	Bad	10	15:14	
Pekahiah	Bad	2	15:22	
Pekah	Bad	20	15:25	
Hoshea	Bad	9	15:30	
ASSYRIAN CAPTIVITY			17:1	

Yet, for all his success, Solomon did more than any other king to denationalize Israel. His greatest mistake was in seeking to cement alliances with surrounding kingdoms by marrying daughters of their kings. That in itself was illegal under Israel's constitution. Worse than that, he allowed his heathen wives to erect altars to their pagan gods in Jerusalem and, in his old age, even went and groveled before those outlandish and abominable idols himself.

Solomon reigned, not in simplicity as David, but with oriental luxury and magnificence. To support his ambitious schemes for making Jerusalem one of the wonders of the world, he overtaxed his people. He wrote three of the books included in the sacred canon, he built a magnificent Temple to Jehovah, he made Israel famous, but he did more to destroy the nation's true foundations than he ever knew.

THE DIVIDED KINGDOM

Upon Solomon's death the kingdom split in two. One of his former officials seized the lion's share of the kingdom and set up a rival monarchy made up of ten of the tribes. The tiny kingdom of Judah and Benjamin was all that remained to the house of David (1 Kings 12).

The Northern Kingdom lasted for about 250 years. It was known as Israel, and its capital was ultimately Samaria. The epitaph written over every one of its kings was, "[he] walked in the sins of Jeroboam, the son of Nebat, who made Israel to sin" (1 Kings 15:34, for example). Jeroboam, Israel's first king, was the yardstick by which all subsequent kings were measured, and a crooked yardstick he was.

An exception was made in the recitation of that sad formula in the case of Ahab and his sons. Ahab, not content with the wickedness of Jeroboam, went even further and plunged Israel into the abominations of Baal worship (1 Kings 16:30-31). Every one of the kings of the Northern Kingdom of Israel was evil.

The Southern Kingdom of Judah had a somewhat better record. Half a dozen of Judah's kings were outstanding for their godliness—Asa, Jehoshaphat, Uzziah, Jotham, Hezekiah, and Josiah; two others (Joash and Amaziah) continued true to the faith for a considerable time, and one (Rehoboam) for a short time. On the other hand, five of Judah's kings acquired a fearful reputation for daring blasphemy. Abijam, son and successor of Rehoboam, quickly adopted all the pagan practices introduced by his father during the last fourteen years of his reign (1 Kings 15:3). During the reign of Jehoram, Baal worship was introduced into Judah, to be continued under Ahaziah and brought to a climax under Ahaz (2 Kings 16). Hezekiah's noble reforms were swiftly swept aside by Manasseh, who distinguished himself as Judah's worst and longest-reigning king.

The reigns of the wicked kings of Judah were offset by several factors that distinguished Judah from Israel. The Temple exerted a positive influence for good. The worst of the idolatrous Judean kings were each succeeded by rulers outstanding for their piety, who at once sought to purge the land of its abominations. On the whole, the reigns of the evil kings were relatively short compared with those of the good ones. For instance, from the time of Rehoboam to the time the Northern Kingdom of Israel was deported into captivity (a period of 250 years), the throne of David was occupied for nearly two centuries by kings who maintained the Mosaic religion, whereas it was occupied for only fifty years by kings who discarded the ancestral faith. That proportion was changed, of course, once Manasseh ascended the throne. The nation never recovered fully from the disastrous effects of his vile reign, despite the noble attempts of Josiah to bring it back to God.

COLLAPSE OF THE NORTHERN KINGDOM

The last king of Israel was Hoshea (2 Kings 17). The petty wars of the past, wars with Syria and Edom, Ammon and Philistia, were now to give way to war on an ominous new scale. A world empire was being gathered into the ruthless hands of the Assyrians, whose very name was fast becoming a byword in that ancient world for cruelty and atrocity. Shalmaneser sent Assyrian troops into Israel, and Samaria was beseiged. Shalmaneser died, and Sargon continued the siege. After holding out for three dreadful years, Samaria fell. The hour of Israel's doom had come.

The Assyrians uprooted the tribes and hauled them away into captivity. They brought in settlers from other parts of their empire to take their place. The new arrivals adopted a debased form of Judaism—a mixture of truth and tradition, of the corrupted religion of the northern tribes mixed with the pagan rites they had brought with them from foreign parts. Those settlers became the "Samaritans," who later harassed the Jews who returned from the Babylonian exile and who were cordially detested by the Jews to the time of Christ.

COLLAPSE OF THE SOUTHERN KINGDOM

Meanwhile, in the Southern Kingdom of Judah, a similar if slower pattern of events began to emerge. Manasseh was undoubtedly the worst and wickedest king ever to sit on the throne of David. He was only twelve when he took the throne. He was selfish, reckless, willful, weak, and cruel. Even in his belated repentance he was barely respectable.

Manasseh crowded the Temple site with altars to the hosts of heaven. In the sacred house itself he blasphemously set up the graven sex symbol that played so prominent a role in the vile worship of Astarte. He instituted a new kind of priesthood, one dedicated to occult practices. He revived the cruel worship of Moloch. He silenced brutally those who raised their voices in protest. Tradition has it that Manasseh actually put Isaiah into the hollow trunk of a tree and had him sawed in half.

In the end he was carried away into captivity by Esarhaddon, the Assyrian monarch. Thereupon he showed signs of repentance, and God allowed him to be restored to his throne. He made desultory efforts to reform the country, but without lasting effect. In any case his son, Amon, simply resumed all his father's former apostasies when he briefly took the throne. Manasseh reigned longer than any other Judean king and did more than any other single king to set the sails of the ship of state permanently toward shipwreck.

REVIVAL UNDER JOSIAH

Manasseh's grandson Josiah was cut from a different piece of cloth (2 Chronicles 34-35). In his reign the last flicker of revival took place before the night came. The prophet Jeremiah stood shoulder to shoulder with him but had no optimism about the ultimate results. Nothing could save the country now from the Babylonians. Still, Jeremiah and Josiah did their best. The Temple was cleansed and repaired, and when a copy of the Mosaic law was unearthed and read, it brought the king down on his face before God. So thorough had been the apostasies throughout the land that God's Word had been completely lost, and its discovery and an investigation of its contents prostrated Josiah in dismay in the presence of God. More vigorously than ever the reforms were pressed, culminating in the celebration of the Great Passover. The hearts of the people were not in the reforms at all, however, as Jeremiah could clearly see. Increasingly his prophecies took on an ominous note. God would punish Judah as He had punished Israel. Captivity to the Babylonians was inevitable. It would last for seventy years.

Josiah's reign was cut short when he attempted to halt an Egyptian military expedition that was crossing the country on its way east. On the fateful plains of Megiddo the king suffered a mortal wound. His death sounded the bell of Jewish independence. Thereafter the little land was but a puppet in the power plays of Egypt and Babylon.

THE LAST DAYS OF JUDAH

The people crowned Jehoahaz upon the death of Josiah, but Pharaoh Necho was not going to have that. Necho deposed him and carried him off as a hostage. He put his brother Eliakim on the throne instead and, in order to remind the people who really ruled the land, he changed Eliakim's name to Jehoiakim (2 Chronicles 36:1-7). Louder and louder grew the voices of the prophets. The land groaned beneath the weight of its apostasies and social injustices.

By now Nineveh and Assyria had fallen, and Pharaoh Necho decided it was high time he put in his own bid for world supremacy. The fate of the world was decided at Carchemish, where the Egyptians went down to defeat and their possessions in western Asia became Babylonian spoil. In the fifth year of Jehoiakim's reign the victorious Babylonians advanced toward Judah, and in terror the king proclaimed a national fast. His sincerity is doubtful, for when Baruch read a book of Jeremiah's prophecies on that occasion, the infuriated king seized the book, cut it to pieces with a knife, and threw it on the fire. Baruch and Jeremiah barely escaped with their lives (Jeremiah 36).

In 605 B.C. Nebuchadnezzar appeared in Jerusalem and bound Jehoiakim in fetters with the intention of carrying him off to Babylon. Daniel (then a youth, but destined to become one of the greatest of the prophets) was taken then to Babylon.

Opinions differ as to whether or not Jehoiakim was also taken at that time. Edersheim thinks that he was allowed to remain on as king under tribute to Nebuchadnezzar.[1] Heedless, as ever, of Jeremiah's warnings, the foolish king, urged on by Egypt, raised the standard of rebellion. Again the Babylonians overran the country, and in the midst of those disasters Jehoiakim appears to have died unmourned and dishonored (2 Chronicles 36:1-8).

He was succeeded by his son Jehoiachin, who was but a youth. He lasted only three months, at which time the Babylonian king appeared in Jerusalem for the second time (597 B.C.). This time Nebuchadnezzar was more thorough (2 Chronicles 36:9-10). He carried Jehoiachin into captivity with most of the people of importance, including Ezekiel the prophet. Only a remnant, and that made up of the poorest of the people, was left behind.

With astounding generosity, Nebuchadenezzar placed another king of David's line upon the throne in Jerusalem. He chose an uncle of Jehoiachin, a man named Mattaniah. Having changed his name to Zedekiah, and having taken from him an oath of allegiance, the Babylonian king departed (2 Chronicles 36:10-21).

It was no good. Zedekiah was as faithless as those who went before him. He rebelled against Nebuchadnezzar, forcing that patient monarch to make a final end. Back he came for the last time (586 B.C.) to reduce Jerusalem to rubble and send the Temple up in flames. Zedekiah was forced to witness the slaughter of his sons, then his own eyes were put out, and he himself was carried off to Babylon. The monarchy was over. The times of the Gentiles had begun.

NOTE

1. Alfred Edersheim, *The Bible History: Old Testament,* 7 vols., reprint (Grand Rapids: Eerdmans, 1956), 7:203.

3

THE OLD TESTAMENT JEW:
THE DEPENDENCY

THE CAPTIVITY

The Babylonian captivity lasted for seventy years, as Jeremiah had foretold. In Babylon, the homeland of idolatry, the Jews learned to loathe idolatry. It was burned forever out of the Jewish soul. In Babylon many of the exiles prospered, some reached positions of great rank in the government, others became successful in business and developed those commercial instincts that have marked many Jews ever since. The more religious Jews began to experiment with Judaism itself. They substituted the synagogue for the Temple, prayers for the Levitical rituals, scribes for the priests.

Elsewhere in the world new religious philosophies were taking root. In India, Siddhartha of the clan of Gautama, was about 500 B.C. laying the foundations of Buddhism. Further east still Confucius was expounding a system of rational ethics later to be known by his name. The great Eastern religions, destined to enslave millions, were taking form. The Jewish people, raised up by God to be an elect nation and His witness to all mankind, had thoroughly and dismally failed.

In Babylon the prophets Ezekiel and Daniel sought to keep the true faith alive. Jeremiah had expressly stated that the captivity would last for seventy years. So, while it was sensible to make the best of things in Babylon, the Jews must not forget that they were exiles there (Jeremiah 29:4-10). Babylon was not their home. Great world changes were coming, and, with the rise and fall of empire, the chance would be given for them to return and rebuild the promised land and await the coming of the Messiah.

33

THE DECREE OF CYRUS

The deportations to Babylon took place in three stages. The end of the captivity and the return likewise took place in three stages. The first move came about the year 538 B.C. The Babylonian Empire passed into history, and the Medo-Persian Empire took its place. Cyrus the Persian then issued the momentous decree that gave the Jews the right of repatriation. They could go back to their land with the blessing of the Persian Empire and under the shadow of its wing.

Most of the Jews were unimpressed at this remarkable fulfillment of prophecy. Many of them had been born in Babylon and had made it their home. Others felt, no doubt, that they were too old to start life anew. Not for them were the rigors of a four-month march across the pitiless desert, to be followed by the incredible hardships of pioneer life.

The majority of Jews had made the world their home. They were satisfied to stay where they were. Of the vast host of exiled Jews in Babylonia and elsewhere throughout the vast Persian domains only 42,360 returned at that time (Nehemiah 7). With them they took about 7,000 slaves, of which about 200 were trained singers.

About 4,000 priests returned, but those came from only four of the twenty-four priestly "courses" into which their order had been divided since the days of David. It says much about the general backslidden state of the Jewish people, too, that of the Levites, a tribe supposed to be distinguished for its dedication to the things of God, only 74 bothered to return to the promised land.

ZERUBBABEL

The first move back to Palestine was led by Zerubbabel, a prince of the house of David, and by a priest named Jeshua (Ezra 2). Zerubbabel was the only person of royal blood to pay any attention to the decree of Cyrus. The little band of pioneers descended upon the promised land and found it a land strewn with the debris of war. There was no Temple. Jerusalem was a heap of rubble, its magnificent walls tossed here and there as testimony to the thoroughness of the Babylonian destruction. The Edomites had seized much of the land, and the entire central portion of the country was in the hands of a people of mixed blood, the Samaritans. But the mysterious hour had struck in the purposes of God, and the time was big with potential and the fulfillment of prophecy.

The returned remnant was very much aware of the national sins that had wrought all this ruin. They were going to make sure that first things were put first, so their primary concern was to set up an altar upon its ancient site and reinstate the sacrificial system and the worship of Jehovah. In April or May of 536 B.C. they laid the foundations of a new Temple (Ezra 3). That foundation was laid amid the mingled sobs and songs of the people. The young people raised their voices in song; the old people who remembered the vanished glories of Solomon's Temple lifted up their voices and wept.

Work on the new Temple had not proceeded far before the Samaritans asked to have a share in the work (Ezra 4). The Jews refused to hear of any such thing, and from then on the Samaritans did all in their power to oppose and hinder the work. They were so successful that the building of the Temple came to a halt, and no further progress was made during the reign of Cyrus or the reigns of the next two Persian kings. The Jews, however, although neglecting the Temple for sixteen long years, pressed ahead with building elaborate homes for themselves.

On August 29, 520 B.C., the prophet Haggai began to urge the Jews to get on with the Temple.[1] The consciences of Zerubbabel and Jeshua were pricked, and the work began again. At that time, too, Zechariah the prophet began his ministry, but with a prophetic vision that reached far beyond the immediate times. The work had hardly started again before the Persian governor wrote to Darius I to challenge it. A search was made of the state records, and back came orders to the governor to expedite the work with all the means at his disposal.

In 519 the priest Jeshua was crowned by the prophet Zechariah in a symbolic ceremony that looked forward to the day when the Messiah would come and unite the offices of priest and king in His Person. Work on the Temple continued and was finished in 516 B.C., in the sixth year of Darius.

EZRA AND NEHEMIAH

Fifty-eight years later, in 458 B.C., a second contingent of Jews ventured back to the promised land (Ezra 7). The reign of the mighty Xerxes had come and gone, and Artaxerxes I was on the throne. This king gave Ezra the scribe a mandate to lead another group of exiles back to their land. Twelve years later, Nehemiah, a high official in the court of Artaxerxes, was also given permission to return (Nehemiah 2). His mandate was to rebuild the walls of Jerusalem and to govern Judea. He arrived in Jerusalem in 444 B.C. and threw himself zealously into the work. Despite the discouragements and threats that faced him from the hostile tribes around, that remarkable man was able to complete his monumental and seemingly hopeless task in fifty-two days.

Once the wall of Jerusalem was built, attention was given to the instruction of the people in the things of God, and a great religious revival followed (Nehemiah 8).

Ezra and Nehemiah instituted the practice of reading aloud to the people the canonized books of the Old Testament. They also began the practice of interpreting the difficult passages. The average man no longer spoke Hebrew. Aramaic had replaced it as the language of culture and commerce, and that in itself made the common people dependent on the instruction of their more scholarly peers.

The last prophetic voice to be raised in Old Testament times was the voice of Malachi. Little is known about Malachi. He seems to have prophesied about a century later than Haggai and Zechariah. It was long enough, at any rate, for a sharp moral and religious decline to have set in. The formalism and skepticism of his day were to flower into full bloom in later years in Pharisaism and Sadduceeism of the time of Christ.

THE SOPHERIM

In this intertestamental period a new breed of interpreters, the *Sopherim*, or scribes, emerged and took over the interpretation of Scripture. Their commentaries gradually assumed semi-inspired status and eventually practically replaced the Word of God altogether. Those commentaries were the first tender shoots of the Midrash. In time that exegetical growth flourished into the vast, tangled jungle of the Talmud, that enormous body of writings that constituted the body of extrabiblical Jewish civil and religious law.[2]

HELLENISM THREATENS JUDAISM

The conquests of Alexander the Great changed everything. The

massive Persian Empire fell into his capable hands, but that was
the least of his accomplishments. Alexander had the vision of a
statesman. He could see that the only way to hold together the
enormous domains he now ruled was to unite the heterogeneous
peoples by means of a common culture. He deliberately sought
to marry East and West. The result was Hellenism, a blend of
Greek culture and oriental opulence and pornography. Alexander
did not live long enough to achieve his ambitions fully, but the
impact of Greek thought was to be long lasting. Hellenism became
the major cultural force in the world. Greek cities such as Antioch
and Alexandria sprang up everywhere, many of them totally
eclipsing the native Greek cities of Alexander's homeland.

Hellenism posed a major threat to the Jews and continued to
challenge the world of Judaism for many centuries. Many Jews
became outright Hellenists and openly embraced the liberal ideas
of the day. Others dug stubbornly into their Judaism, determined
to maintain their strict orthodoxy in the face of the dazzling attractions of the Hellenistic world. The Hellenistic Jews added the
new ideas to their approach to biblical truth. They replaced the
old and approved allegorical approach with a new, exciting, logi-
cal approach. It was not long before a lush new tangle of exegetical undergrowth began to emerge to add to the already spreading
Talmud.

THE SYRO-EGYPTIAN ERA

When Alexander died, his empire was divided by four of his
generals. Two of those, Ptolemy Lagus, who seized Egypt and the
surrounding countries, including Palestine; and Seleucus, who
took Syria, many provinces in Asia Minor, Mesopotamia, and
Babylon, set in motion events that were to trouble the Palestinian
Jews for centuries.

The Ptolemies and the Seleucidae viewed each other with mutual envy and mistrust. Judah, which had happily stagnated for
centuries in the backwaters of history, was now thrust violently
into the turbulent mainstream of events. The unfortunate country
now occupied the unenviable position of buffer state between
Egypt and Syria. The two countries were constantly at each other's
throats, and wretched Judah felt the brunt of it all as the furious
armies marched back and forth across her fields and farms.

Matters came to a head when the Syrian tyrant Antiochus Epi-

phanes came to power in Syria and determined to force the Jews to
convert to Hellenism. There were some in Judea, notably Jason
the high priest and Menelaus, his successor, who sided with Antiochus. Most Jews, however, looked with abhorrence upon both
Antiochus and his plans. Antiochus treated those who resisted him
with such ferocity that he has gone down in history as the very
archetype of the coming Antichrist. Many of his activities were
predicted with amazing accuracy centuries before by the prophet
Daniel. The tormented Jews eventually rallied round a new breed
of leaders, the Maccabees, and rose in rebellion against their
enemy. The struggle for independence went on for a quarter of a
century.

THE SEPTUAGINT

During that period one important event took place that was to
have lasting results, not only for the Jews but for all mankind as
well. The Hebrew Bible was translated into Greek. Many Jews of
the Diaspora (the Dispersion) had forgotten their native tongue
as Greek became increasingly the lingua franca of the ancient
world. Worse still, the seductive and secularizing ideas of Hellenism were beginning to make deep inroads into Jewish thought.
Judaism was about to be destroyed from within.

The answer was a Bible in Greek the Hellenized Jews could
read for themselves. Jews from Palestine were settled in Alexandria and commissioned to do the work. The resulting translation, the famous Septuagint, was finished between the years 285
and 130 B.C. It was an effective answer to Greek rationalism. The
Septuagint is the version quoted throughout the New Testament.

JUDEA BECOMES INDEPENDENT

The independence won for the Palestinian Jews by the Mac-
cabees led to the establishment in Palestine of the rule of the
Hasmoneans, a family of Jewish priest-kings descended from the
Maccabees themselves. The Hasmoneans remained in power until
the Romans came and incorporated Palestine into the Roman
Empire.

During that period a number of important Jewish sects began to
flourish. First there were the Pharisees, a party devoted to up-
holding the law in its integrity. They first came to prominence

during the days of the Maccabees and were essentially a religious party.

The Pharisees were devoted to the oral law of the great rabbis, which later would be inscribed as the Mishna (an early form of the Talmud). They were convinced the Mishna held the key to all the hidden depths of the Torah as well as having the answer to all the needs and problems of mankind. Their lofty aspirations degenerated eventually into dogmatism, their patriotism into partisanship, and their fidelity into fanaticism. It was perhaps inevitable that in time they would come to regard the oral tradition of the rabbis as of equal authority with the written law of Moses. It was the Pharisees who provided Judaism with its rabbis. By the time of Christ rabbinic Judaism, the synagogues, and the chief outward forms of Judaism were in their hands. The Lord denounced the Pharisees for their hypocrisy and for diluting divine truth with human tradition.

The great rivals of the Pharisees were the Sadducees. The Sadducees were never a large party numerically, but they made up for that in other ways. They were, for the most part, wealthy, aristocratic, and influential. They were the materialists, the secularists of the day, and in rabbinic writings are sometimes spoken of as heretics. They opposed the Mishna and had no use for the cumbersome oral tradition so dear to the Pharisees. They interpreted the law literally and severely.

In theology, the Sadducees denied the existence of angels, the truth of resurrection, the immortality of the soul, and a future life. The Sadducees were the priestly caste in Israel, and their interest focused on the Temple and the sacrifices. They were Hellenistic in outlook and sympathy and, like the Pharisees, ran into conflict with Christ.

The sect of the Essenes also flourished at that time. The Pharisees were the separatists, the Sadducees were the moralists, and the Essenes were the mystics. They were essentially a monastic order given to living in small, exclusive communities. They were never numerous, and membership in their order was granted only after the candidate had passed through severe initiation. The Essenes wore white dress to symbolize purity and a leather apron to depict defense from impurity. They were given to frequent washings. They were conscientious objectors and would touch nothing harmful such as weapons of war. They believed their word should be their bond, venerated Moses and the law, strictly observed the Sabbath, served one another, and were inclined toward celibacy.

The Romans Take the Stage

As those and similar sects were developing among the Jews, history was hurrying on its way. The Romans had come and were hammering loudly at the door of the empire. Three Punic wars had reduced Rome's ancient enemy Carthage to rubble, making Rome mistress of Africa and Spain. Four Macedonian wars had added Greece to the growing empire; the Mithridatic wars had brought in the Seleucid kingdom, and, with the annexation of Egypt and Palestine, the whole Mediterranean became a Roman lake.

Gaul and Britain were conquered, and Europe became one great community bound together by Roman law, Roman roads, and Roman troops. The republican form of government in Rome gave way to the imperial government as the day of the caesars dawned. And, most important of all, in a tiny corner of the spreading empire of Rome, in a little Judean town called Bethlehem, Jesus was born.

Jesus and the Jews

The greatest single tragedy in the story of the Jew is his national rejection of Jesus as Messiah, Savior, and Lord. The throne rights of Jesus ran back to David both through His mother, Mary, who so miraculously conceived Him, and through His foster father, Joseph, who adopted Him (Luke 3; Matthew 1). He was Israel's true Messiah, the only Messiah she will ever have. His claims to be both Messiah and Son of God were substantiated by the sinlessness of His life, by the countless miracles He performed, by the pungency and purity of His teachings, and by His clear fulfillment of many Old Testament prophecies.

The religious Jewish establishment, however, wanted no part of it. The rabbis were jealous of the teaching of Jesus, which was so memorable and authoritative and which was so enthusiastically hailed by the common people. The Pharisees were infuriated by the way He attacked their precious oral law, their entrenched and cumbersome traditions, and their evident hypocrisy (Matthew 12:1-14, for example). The Sadducees saw their vested interests in the Temple threatened by Jesus, and they took umbrage at His teaching concerning the spirit world and the life to come (Matthew 22:23-32).

The priests feared that His Messianic teachings would bring down on the nation the wrath of Rome. The scribes and the Levites were scalded by His exposure of their insincerity. The common people flocked after Him, thrilled by His miracles, astonished at His preaching, delighted with the forthright way He exposed error, hypocrisy, and pride. A crowd, however, is never anything else but a crowd: fickle, unstable, and easily swayed. Jesus never committed Himself to crowds.

The Jewish establishment became increasingly hostile to Jesus. The various factions stopped their infighting long enough to make common cause against Him. They presented a united front to the Roman governor, Pilate, and, using all the pressure plays at their command, forced him to sign the order for Jesus' crucifixion. "If you let this man go you are not Caesar's friend" (John 19:12). "His blood be on us and on our children," they cried at one point when they thought he might draw back (Matthew 27:25).

Jesus was crucified while the people stolidly watched. Yet Jesus prayed from upon the cross, "Father, forgive them; for they do not know what they are doing" (Luke 23:34). Christ's prayer will someday be answered nationally. In light of that prayer no true Christian can ever join those who persecute the Jews. Many Jews believed on Him and wept at His death—and, of course, He Himself was a Jew.

Pilate, the Roman governor, admitted Christ's innocence. Nevertheless, to avoid endangering his position with Caesar, gave the death order, and the Romans put Christ to death. God, knowing the sin-guilt of all mankind, allowed both Jew and Gentile to have a hand in the crucifixion. Anyone who accuses "the Jews" of killing Christ forgets that the Father sent Jesus, who was willing to die for our sins. The Jews delivered Him up, the Romans crucified Him, and all of us today share in the necessity and cause of His death (Mark 10:45; Romans 3:9-12).

He was buried in a guarded tomb, but on the third day He rose from the dead. The resurrection of Christ is a well attested historical fact. He showed Himself alive to a score of credible witnesses, and then on one occasion to over five hundred people at the same time.

The early evangelists were mostly Jews. When they arrived in a new city they naturally made straight for the Jewish community, and their message was invariably first proclaimed in the local synagogue.

That was particularly true of the preaching of the apostle Paul (Acts 12:14; 14:1; 17:1). He himself was a trained rabbi. His education had been at the feet of Gamaliel, one of the most renowned and respected rabbis of the day (Acts 22:3). At one time Paul had been a committed enemy of Christianity and had dedicated himself to stamping out the infant church. His conversion to Christ had been no light thing, and it had far-reaching results. Even though he was bitterly persecuted by his fellow Jews, Paul never lost his love for the Jewish people and invariably made it his practice to go to "the Jew first" wherever he went with the gospel.

Throughout the period covered by the book of Acts, opposition to the preaching of the church arose nearly always from a segment of the Jewish communities in the various cities where Christ was proclaimed. The world of the Jew closed its doors to Jesus the Christ.

NOTES

1. George Adam Smith, "The Book of the Twelve Prophets," in *The Expositor's Bible,* 6 vols. (Grand Rapids: Eerdmans, 1956), 4:613.
2. See chapter 5.

4

THE WANDERING JEW

In Charles Dickens's novel *Bleak House* the policeman ordered Joe to move on. Loiterers were frowned on by the law. Poor Joe had nowhere to go.

"I'm always a-moving on, sir," cried the boy, wiping away his grimy tears with his arm. "I've always been a-moving on ever since I was born. Where can I possibly move to, sir?"

"My instructions don't go to that," replied the constable. "My instructions are that you are to move on. I have told you so five hundred times."

Down through the ages, life, like the policeman in *Bleak House,* has kept the Jew moving on. He has been regarded as an unwanted loiterer in the countless lands of the world where he has tried to settle down. He has managed, at times, to make himself believe that, at last, he has found a place where he can rest. But ever and again the order has come for him to move on.

Eugene Sue has used a phrase for the title of a book that somehow captures the whole spirit of the plight of this people. He called it *The Wandering Jew.*

In this chapter we are going to briefly summarize the history of the Jewish people from the time of the Romans to modern times. Later chapters will fill in many of the details, but first we must have before us a general survey of Jewish fortunes in Gentile lands. The historical time chart at the back of this book will help you paint in the broad background of Gentile world history against which this summary is displayed.

THE FIRST REVOLT AGAINST ROME

Jews had been dispersed among the nations for centuries before Titus destroyed Jerusalem and burned the Temple. The ten tribes had been scattered from the time of the Assyrian invasion and the

people of Judah since the Babylonian invasion. The countless
thousands of Jews who chose to remain in Babylonia after the end
of the captivity turned the exile into the Diaspora, the voluntary
Dispersion. The Jewish revolt against Rome, however, marked the
end of an era and the beginning of an exile that has lasted to
recent times. The blazing Temple in A.D. 70 put an end to biblical
Judaism in practice just as Christ's death at Calvary had put an
end to it in principle.

The Jews fought against the Romans with the courage of de-
spair. Despite the internal squabbles that tore out Jerusalem's
heart, the valiant defenders almost won. The Romans were forced
to bring enormous pressure to bear before the city finally fell.
When they did take the city they showed no mercy. They left
behind them total ruin, a smoking Temple, and a people either
dead or in chains.

BAR KOCHBA'S REVOLT

The Jews, however, were by no means through. Forty years
later, led by a pseudo-Messiah by the name of Bar Kochba (Son
of the Star) they tried again (A.D. 132-135). Once more they
tested the Roman military prowess to the utmost. When the Jewish rebellion was finally quelled, the infuriated Romans decided
that never again should the Jews be allowed to cause them so
much trouble. They banished all Jews from the country and
posted it out of bounds to them. They changed the name of the
country to Palestine in honor of the Philistines, the ancient heredi-
tary foes of Israel, and they changed the name of Jerusalem to
Aelia Capitolina.

THE JEWS BECOME A STATELESS PEOPLE

That brought an end to Palestine as a national home for the Jew
for nearly two thousand years. The world of the Gentile henceforth had to be the world of the Jew. The homeless, stateless people became indeed the wandering Jews.

Many of the refugees who fled from the Romans made for
Parthia, where they were welcomed with open arms. There were
already large colonies of Jews in that area, generally called "Babylonia" by the Jews themselves. The fugitives would be secure
there, for the Roman Empire ended at the Euphrates. The Romans had never been able to subjugate the lands beyond. Jews
had dwelt happily in Parthia since the days of the Babylonian

exile, and, by the first century of the Christian era, some two million of them were at home there. The Parthians respected them, granted them home rule, and bestowed the title Exilarch upon their leaders (c. A.D. 190).

With their homeland denied them the Jews had become truly a stateless people. They could be found from India to the Atlantic Ocean. They lived on three continents, in two empires, and in scores of countries. Never again would they have a permanent home until the rebirth of their state in modern times. The world-wide dispersal posed some immediate problems for the Jewish people. So long as Jerusalem and Judea stood intact there had always been a visible center around which some form of national life could revolve, but now that their former homeland had vanished, how could they possibly survive? Even the ghost of Jewish nationality could now be expected to be exorcised from the earth. In time the Jews could be expected to disappear as a people in accordance with the relentless laws of history. It had happened to countless other peoples. Why not to the Jews?

PLANS FOR SURVIVAL

As some of the more farsighted Jewish leaders saw it, the only hope for national survival lay in producing a counterculture, something distinctly Jewish, something that would match, rival, and outlast the culture of the various Gentile countries in which the dismembered parts of the Jewish nation now lay buried.

To some extent, the Jews had already become adept at surviving in alien lands. The Babylonian captivity had taught them the basic techniques. Their voluntary dispersal up and down the Persian, Greek, and Roman Empires, over many centuries, had immunized them against alien cultures and had given them a remarkable resilience and adaptability. That was all well and good, but something more would be needed to face the ages that now lay ahead.

The architects of the new Judaism carefully assessed the situation. For the centuries ahead, perhaps indefinitely, the Jews would have to survive without a land, a capital, a national government, or an army. They would have no Temple, and the sacrifices had ceased. They did not know it then, but not just the Roman world, but the Parthian world, the Islamic world, the feudal European world, the ghetto world, and the modern world, would all have to be, in turn, the world of the Jew. There would be pressure from the forces of both extermination and assimilation. Yet in every country, in every age, no matter what the pressure from without or within, if they were to survive as a people they must become a Gulf Stream in the ocean of mankind. They must be able to adapt and change and yet remain the same.

The means of survival that the Jews adopted was unique. They had already begun to invent a form of Judaism that could cope with their loss of the biblical essentials such as a homeland, a Temple, and a sacrificial system. The basic concepts had already been hammered out in the Midrash and the Mishna. The thing to do was to keep on adding to that religious system and make *it* the true home of every Jew no matter where he lived, what language he spoke, or what cultural forces pressed upon him.

The designers of the new Judaism, of course, did not know just how far it would eventually go. They only knew that Judaism, if it was to survive, must be capable of being reshaped and adapted, and that it must become the means of Jewish national identity and survival no matter where the Jew pitched his tent in the wilderness of the world. How they did that we shall explore in another section of this book.

A Breathing Spell

While the new architects of Judaism were drawing up their blueprints for survival, the Jews themselves were given a welcome breathing spell. For centuries they had been the convenient scapegoat for anything that went wrong in the world. Jews now saw the Christians step into their uncomfortable role. The follies, failures, insanities, and jealousies of the caesars of Rome had to be blamed on someone. The Christians were a much better whipping-boy than the Jews, from the Roman viewpoint. They were even more strange in their beliefs than the Jews. For the next three hundred years whenever the caesars felt it necessary to vent their spite and frustration on someone, it was the Christians rather than the Jews who bore the brunt of their malice.

In the east, the old Parthian kingdom was replaced by the Sassanid Empire (A.D. 227), which, in turn, was a revived form of the old Persian Empire. The Sassanids maintained the area's traditional hostility toward Rome and friendliness toward Jews. The Jews in the Sassanid world either ventured farther and farther eastward, planting new trade outposts in the distant Orient, even as far afield as China, or else they stayed home and enjoyed themselves haggling over the ever growing Talmud. The Sassanid Empire continued to the days of Mohammed and the coming of Islam.

ROME FACES THE END

Meanwhile, the old Roman Empire creaked on its dreary way through history. The persecuting caesars gave way to the patronizing caesars (A.D. 306), and the Christian church rose to power in the world, a circumstance that was eventually to have ominous implications for the Jews. By the time of Theodosius (A.D. 379) the church had grown so strong that Ambrose, Bishop of Milan, was able to force even the emperor to do penance for putting down a rebellion with too much cruelty.

With the death of Theodosius, the Roman Empire split in two, and his two sons carved up the world between them. Arcadius took the East and Honorius took the West. A greatly weakened empire woke up too late to discover that it was unable any longer to hold its frontiers against the savage northern tribes. The Huns, the Goths, the Vandals, and the Visigoths laid the once proud empire in the dust. In 455 the Vandals sacked Rome, and in 476 the western empire came to an inglorious end.

THE BIRTH OF ISLAM

History never stands still. A new voice was now to be heard in human affairs, the voice of an eastern prophet by the name of Mohammed (A.D. 622). In Mohammed's day, Arabia was a miscellaneous assortment of Semitic tribes. There were the desert Arabs, wedded to their camels and tents. There were the city Arabs in places like Mecca and Medina, who had long since absorbed both Greek and Jewish ideas. In Mohammed's day there were more Jews in Medina than there were Arabs. The prophet himself was not above borrowing from Judaism for some of his religious ideas.

The Arabs spread their faith with fanatical zeal and, in its wake, came a new and dynamic civilization. The Islamic culture was bursting with new ideas and with vigorous economic life. Whereas Christian civilization was sinking slowly into the Dark Ages, the Arabs were making great advances in mathematics, medicine, science, and architecture. In that exciting, exotic world the Jews flourished, and many of them rose to positions of great power. In that world, too, they were able to put their Talmud to the test. They found that it worked. Henceforth they could march in step with the new enlightenment without sacrificing their essential Jewishness.

The Roman Church Takes Over

In the west, the Vandal tide ebbed, leaving the church as the only organized force in European society. The Roman bishopric had long been powerful and rich, and its bishops had come to see themselves as lords of the church, the true custodians of the apostolic tradition with the right to universal jurisdiction over church affairs. Pope Leo the Great (440-461) persuaded the Emperor Valentinian III that it should be passed into law that all papal decisions must be regarded as binding. With the collapse of the Roman Empire the church had the machinery ready for taking over governmental affairs outside as well as inside the church The popes realized, however, that the church needed a strong secular arm upon which to lean. It found what it wanted in Charlemagne (771).

Charlemagne's reign was one of great importance in the post-Roman world. He united Germany and France, allied himself closely with the papacy, supported church reforms, and held out a friendly hand to the Jews. He allowed them into his kingdom and encouraged them to build up great mercantile enterprises in Europe. His empire did not last, but it did pave the way for the conversion of Europe to papal Christianity. It also laid the foundations of the four medieval kingdoms of Italy, France, Germany, and Spain, followed later by England. For the next four or five centuries the fortunes of the Jews were to be bound up with those kingdoms.

The Feudal World

The Jew was unique in the feudal world. In the feudal systems There was only a small middle class or merchant class. Here the Jew found a niche for himself. He was denied admission to both nobility and the medieval craft guilds. Castles that would permit his presence were few. But when the popes forbade "usury" (money-lending) by "the faithful" but permitted it to the out-of-the-fold

Jew, the Jew became the European moneylender and eventually
its banker. Both the Jew and his trade were completely despised,
but from the time of Pope Gregory (590) until the time of Innocent III (1198) the Jew's services were indispensable, and he was
more or less left alone. Bishop and baron alike found themselves
at times approaching the Jew for help.

The Crusades were an exception to the general tolerance of the
Jew in the feudal world. The Crusades themselves began in 1096
and were popular, somewhat aimless, and somewhat ineffective
efforts to free the Holy Land from the Muslims. They were, for
the most part, inspired by fanatics (there was even a Children's
Crusade), blessed by the popes, and marked by general incompetence and lack of organization.

Wherever they went the Crusaders did "accomplish" one thing.
They whipped up sentiment against the Jews. After all, they
thought, what was the sense of marching off to trounce the Saracens if the Jews were left in peace? They labeled them "Christ-
killers," forgetting that Jesus Himself was a Jew and that the beloved apostles were also all Jews. In the wake of the Crusaders,
Jewish communities were left ravaged and horror-struck by the
atrocities that had been committed. It was a sobering reminder
to the Jews that their presence was merely tolerated and that they
lived in a Gentile world that could turn against them at any time.

OLD ORDERS CHANGE

The Islamic Empire ran its course and fell into decline. It was
not so much the efforts of the Crusaders that brought about the
fall of Islamic power as the hammer blows that fell upon the
Muslim world at the hands of the Mongolians (1218). Again it
was time for the Jew to recommence his wanderings. The Islamic
world was no longer to be the comfortable place it had been for
many centuries. Many Jews, frightened by the changes taking
place, trekked into Europe in the hope of finding new homes there.

Europe, however, was changing too. The Renaissance was
challenging customs and institutions that had held the continent
in darkness for centuries. The power of the church was being
weakened as the ignorance and superstition it had fostered for so
long were attacked. Greek and Arab learning was rediscovered,
and men began to think for themselves again. The feudal system

was falling apart as kings seized power from the barons. Stronger central governments emerged, and, as trade and commerce began to spread, a thriving middle class appeared.

The Jews were now about to be forced out of the niche they had filled for so long in the medieval world. For three hundred years they had survived and some even flourished in the business side of things in the feudal system. The trade cartels of a handful of the most prosperous reached all the way from China to Spain. It did not take the emerging Gentile business class long to realize that something would have to be done to dislodge the Jews from areas now seen to be lucrative.

At the same time, the church was thoroughly alarmed at the intellectual attacks being made upon its archaic traditions and unfounded dogmas by thinking people. The Jew proved to be a handy scapegoat for those new troubles. It soon became evident that if the Jews were eliminated from society two birds could be killed with the same stone. The church could divert attention from its own inadequacies by focusing attention on the Jews as heretics, and the business world could profit from the elimination of competition. Thus, beginning with England in 1290 and ending with Spain in 1492, the Jews found themselves driven from country after country in which they had made their homes for hundreds of years.

JUDAISM IN THE MIDDLE AGES

The Middle Ages had seen the rise of two very different forms of Judaism. The first of those was Sephardic Judaism centered in Spain. Jews had lived in Spain since Carthaginian times. They had produced a virile culture in which Torah and Talmud were blended with Greek and Islamic ideas. They had flourished exceedingly during the Muslim period in Spain, entering the mainstream of Spanish life and rising to positions of wealth and power. They excelled in mathematics and astronomy. They became landowners, financiers, physicians, and courtiers. One such Sephardic Jew was Maimonides to whom, long after his death, such diverse figures as Spinoza, Mendelssohn, and Thomas Aquinas acknowledged their intellectual debt.

When the Spanish people threw off the Moorish yoke and marched back into Christendom, they instinctively turned against

the Jews. Before long the new leaders of Spain, encouraged by an
intolerant papacy, were clamoring for repressive measures against
the Jews. By the end of the fourteenth century, anti-Semitism was
epidemic all across the Iberian peninsula.

At first the Spaniards tried to force Jews to convert to Christianity, making the alternatives very simple—convert and prosper
or remain a Jew and perish. Thousands of Jews converted to
Christianity as the expedient thing to do. They became known as
Marranos. They prospered, entered the universities, took up high
positions at court, married into aristocratic families, and incurred
the jealousy of the Spanish neighbors. They were suspected of
phoney conversion, of still being secretly Jewish, of paying only
lip service to the church.

Before long the fires of persecution were kindled in Spain. Isabella of Castile and Ferdinand of Aragon became joint rulers of
the country (1469). Isabella's father confessor was Torquemada,
who was appointed Grand Inquisitor of the Inquisition with full
powers to root out all heresy and with instructions to pay special
attention to the Marranos and the Jews. Terrible and thorough as
were the methods of the Inquisition, they were not enough. Spain
finally expelled all the Jews from the country, ending fifteen hundred years of Jewish life in Spain.

The Ashkenazi form of Judaism took root in eastern Europe.
There the Jews, faced with growing hostility from their Gentile
neighbors, retreated more and more into the Talmud. It became
their home, their fortress, their strong tower against a threatening,
treacherous, hostile, proselytizing world. The world of the Ashkenazi Jew shrank into an ever smaller and smaller compass. The
price the Ashkenazis were eventually to pay for retreat into their
unreal, make-believe world would be high, but there was no doubt
that the outside world was a dangerous and hostile place for Jews.
In most places they were forced to wear a distinctive garb or a
special, ugly badge.

The European Jew soon lost what was left of his dignity. In
Gentile eyes he was a sly, contemptible creature slinking down
back alleys and not fit for the company of mankind. Almost every
European country took it for granted that Jews should be persecuted. It is small wonder that the Jews themselves wished to
retreat from such a world into an artificial one, bounded by the
comforting, familiar phrases of the beloved Talmud.

WESTERN HOSTILITY TOWARD THE JEW GROWS

In the fourteenth century, the Black Death marched across Europe. People were smitten with the dreadful symptoms of the plague, and they died like flies (1347). The cities were choked with the dead, and in the country farms were left without a man to till the soil. A quarter of the population of Europe perished. Insane with fear, people tried every quack remedy the medicine men could suggest. Then someone ignited the dry grass of ignorance, and a conflagration swept across the stricken continent, driven by the high winds of prejudice, fear, and hate. The Jews were responsible! They were the cause of the plague. Heaven was angry because "Christians" allowed these "Christ-killers" to dwell in their midst. Massacres of Jews became commonplace throughout Europe.

ASHKENAZI AND SEPHARDIC

As western Europe drove out its Jews, they crowded into eastern Europe, hanging tenaciously onto life. When the Protestant Reformation came along and the Roman church girded for the fight, Jews everywhere were regarded as a nuisance. They were banished into the ghettos. The ghetto itself was a walled enclosure, a heavily-populated warren of streets and alleys and cheap houses. Had it not been for the Talmudic laws of hygiene, the ghettoes would soon have become slums. It was ghetto life in particular that produced the Ashkenazi Jew. *Ashkenaz* in Hebrew means "German." Thus the Ashkenazi refers to those Jews who made their homes in Germany and in central and eastern Europe.

Just at the time when the rest of the world was booming, when science was opening up new frontiers, when explorers were adding new worlds to be explored and colonized, the Jews of eastern Europe straight-jacketed themselves in the Talmud and meekly accepted the restrictions imposed upon them by the world outside. Life passed those Jews by. In western Europe they would eventually be permitted to filter back into the real world, but in the east they would continue to stagnate.

In time a bitter feud developed between the Sephardic (Spanish) and Ashkenazi (European) Jews. For centuries the Spanish Jews had been Judaism's aristocracy, and the Ashkenazis had been the serfs. When education became available to Ashkenazi Jews, however, the situation reversed itself. The very name *Sephardi*, once a title of honor, became a term of contempt. It was ultimately applied indiscriminately to any Jew who was not an Ashkenazi, regardless of whether or not he was born in Spain. In time it became a general term for all oriental Jews as opposed to European Jews.

Prior to the rise of Hitler and the establishment of the state of Israel, differences between Ashkenazi and Sephardic Jews had been decreasing. Of some 16,500,000 Jews in the world about 15,000,000 were Ashkenazi. But the extermination of 6,000,000 Ashkenazi Jews and the isolation of a further 3,000,000 in Russia meant that the Sephardis became proportionately more important. The tide of immigration into Israel brought in more Sephardi, oriental Jews than it did European, Ashkenazi Jews. The Sephardi Jews were backward in terms of Western culture, emotional, and easy-going. The Ashkenazi Jews were the elite of Europe and America. As a result, in the highly industrialized, Western culture of Israel, a clash soon developed. The Sephardic Jews made up about half the population, but they occupied less than 5 percent of the good positions in the country. This has been a cause for friction.

Some Ashkenazi Israelis fear that much more immigration from the wrong countries could turn Israel into a Sephardic state. The pragmatic Ashkenazis know full well that such an Israel could not survive in a coldly competitive world. The Sephardic Jews naturally believe that they are discriminated against.[1]

The eighteenth century dawned upon a Judaism that had degenerated into meaningless formulas and religious mutterings. The Hasidic revolt shook the rabbis to some extent out of their senseless hair-splitting, but their devotion to their beloved Talmud did not die easily.[2]

The rabbis eyed with great suspicion men like Moses Mendelssohn, for instance, who tried to break down Jewish dependence on Yiddish as a language of communication. The rabbis were especially alarmed at the cracks showing up in the ghetto way of life. They saw the Jews being drawn into the vortex of the fascinating Gentile world just as centuries before they had been caught up into the Hellenistic world.

They watched with horror as increasing numbers of Jews renounced their Judaism only to be swallowed up by the Gentile world of commerce, culture, opportunity, and heretical patterns of thought. They bitterly denounced education as a curse and opposed it with all their power, but it was no use. The old way of life was about over. The reign of the Talmud as the supreme arbiter in all matters of faith and morals for Jews was over.

THE FRENCH REVOLUTION

The French Revolution (1789) brought in its wake political emancipation for millions of European Jews. It broke the power of the aristocracy, trimmed the church down to size, and gave the middle classes a chance to seize power. In the French world all restrictions against the Jews were abolished, and they were given their freedom along with everyone else. Napoleon, a strategist and a pragmatist, knew well that in the countries he wished to conquer there resided countless Jews. He saw them as useful allies. In a bold move he reconvened the Sanhedrin in Paris in 1807 and hoped by that move to rally the world of Jewry to his cause. He planned a national home for the Jew in Palestine (under French protection, of course) as a means of cutting Britain's lifeline to India.

Napoleon's ambitions were finally crushed at Waterloo (1815). There was an immediate reaction throughout Europe. The Jews were blamed for the unemployment and chaos that reigned everywhere and were herded back to the ghettos. In Italy and Spain the Inquisition, abolished by Napoleon, was restored and a fresh baptism of misery was administered to the Jew. The Jews, however, were no longer docile as once they had been. They had been given a taste of freedom, and they liked its flavor. They threw themselves avidly into every movement that promised them any hope of redress from their sufferings and became active in all the underground movements that led to the further revolutions of 1830 and 1848.

A NEW DAY DAWNS

By 1870 almost every country on the continent had been reorganized and was governed under a constitution that guaranteed civil rights for all. It was a new day. Jews rapidly began to climb the ladder of success. Their financial genius was soon felt in the world as they gained control of giant corporations and financial institutions. Some Jewish families, such as the Rothschilds, became powerful enough to change the whole course of history. In England, Jews rose to the highest posts in the land. Benjamin

Disraeli became Prime Minister, Lord Reading (formerly Sir Rufus Isaacs) became Viceroy of India, Sir Herbert Samuel became His Majesty's Commissioner for Palestine.

JEWS IN AMERICA

Jews arrived in America in four waves. First came the Spanish Jews between 1621 and 1825, many of them Marranos. They settled in both Spanish and Portuguese territories. When the Inquisition arrived in the New World many of them fled once more, this time north to New Amsterdam. Those Jews became merchants and traders.

In 1825 and 1880 fresh waves arrived fleeing from a Europe inundated by revolution and war. The two hundred thousand Sephardic Jews already in this country were swamped by the arrival of nearly two million Jews from eastern Europe and Russia. The new arrivals settled down to business. They became peddlers, storekeepers, and businessmen. Indeed, many of the modern, complex department stores in America evolved from the enterprising activities of those early Jewish peddlers. Jews became very prominent in America's retailing business.

Between 1880 and 1920 came a massive new influx of some two million Polish and Russian Jews fleeing the pogroms of the Czars. Despised and beggared though they were, surprisingly enough they gave fresh stimulus to Jewish consciousness in America. The United States was willing to open its doors to large numbers of refugees because the country, at that time, needed unskilled workers to man the giant industrial complexes springing up all over the country. Jews filtering into American industry were not long in seeking advancement in that field.

Nor did it take Jews in America long to realize that great opportunities for the future were open in the professions, in art, and in science. Jewish parents living in the slums of New York, Chicago, Cleveland, and Detroit, saw to it that their children took full advantage of the American educational system. Before long Jews in ever increasing numbers were pouring into the country's colleges and universities.

After 1920 the American labor market reached its saturation point, and in 1924 the government put the brakes on further immigration. That sealed the fate of millions of Jews still living in

Russia and Poland and other countries soon to be overrun by the Nazis.

The fourth great wave of Jewish immigration came in 1935 when the United States Congress relaxed its immigration laws to permit the immigration of 300,000 refugees from Nazi terror. Many of those who came were the cream of European Jewry. Jewish intellectual life found a new home, and America became a capital of Jewish opinion and thought.

JEWS IN RUSSIA

In Russia, the history of the Jews has been one of unrelenting persecution. It began in the beginning of the sixteenth century when the Russian Orthodox church took alarm at the defection of so many Russians into Judaism, which they found much more attractive than the Russian brand of Christianity. The church had the Jews expelled from Russia. In 1655 Russia annexed Lithuania, and once more the Russians were saddled with a large and unwanted domestic Jewish population. They expelled them again.

In 1721 Peter the Great took over the former Swedish territory along the Baltic Coast, and the Russians discovered that once more they had a large Jewish population on their hands. In 1762 Catherine the Great proclaimed Russia to be out of bounds for all Jews. Jews could live in Poland, in Lithuania, and in the Ukraine, but not in Russia itself. The territory along Russia's western border, where the Jews were allowed to reside, was called "The Pale of Settlement."

Russian hatred of the Jews was the fruit of Czarist incompetence, peasant ignorance, and church intolerance. When the Jews sought to resist the intense Russification of the Slav Empire, the Czars tried to crush them with unbelievable ferocity. The five Romanov Czars in particular were unrelenting in their persecution of the Jews. For a century and a half the Russian Jews lived under the most brutal tyranny. For twenty years Czar Nicholas II subjected them to the worst persecution they ever had to face in Russia. The Jews, millions strong, resisted all attempts to assimilate them, and the Czar reacted with even worse persecutions.

KARL MARX

It is small wonder that from the time of Karl Marx (1848), many Jews in Russia allied themselves with the socialist, radical, and

Bolshevik movements. Trotsky, Zinoviev, Kamenev, Radek, Litvinov, and numerous other Bolshevik leaders were Jews. The outbreak of World War I brought frantic promises from the Czar of better treatment for everyone, of religious freedom, and of racial equality if only everyone would unite and support Russia in her hour of need. It was too late. Russia was badly mauled by the Germans, signed an armistice agreement, and then plunged headlong into a massive revolution.

The Jews remained a force in Russian Communism for a period. It was not until the Trotsky-Zinoviev-Kamenev group was purged by the Stalin-Bukharin-Rykov faction (1935) that the Jews ceased to be an influential factor in Soviet Russia. As the Bolshevik revolution continued to attract radical elements abroad, the Communist International was formed to speed the work of uniting the world under a Communist regime.

THE HOLOCAUST

Then came the Nazis. Anti-Jewish feeling, ever fluid beneath the surface in Europe, hardened into the most vicious form of anti-Semitism the world had ever seen. Hitler set out to exterminate the Jews and failed, not because he lost sight of his goal but because he lost the Second World War. The Nazi holocaust gave tremendous impetus to Zionism, a movement that had been gathering momentum among European Jews and aimed at establishing in Palestine a national home for the Jew. The British had been active in that direction ever since the end of World War I but had been greatly hampered by Arab opposition. The Nazi atrocities, however, brought matters to a head, with the result that the state of Israel was created under the sponsorship of the United Nations in 1948.

ARAB HATRED OF ISRAEL

The Arabs have never ceased in their efforts to get rid of the unwanted Jewish state created in their midst. From their point of view it is a monstrous crime that they should be forced to make expiation, with their land, for a crime committed by somebody else. As the Arabs see it, crimes against the Jews were committed by Europeans. It was "Christian" Europe that fired the ovens of Auschwitz, Treblinka, and Belsen, not the Arabs. In Arab thinking the British had no right to give Arab land to Israel. The Arabs

have greatly oversimplified the problem, of course, and have understandably ignored other sides to it, but that is how they saw it
when partition was voted in the United Nations, and that is how
they see it still.

Israel is a nation whose time has come. The Jew now has a home
beckoning to him wherever his wanderings have taken him to the
ends of the earth. The wandering Jew need wander no more.

NOTES

1. See for instance Mayo Mohs, David Aikman, and Marlin Levin, "Troubled Land of Zion," *Time*, 18 May 1981, p. 43.
2. See chapter 7.
3. When General George S. Brown, chairman of the Joint Chiefs of Staff,
made a remark which the Jews regarded as anti-Semitic about Israel and
Jewish pressure on the Congress, he was instantly called on the carpet.
President Ford took him to task, as did James Schlesinger, Secretary of
Defense. He was sharply criticized in Congress, and he was forced to
make a public apology. See *Time*, 25 November 1974.

5

THE RELIGIOUS JEW:
THE BEGINNINGS OF THE TALMUD

If we are to understand the world of the Jew, we must try to understand the Jew's religious background. To do that we must know something about the growth, the contents, and the influence of the Talmud, the encyclopedic collection of extrabiblical Jewish religious and civil law.

THE TORAH VERSUS THE TALMUD

The *Torah* is the Jewish name for the Pentateuch, the five books of Moses. It is their word for the law. Jewish life for centuries has revolved around the Torah, but, for the most part, it has been a Torah buried beneath vast accumulations of tradition and encrusted with enormous deposits of human interpretation. The Torah itself has been largely superceded in Judaism by the Talmud. The five books of the Torah can be written out in 350 pages. The Talmud takes up 523 *books* printed in 22 volumes.

The Torah is clear and concise, part of the inspired Word of God. The Talmud is wordy, rambling, argumentative, inconsistent, sometimes witty, sometimes boring, sometimes brilliant, sometimes inane. The laws of the Talmud comprise a cold concrete poured over Jewish life and hardened by time into a rigid prison for the soul. Had the Talmud contained only cold laws it would never have survived the centuries. The people it has shaped would have perished long ago from the earth.

The Talmud contains more than law, however. It has swept into its pages a miscellaneous assortment of songs and sayings, a brew of fables and fancies, a treasure trove of wisdom and wit.

In the process of time, the Talmud became the race memory of the Jewish people and a distillation of their joys and sorrows. It was the one unifying factor the Jews possessed with which to face the baffling equation of life in which the chief ingredients seemed to be homelessness and hopelessness. For the scattered, persecuted Jews the Talmud became a talisman. Side by side with arrant non-sense it contains the sagest wisdom. It is a uniquely Jewish brew. Jews everywhere in every age have been able to find identity in the Talmud. Humanly speaking, it has done more to shape and preserve the Jew than anything else in his long and remarkable history.

THE TALMUD'S SLOW EVOLUTION

The designers of the Talmud were never in a hurry, and, to begin with, they had no idea they were writing such a book. It began with the *Midrash*, a series of verbal expositions of the Torah; it developed into the *Mishna*, further repetitions and ac-cumulations of rabbinic commentary; it evolved into *Gemara*, another series of supplements. Those three, Midrash, Mishna, and Gemara, made up what was called the *oral law*, a vast body of literature which, for centuries, was passed on verbally. By the time the rabbis decided to write the whole thing down it had grown to some 2,500,000 words—all of which up to that time, had been memorized. Some infant prodigies mastered it before their teens.

The writers of the Talmud worked slowly. They took centuries to perfect their art and to hammer out their ideas. The growing Talmud, like some sluggish stream, meandered through the world of thought from the days of the Babylonian captivity (586 B.C.) until the dawn of the nineteenth century A.D. During that long period its creators haggled over every phase of Jewish life and argued over every word and comma. In the process of mulling over every possible facet of Jewish life and thought they created a mandate for survival in a hostile, alien world.

Efforts might be made to exterminate the Jews, and weaker Jews might yearn for assimilation as the answer to their woes, but the Talmud was ready—ready to soften the blow from without and ready to stiffen the will from within. The Assyrians, Babylonians, Persians, Phoenicians, Hittites, and Philistines have vanished, leaving but a few markings in the sands of time. Empires have waxed and waned. Egyptians, Assyrians, Babylonians, Persians, Greeks, Romans, feudal kings, Islamic caliphs, European democ-racies, and modern dictators have all held the Jews in thrall. The

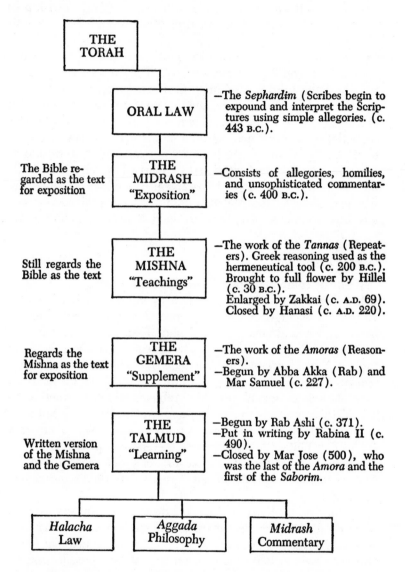

Fig. 5.1

Jew outlives them all. The chief instrument of both Jewish political survival and blindness to true biblical truth has been the
Talmud.

With the conclusion of the Old Testament canon the Jews concluded that God had no more to say. They were wrong. In the
person of the Lord Jesus Christ, God was going to say far more
than He had ever said before, and in a far more eloquent and wonderful way. The Word was to be made flesh, God was to become
Man, deity was to be manifested in humanity. Moreover, He was
to inspire the writing of the twenty-seven books that constitute the
New Testament, a fact intimated by Christ Himself (John 15:26-
27; 16:12-15). Still, the Old Testament canon *was* complete, and
between Malachi and Matthew there ensued a silence of some
four hundred years. The Jews assumed God had no more to say.

THE MIDRASH

With the completion of the Old Testament canon, the Jews decided that it was their prerogative to interpret what God had
written. The *Midrash* was developed out of a sincere desire to
better understand what God had said. Ezra and Nehemiah (443
B.C.) paved the way for it as we have seen by reading the Scriptures to the repatriated Jews of Palestine and by expounding to
them the significance of the Scriptures. The Jews decided that
since the solutions to all possible problems were contained in the
Torah, their task was to seek out and explain those solutions.

The destruction of the Jerusalem Temple by Nebuchadnezzar
(586 B.C.) diluted the authority of the Aaronic priesthood to the
point where a new elite class arose and took their place, the rabbis.
The word *rab* originally meant "great one"; *Rabbi* means "my
superior."

During the captivity in Babylon those new teachers assumed
the custodianship of divine truth. In the process of time they
evolved a principle: At Sinai, God had handed Moses *two* sets of
laws; the *written* law, inscribed on the tablets of stone, and the
oral law, which, so they said, gave specific elaboration of the
Torah. For instance, God said: "Remember the Sabbath day to
keep it holy," but He did not elaborate on that law. It was up to
the rabbis, depending on the oral law supposedly given to Moses,
to determine the exact boundaries of that specific command and

then to clarify that injunction to the people by setting it out in all its ramifications.

That mythical oral law, of course, was known only to the rabbis. They knew it because they were the spiritual heirs of Moses. Moses had received it from God at Sinai, they declared, and had passed it on to Joshua; Joshua had bequeathed it to the elders, and the elders had given it to the prophets. It was passed on in this way to the Sanhedrin, then to the men of the Great Assembly. Just before the birth of Christ it became the special property of the rabbi Hillel. It would continue to be handed down to Gamaliel, to the renowned Akiba, to Maimonides, the greatest rabbi of all, to the Vilna Gaon of Lithuania, to the rabbis of today. The Jews thus anticipated, by many centuries, the myth of apostolic succession and the sacredness of oral tradition.

THE MISHNA

It was in the Midrash that the seeds of the Talmud were sown. The conquests of Alexander the Great and the subsequent Hellenizing of the world faced the Jews with a tremendous survival challenge, as we have already seen. The naive and artless interpretations of the Torah, offered by the Midrash, would no longer suffice in an age of intellectual vigor. The rabbis began to add Greek reasoning to biblical revelation. The result was the Mishna, the work of a new set of Jewish scholars known as the Tannas. Instead of the allegories and homilies of the Midrash, the Tannas employed logic and reasoning borrowed from the Greeks. The Mishna first began to make its appearance within Judaism about 200 B.C., surfacing both in Babylonia and Palestine. Like the Midrash it was a somewhat jumbled exposition of truth, and, like the Midrash, it kept on diluting the Word of God with liberal quantities of fallible human opinion.

It would keep on flourishing and growing for some four hundred years until about A.D. 200. Its popularity was so great that the rabbis ruled that it must not be written down lest it should overshadow the Scriptures. It became known as the oral law because it had to be memorized and passed on orally.

SHAMMAI AND HILLEL

Two schools of Mishna became popular around 35 B.C. One school was developed by Shammai, a strict legalist. The other was developed by Hillel (whose pupil Gamaliel became the teacher of Saul of Tarsus). Hillel's school was the more liberal of the two, but in his day Shammai had by far the greater following. In the years that followed, however, Hillel's disciples became the more numerous. Hillel became the father of rabbinical hermeneutics.

By the time of Christ the Mishna had already accumulated vast prestige, and its custodians, the rabbis and the scribes, were held in veneration by the common people. Jesus swept the whole Talmudic myth aside as "vain tradition," useless verbiage that "made the law of God of none effect" (Matthew 15:1-9). It was for that, as much as anything, that the designers of Judaism determined to get rid of Him.

For instance, in place of the concise statement of the Mosaic law regarding the Sabbath, the Mishna spelled out some forty different kinds of labor that were forbidden. It was forbidden to untie a knot, to sew two stitches, to light a fire, to carry anything from one place to another. We have an example of that kind of "exposition" in the gospels.

The Lord's disciples were accused of breaking the law because they plucked some grain while passing through a field (Matthew 12:1-8). In the rabbinic view they had thereby violated the Sabbath prohibition against *reaping* because they had plucked some grain, and they had broken the Sabbath by *threshing* because they had husked it.

Such prohibitions connected with the Sabbath were taken by the rabbis to fantastic extremes. A tailor must not take his needle into his hand just before nightfall on Sabbath eve because he might forget he has it and go out with it. Carrying his needle would be work and a violation of the Sabbath. It was forbidden to read by lamplight on the Sabbath because the reader might tilt the lamp, and that would be work. A person could go out sucking a candy on the Sabbath day *only* so long as he placed it in his mouth before the Sabbath began, and so long as it was done only to keep the breath sweet.

Should the candy fall out, however, it could not be put back into the mouth again, for that would be work. The rabbis would debate for months over whether a person could wear a false tooth on the Sabbath; whether he could wear it if he needed it to eat better; whether he could eat just as well without it; whether it was to be worn solely for cosmetic purposes, and if so whether such wearing was permitted by the law.

They discussed for nine years one simple statement in the Mosaic law: "Thou shalt not seethe a kid in his mother's milk." No doubt the prohibition was originally aimed at some idolatrous Canaanite practice. The rabbis decided the simple prohibition needed expansion. In the end they concluded that milk and meat must forever be kept separate, for the slightest trace of one could contaminate the other. Even vapors from a pot containing beef could contaminate the very kitchen where the milk was being used. Milk carelessly spilled into a pot used for boiling beef meant that the pot thus defiled must be destroyed.

Consciously or not, the rabbis were creating a cumbersome legal code that would effectively seal off Jews from all other peoples and that, by its uniform application, would bind the Diaspora together. No matter where he went a Jew would be bound by the rabbinical code. By living within its prescribed limits, he would become part of a community far more permanent in character than those that surrounded him. The Talmud would become the Jew's home no matter where he lived. It became the tough adhesive that joined Jews together in one social and religious community.

The Mishna received new impetus just before the birth of Christ when Hillel became the president of the Sanhedrin in Jerusalem. A gifted scholar equally at home in both Greek and Hebrew thought, he postulated seven rules for applying logic to old concepts so as to come up with new ideas. One begins, he taught, with a divine proposition. To that one applies the laws of reason. If the resulting deduction can be shown to grow logically out of the proposition, then the deduction is just as divine, just as inspired, as the original proposition. Not all Jews were impressed. The Pharisees of Jesus' day followed Hillel's arguments and espoused them; the Sadducees rejected them.

ZAKKAI AND VESPASIAN

When the Roman armies surrounded Jerusalem in A.D. 70, and a fresh dispersion seemed likely, the Jews were faced with a new challenge to their survival. It was met by Jochanan ben Zakkai, destined to become one of the most revered of all the architects of the Talmud. He deserted the besieged city and contrived a meet-

ing with the Roman general Vespasian. He boldly prophesied that
Vespasian would become the next Caesar of Rome, and he ex-
tracted a promise from the general that he be permitted, after the
war, to establish a small school of Jewish learning in Palestine.
Vespasian agreed. What harm could a doddering old Jew do,
anyway?

As a result Zakkai founded a small Jewish academy at Jabneh,
just north of Jerusalem. Within ten years he made it a center for
rabbinic Judaism. Zakkai was convinced the Jews needed the oral
law for their survival. They needed the Mishna as a source of
national identity in the dark days ahead. Deprived of their Temple, the Mishna would be their Temple. Hillel's brightest pupil
now became his heir. What a pity that Jochanan ben Zakkai failed
to see that Jesus was the real answer to his people's needs.

Zakkai found the text he needed, on which to base his bold
ideas, in Hosea 6:6—"for I desired mercy, and not sacrifice." Zakkai
set aside the Temple and the sacrificial system in his theology, not
because it was all fulfilled in Christ and rendered obsolete by Him,
but because the destruction of Jerusalem demanded some other
gathering center for Judaism.

With the fall of Jerusalem, the Sanhedrin was moved to Jabneh
in Palestine. Zakkai eased himself into its presidency, changed its
name to the Great Assembly, and then took over the developing
Mishna, hammering it out to suit himself.

In order to have a proper congregation, the rabbis decided it
was necessary to have ten Jewish males living within commuting
distance of each other. Wherever ten such Jews were to be found
it was incumbent upon them to form a synagogue. The maxim
arose: "God is willing to meet with ten street sweepers, but not
with nine rabbis." A male was defined as any youth who had
reached the age of thirteen. When any Jewish religious community acquired 120 members it must establish a school and a court.
Furthermore, the community must tax itself to support its institutions, and it must not accept financial aid from outsiders. No Jew
was to marry a non-Jew. Those were sensible and practical rules.

Zakkai then swept away obsolete and irrelevant Jewish laws,
decreed that all oaths and documents, whether Jewish or not, were
to be honored, ordered Jews to obey all the laws of the lands in
which they lived, and said they should even fight for those countries. Moreover, charity must be extended to all. It is no wonder

Zakkai is revered in the religious world of the Jew. Sensible laws such as those were the very material of which Jewish survival in alien cultures was made.

But, basic as those laws were, they had little to do with the Torah. The rabbis, while professing great reverence for the Mosaic law, had buried that beneath their oral traditions. Jews were required to consider themselves bound by the Torah but bound even more by the Talmud.

Expediency ruled in many of the conclusions reached by the rabbis, and some of their exegesis was devious in the extreme. For example, the law decreed that no bastard could enter the congregation of the Lord "even to his *tenth generation*," which the rabbis regarded as a figure of speech meaning *forever*. In Palestine the law was rigidly enforced, and illegitimate children were outcasts forever, were denied the services of the synagogues, and were not allowed to marry other Jews.

The rabbis frequently went to one extreme or another in expounding that Mosaic law. Some were slavishly literal; others explained the passage away. One expedient went like this: Let the bastard, when past the age of twelve, steal something inconsequential; have him arrested and sold into slavery to another Jew; while in slavery let him be married to another slave and, after a few years, let the pair be emancipated. In this way the bastard could acquire a Hebrew mate, something normally denied to him. Moreover, because he was now a free man, his children could be welcomed into the congregation even though he himself, as a bastard, could never be so received.[1]

RABBINIC LAW AND THE DIASPORA

Within ten years of the fall of Jerusalem, Rabbinic law had established itself firmly at Jabneh. But what about the Diaspora? The task of spreading the Rabbinic gospel fell to Gamaliel II. He travelled far and wide with the Jabneh message, urging the Jews to close ranks, urging them to adopt Zakkai's principles, urging them to keep Christians out of their synagogues, even inserting a curse into the Jewish liturgy against those who allowed Christians to use synagogues as platforms for evangelism.

NOTE

1. Rabbis Tarfon and Shamma, cited in James Michener. *The Source* (New York: Random, 1965), p. 457.

6

THE RELIGIOUS JEW:
THE COMPLETION OF THE TALMUD

We have traced the initial growth of the Talmud. The artless
commentaries of the Midrash were seen by the Jews as inadequate
in an age of Greek enlightenment. Adding Greek logic to their
hermeneutics, the rabbis overhauled their views and developed
the Mishna. After the fall of Jerusalem and the destruction of the
Temple, leaders of Jewish thought decided that it was more im-
perative than ever that Jewish people everywhere be given a unifying code. Thus enlargement of the Mishna to include practical,
down-to-earth legislation followed as a matter of course.

During the following century the Mishna continued to grow.
Initially the rabbis focused on practical questions, and they overhauled the Torah by applying Hillel's laws to divine law. With
the passage of time, however, the whole process of interpretation
and commentary degenerated into foolish hair-splitting with each
rabbi trying to outdo his fellows in wresting new absurdities from
the Mishna. Various schools of thought sprang up, each one
claiming to have arrived at ultimate truth.

HANASI CLOSES THE MISHNA

When Judah Hanasi (135-220 A.D.), the great-grandson of the
illustrious Hillel, became president of the Great Assembly, he decided to put an end to the confusion and personally took the
Mishna in hand. He sorted it out, tossed out matters he considered
nonsense, systematized it, codified it, and rearranged it according
to subject matter, historical development, and relevance. Then,
arbitrarily, he announced the Mishna closed. It was finished. No
more must be added to it. He hoped thus to put a stop to further
accretions to the oral law.

Hanasi's colleagues resented his despotism, but he wielded such influence that during his lifetime they dared not oppose him. As soon as he was dead, however, they gathered up the sections of the Mishna that Hanasi had discarded, looked them over lovingly, and added most of them back in as footnotes. So much for Hanasi's hopes for putting an end to further additions to the Mishna. But at least he did succeed in standardizing the work.

The center of interest now moved away from Palestine to Babylon (Parthia), where some two million Jews were residing. Up to that time the Palestinians had more or less controlled the Mishna and had jealously guarded their copyright. Three of Hanasi's disciples broke that monopoly by moving out to Parthia, carrying the whole of the Mishna in their fantastic memories. In Babylonia Abba Arrika and Mar Samuel, Hanasi's former pupils, opened academies of their own. They were enthusiastically received by the Eastern Jews, and many eager students crowded to their schools.

THE GEMARA

The Babylonian Jews soon found that the Palestinian Mishna was awkward since it had not been designed originally for their particular situation. Despite Hanasi's formal closing of the Mishna, it was obvious that changes would have to be made. A new exegetical system was now developed to become known as *Gemara* (supplement).

The Gemara was a rehashed Mishna, but propagated in Aramaic rather than Hebrew. Under cover of clarifying the Mishna, the new custodians, known as the *Amoras* (reasoners) boldly amplified it and initiated more new departures from divine truth. The Tannas of the Mishna had regarded the Bible as the text and their Mishna as the commentary; the Amoras took the Mishna as the received text and the Gemara as the commentary. Thus, at one swoop, all the encrustations of the Mishna were raised to quasi-divine status. In due course the Gemara was looked upon as being as authoritative as the Torah itself. From A.D. 300 to 600 all Jewish thought was dominated by the new Babylonian academies, and, like the Mishna before it, the Gemara kept growing and expanding with the passage of time.

It seems incredible to us today, but it is a fact that, for the most part, the entire body of the oral law, vast and complex as it had become, was transmitted by memory. For hundreds of years, from

long before the birth of Christ, the Mishna and then the Gemara
had been committed to memory by the rabbis and had been taught
orally. To make sure that no mistakes crept in, and to safeguard
the oral law against the insertion of the private opinions of the
scholars, it was required that each opinion quoted be supported
by reference to the appropriate authority.

THE EMERGENCE OF THE TALMUD

In the fifth century a time of upheaval overtook the world, and
persecution once more threatened the Jews. What would happen
if those who carried the oral law in their prodigious memories
were to be killed? The beloved oral law would be lost to posterity.
Despite an ancient ban, it must be written down. The process took
nearly two centuries. The completed work was called the *Talmud*
(Learning).

The idea behind the Talmud itself had been conceived a century
before by the Palestinian rabbis. Although the Babylonian Gemara
had been growing and expanding, the Palestinians had not been
idle. They began work on their own Gemara. Their Talmud was
finished about 395, about a century before the Babylonian Talmud.
The Palestinian Talmud ended about the fifth century when
Jewish life in Palestine virtually came to an end.

The work of combining the text of the Mishna and all existing
Gemaras, of reconciling them and of committing them to writing,
was no small task. A school of experts, familiar both with Aramaic
and Hebrew, was chosen. It was led by a genius named Ashi
(352-427), the head of the Sura academy. Ashi followed the example of the Palestinian rabbis who had anchored their Talmud to
Hanasi's Mishna. Ashi's work was done so thoroughly that the
very word *Talmud* is associated with him. His successor, Rabina II
(474-499), published the Talmud as one standard text for the first
time.

The Talmud is divided into three parts. It comprises the
Halacha, the law, which is concerned with a variety of complicated
legal matters; the *Aggada*, a series of philosophical discussions on
morals and piety; and *Midrash*, the sermons, made up of Bible
stories, memorable sayings, and stories of various kinds.

The Talmud was declared closed in the year 500 by Mar Jose,
about whom little is known. But that did not mean that the rabbis
were through tinkering with the truth. There now arose a new

school of experts known as the *Saborim*. Those scholars made it
their business to deliver opinions about the Talmud. Not content
with that, they also edited it, expounded and restyled it, added
their opinions to it under the pen names of departed authorities,
and reorganized the whole thing.

THE GAONS

By the year 700 there were two leading academies, one at Sura
and the other at Pumbaditha in the Muslim empire. The Muslims,
who had given recognition to the Jews in their midst, granted lim-
ited *political* power to the exilarchs, the Jewish leaders, and a
measure of *judicial* power to the Saborim. Those judicial leaders
were known as Gaons (Your Eminence) and were to flourish for
about three and a half centuries (689-1038). Before long the
Gaons became international jurists for Jews all over the Diaspora,
and questions were brought to them from various parts of the
Jewish world. The result was that, by the tenth century, the
Babylonian Talmud had become the common law of the Diaspora.

History was still on the march, and the Jews were squeezed out
of the Islamic world into feudal Europe. There they came in contact with Jews who had managed to survive somehow without the
Talmud. Confronted with the Babylonian Talmud, the European
Jews had a decision to make. Should they adopt the Talmud, or
should they continue as they were? It was Rabbi Shlomo Itzhaki,
commonly known as Rashi (1040-1105) whose influence swung
the balance.

THE TOSAPHAT

Rashi could clearly see that the Babylonian Talmud, as it stood,
did not relate to European Jews because, for one thing, they did
not know Aramaic. What was needed was a Talmud the Jews of
Europe could understand. He set to work to translate the Talmud
into Hebrew, unblushingly tossing in French words where the
Hebrew vocabulary failed. He sparked a new interest in the Talmud and, once again, the riggers and innovators got to work. A
new series of Talmudic commentaries emerged known as *Tosaphot*
(Additions). Then, at that point, the Talmud was finally closed.

No more changes, no more additions, no more footnotes! The Talmud had arrived. It had completely ousted the Torah as the prime source of authority among the Jews.

Next to Rashi, the man who did the most to carry the Talmud into Europe and saddle it on the Jews of the European Diaspora was a Moroccan rabbi named Alfasi (1013-1103), who had fled persecution in Morocco to take up his abode in Spain. He saw that changes would need to be made in the Talmud if ever it was really to suit Europeans. He decided to codify it. He set to work discarding irrelevant laws, abridging, summarizing, and importing views from the Palestinian Talmud. He ended up giving the Jews of Europe a workable legal code.

MAIMONIDES AND THE MISHNAH TORAH

Others followed his lead. The greatest of the later commentators on the Talmud was the Spanish Jew Maimonides (1135-1204), a man who had a warm appreciation for the best of both Islamic and Christian civilization.

Maimonides was court physician to Saladin, caliph of Egypt. He had chosen that over the same position offered him by the colorful Richard the Lionhearted. Maimonides was a powerful thinker. His influence extended far beyond the Jewish world. Among Jews he reigned supreme and was frequently consulted by world Jewry on all matters of law and ethics. Upon his death the Jews coined a proverb about him: "From Moses to Moses, there arose none like Moses" (a maxim based upon his full name, Moses ben Maimon).

Maimonides's great work, so far as the Jews were concerned, was his *Mishna Torah* ("The Second Torah"). That was the name he deliberately chose for his codification of the Talmud in the hope that its readers would be reminded that, ultimately, Talmudic authority rested on the Torah. He stated his objective very simply: "Everyone who will read the *Mishna Torah*, after the Written Law, will know from it the whole Oral Law and will not have to study any intermediate book."[1] He desired to set before the layman an understandable and available Talmud. His finished work ran to fourteen volumes. In the process of writing it, he subjected all the Talmud's allegations and recorded miracles to the searching test of his own rationalistic mind.

PROBLEMS WITH THE TALMUD

By now, however, the horizons of the Christian world were expanding and those of the Jewish world were contracting. The Jews of eastern Europe found themselves herded into ghettos. The narrow horizons of that new, parochial world produced narrow minds. The rabbis who devised Talmudic rules suitable for the ghetto were mediocre men who had a passion for trivia. Jewish life was cast by them into iron ritual. There was a right way to tie a shoelace or kill a chicken; sexes must be segregated in the synagogue; men must cover their heads. That was no time for great academies; what was needed was a handbook, something that would give instant answers to everything.

It was not surprising that there should be such a development. The Talmud was vast, cumbersome, intricate, detailed. It had replaced the crisp 613 laws of Moses with decisions and opinions and rulings running into hundreds of thousands of laws. Even so, given a particular topic, marriage for instance, no Jew could say with authority exactly what the law was. There was need for someone to come up with a miniature Talmud, something that would spell out simply just what the Talmud really did say about marriage, divorce, inheritance, adoption, ownership, business procedures, ritual cleanliness—everything. What was needed was a skilled woodsman who could cut through the tangled undergrowth, hew down the worthless trees, and trim the good ones down to size.

THE SHULCAN ARUCH

The man for the job was Joseph Caro (1488-1575), a Spanish Jew who settled in Safed just north of Jerusalem. Caro founded a small academy and published a book. He was a mystic and claimed he was inspired by an angel. His book was called *Shulcan Aruch* (The Prepared Table). In it he set forth instant answers to all matters relating to ghetto life so that Jews could flip a page and find out just what the Talmud required them to do. Some people thought he was inspired, others ruled him a crank.

His chief critic was Moses Isserles (1525-1572). With their penchant for synthesizing the opposing views of their rabbis, the Jews soon came out with an edition of *Shulcan Aruch* incorporating the comments of Isserles. The combined work is regarded by orthodox Jews to this day as the authoritative legal code of Judaism. One positive thing Caro's work did accomplish was to make it possible for each ghetto to govern itself. One negative result of Caro's work was that Jewish life became more and more circumscribed because everything had to fit within the cramping compass of Caro's code. The Talmud had now become the Bible of Judaism, and any departure from it was apostasy.

NOTE

1. Maimonides, cited in Abba Eban, *My People: The Story of the Jews* (New York: Random, 1968), p. 159. See also Max Dimont, *The Indestructible Jews,* new rev. ed. (New York: New American Library, Signet, 1971), pp. 206-7.

7

THE RELIGIOUS JEW: REVOLTS
AGAINST THE TALMUD

The story of Judaism, as with the story of Christianity or any other faith, is not simple and straightforward. The looms run on day and night weaving the fabric, but here and there are interlaced significant strands, some running with the warp, some with the woof. One such strand, and an attractive and colorful strand it is, can be seen in the *Karaite* revival. It starts off as a colorful strand, but in the end it shades off to a dull and disappointing gray.

Another strand that weaves its way in and out of the fabric is a mysterious one, the *Cabbala*, a sinister strand marked with the occult. We can trace its twisted course, now running off here to produce a series of brilliant philosophers and scientists, now plunging off there into the grossest superstition.

THE KARAITE REVOLT

The Karaite revolt began in Mesopotamia and lasted four hundred years. Its founder was Anan ben David (740-800), the legitimate heir to the throne of the Babylonian exilarch and sometimes called "the Jewish Luther." Because of his known anti-Talmudic views the Babylonian Jews opposed his succession. Anan left Babylonia and settled in Jerusalem, where he founded a new synagogue and set about accusing the Talmudists of corrupting Judaism by adding all their countless and complicated interpretations to the Torah. He called for a rejection of everything the Talmud had foisted on Judaism and a return to simple Bible study. It seemed for the moment that the Karaite revival might restore the Torah to its leading place in Jewish thought.

Since Christ has made "an end to the law," no return to the Torah as such can be a return to reality, as the Karaite revival soon proved. The Karaites called for reinstatement of the Torah's

77

ritualistic obligations, long discarded by the Talmudists. The law of Moses was given some fourteen or fifteen hundred years before the birth of Christ. To expect a people once again to live literally by the Torah was asking the impossible.

Nevertheless, the Karaites tried. Anan abolished the fixed calendar that had been in use since the middle of the fourth century. He demanded that all fires be extinguished prior to the Sabbath—a foolish rule in lands where severe winter climates prevailed. He called for an end to the Diaspora and an immediate return of all Jews to Palestine.

The immediate rabbinic answer was to ignore the Karaite revolt, but that would not do. When Benjamin Nenawendi came along and consolidated Anan's revolt, transforming it into a popular movement, the new sect began to spread. More and more Jews joined "the Children of the Bible." The Talmudists took alarm and denounced the movement, but that did not stop it. What was needed was something to take the wind out of its sails.

THE RABBINIC COUNTERATTACK

They found their answer in the person of Saadiah Gaon (882-942). His attack on Karaism was threefold. First of all he translated the Bible into Arabic so that the common people, those most influenced by Karaism, could read the Bible for themselves and thus be liberated from dependence on Karaite teachers. Next, he admitted that Karaism had a point to make. He picked up its salient features and tacked them onto the Talmud. Finally he brought the weight of his own vast learning to bear upon Karaism itself. He pointed out its errors and exploited its weaknesses. He pointed out that Anan's imposition of a literal application of the rules of the Torah really resulted in the propagation of a new "Talmud." That new Talmud, however, was far more inflexible than the one against which Anan revolted in the first place. The Karaist philosophy did not die quickly, but in time it subsided. Today it is practically extinct.

CABBALISM

As persecutions against Jews increased in severity during the Middle Ages, the Jews retreated more and more into mysticism. The pendulum swung away from the rationalism of Maimonides to the extreme mysticism of the Cabbala.

For centuries Cabbalism had crept down the back alleys of Judaism. It was an exotic blend of superstition, false hermeneutics, astrology, and spiritism. Cabbalists claimed that the *Cabbala* (Revelation) was given at the same time as the Torah. It was not for the common people, however, but for chosen mystics. Like the oral law it grew and grew with the passage of time. It fed on pseudoprophecy, superstition, myth, numerology, and assorted odds and ends of heresy.

Cabbalism surfaced in the form of Gnosticism in the early days of Christianity and was put down vigorously by Paul in his letter to the Colossians and by John in his first epistle. It arose again in the Middle Ages as a welcome narcotic for the fugitive Jews who had been driven out of Spain and who were unwanted misfits in the world and objects of hatred and persecution. Those Jews sought refuge in the Cabbala. They thought its mysticism and occultism would open the door of knowledge and help them understand their strange destiny in the world.

Two sparks ignited that new fire, now to be fanned into a flame in the world of the Jew. The first was the publication of the *Book of Formation* in the ninth century. Supernatural powers were supposed to reside in the letters of the Hebrew alphabet. A mystical significance lurked in the very forms of the letters themselves, in the sounds that resulted when they were spoken, in their numerical value (each letter of the Hebrew alphabet is also a number), and in their position when written on the page.

Cabbalists would juggle with the letters of the Hebrew alphabet for hours on end, moving them this way and that in the hope that they might stumble upon the ultimate secret of God. When the four letters of the tetragrammaton (YHWH—"Jehovah"), the ineffable name of God, would suddenly form on the page before him, the Cabbalist would know he was in the presence of God.

The second spark was also a book, the *Zohar*, written in Spain about 1250. It was written for the enlightened ones, written to offer an ecstatic experience of God. Its teachings could not be grasped with the mind; they had to be perceived intuitively with the heart. Those initiated into its mysteries moved further and further away from the real world into a world of the imagination. Between God in all His immensity and man in all his insignificance the Zohar placed ten spheres of divine manifestation—the old Gnostic heresy. God was said to emerge from His vast, secret, unknowable immensity through those ten spheres, and the initiated man could draw near to God through those same spheres. The *Zohar* was written in the form of a commentary on the Torah, the Song of Solomon, and the books of Ruth and Lamentations. Initiates into the *Zohar* dealt in covert allusions; in magic formulas, in theosophy, and in mystical speculation.

In time, Cabbalism broke into two main streams. One stream was channeled into western Europe, where it took on a saner form and where, eventually, it actually helped inspire modern philosophy and science. The other stream flowed on into eastern Europe, where it plunged over the falls into gross superstition.

HASIDISM

Better than either Karaism or Cabbalism was Hasidism, a charismatic form of Judaism that spread joy and sunshine into the gloomy alleys of Judaism, but which was also seen by the rabbis as just as great a threat to their authority as Karaism or Christianity.

Hasidism first flowered among the Jews of eastern Europe. Pressure from the Gentiles was being brought upon the world of the Jews. Within the Jewish world itself, in the aftermath of the Cabbalistic disaster, the rabbis were tightening the reigns. No wonder the Hasidic doctrine of joy, optimism, and zeal struck fire in the cold lives of Poland's Jews.

The founder of Hasidism was Israel ben Eliezer (1700-1760), better known as Baal Shem Tov (Master of the Good Name), usually abbreviated into the name *Besht*. The actual word *hasid* means "pious man," although the Besht was more of a student of nature and the Cabbala than a great rabbi. He had a magnetic personality, and people attached themselves to him and to his cause with fanatical devotion. Moreover, he was reputed to be a man of great integrity both in his belief and his behavior.

His religious emphasis was on emotion rather than intellect. He urged his disciples to find strength through joy and to seek God in singing and dancing. Away with dry-as-dust studies, away with dead rituals! Find God through prayer. Pray anywhere, anytime, not just at certain required times of the day—and not in formal prayers! Pray from the heart! Let prayer be the soul's spontaneous overflow, and let it be poured out in music and words.

The Talmudists excommunicated the Besht and his followers.

But they might as well have excommunicated the sun. The Besht had struck the right chord. He offered the masses of lower class Jews an escape from inferiority and from their subservience to the rich and learned. His words spread like a prairie fire throughout Poland. People came in thousands to hear him, to receive his blessing, to join him in ecstatic prayer. Soon miracles were attributed to him. Class distinctions were abolished at his meetings. People from all strata of society joined in popular emotional worship.

One of the Besht's disciples was the learned Rabbi Dov Ber. He too surrounded himself with disciples, and, after the death of the Besht, spread Hasidism all over eastern Europe until the revival embraced about half of the Jews living there. Opposition to Hasidism by the rabbinical establishment was unremitting, and in the end the movement died out for lack of organization and leadership.

HASIDISM SUPPRESSED

The fiercest opposition to Hasidism came from Lithuania. The rabbis there were very much afraid that Hasidism would permanently undermine their authority. They found their champion living in Vilna, the capital of Lithuania. In the past, Talmudism had flourished so verdantly in that city that it was known as the "Jerusalem of Lithuania." The city's most respected rabbi was Elijah ben Solomon (1720-1797), better known as the Vilna Gaon (Your Excellency of Vilna). The man himself was a prodigy. He had mastered the Torah by the time he was eight and the Talmud by the time he was nine. He was probably the last of the great Talmudic scholars.

The Vilna Gaon threw himself wholeheartedly into the fight against Hasidism. He considered Hasidic solutions to Jewish problems to be unworthy of Judaism and the rankest heresy. He forced the Hasidic leaders in Vilna to do public penance and to watch as he burned their writings and excommunicated their sect. His methods proved worse than useless. He might as well have tried to stop a flood with a baseball bat. All he did was polarize the rift between the establishment and the masses. He had the sense to recognize that and set off on a new tack. He undertook reforms of Judaism designed to destroy the foundations on which Hasidism was built.

First he called for simpler prayers in the synagogues, throwing out many of the complicated and meaningless poems that had filled the prayer books. He turned his attention to the intricate and senseless arguments dear to the heart of so many Talmudic scholars. He taught his students to concentrate on the true meaning of the Talmud rather than use it as a stage upon which to show off their scholarship. He insisted, too, that Jewish learning include secular subjects, not just religious subjects. From boyhood he had been interested in science, and he encouraged his students to translate scientific works into Hebrew. The Vilna Gaon paved the way for the coming *Haskala* (Enlightenment).

By 1850 the winds of Hasidism had blown themselves out. The Jews found themselves shut up in ghettos and married to a fossilized religion. They themselves had degenerated into caricatures complete with the traditional black hat, caftan, and dangling earlocks. The Jew was no longer the man of affairs, the courtier, the statesman; he was a Shylock, a Fagin, the Jew of Shakespeare and Dickens. The Haskala brought fresh air into the intellectual stagnation of the ghetto.

THE HASKALA

The Haskala was written in Yiddish and Hebrew. Yiddish was a mongrel German written in Hebrew characters, which served as a bridge by which the Jews, imprisoned in the ghetto, could cross over intellectually and make fresh contact with the real world. Those of the Haskala who wrote in Yiddish specialized in escape novels in which they ridiculed life in the ghetto. Those who wrote in Hebrew specialized in poetry and essays that attacked Talmudism as the true source of the unhappiness and the social ills of the Jews. Talmudism, they said, was destroying Judaism's very soul.[1]

There were new stirrings among the youth, who dropped their pacifism and joined underground movements. The Haskala went on for nearly a century until those within the ghetto and Pale of Settlement saw the point. Their persecutions and sufferings were not necessarily an inescapable part of Jewish destiny. The Talmud was not to be equated with God's law, and Hasidism was not the spiritual paradise it was cracked up to be; what was needed was a more realistic Judaism. The Haskala paved the way for modern orthodox Judaism and also for Zionism.

MOSES MENDELSSOHN

One of the early leaders of the Enlightenment was a hunchback, Moses Mendelssohn (1729-1786), and he was certainly its most influential spokesman. He was born in Dessau in the ghetto, the son of a poor Torah scribe. His teacher introduced him to the Bible, to the Talmud, and to Maimonides. Despite his handicaps, Mendelssohn possessed two useful assets—a charming personality and a rare gift for making friends. He became a renowned philosopher and moved in high social circles. He could clearly see the dilemma of the ghetto Jew: if the Jew stayed in the ghetto, he would continue to degenerate, but if he were to be thrown headlong into the Gentile world he would simply be assimilated. Mendelssohn resolved to reform Judaism.

His first step was to translate the Torah into German, but he devised a clever innovation. He wrote in German, but he used Hebrew characters for writing down the translation. With this translation he hoped to prod the Jewish people into a new awareness of the great, wonderful world outside the ghetto walls. His choice of the Torah rather than the Talmud was deliberate. He saw Talmudism as a smothering shroud thrown over everything Jewish. The Torah, on the other hand, pointed to the true foundations of Judaism.

Not surprisingly, the rabbis saw his translation of the Torah as a threat to their authority. Worse, they feared that very contact with the outside world that Mendelssohn espoused. Once Jews made contact with the wicked world of the Gentiles they would certainly be swept away into utter worldliness. Worse, contact with secular education would cause Jews to abandon Judaism. So the rabbis banned Mendelssohn's translation of the Torah. The broad-minded philosopher was undeterred and went right on teaching that the Jewish religion should be concerned with eternal truths and not with archaic rituals and traditions.

REFORM JUDAISM

Thus there developed the three main parts of modern Judaism: Reform, Orthodox, and Conservative. A succession of Reform Jewish writers marched down the trail blazed by Mendelssohn to help clear Judaism of its Talmudic foliage and to allow the light of "modern thought" to stream in. Those men laid the foundations for a modern, streamlined Judaism. They discarded the use of phylacteries and other useless rituals, shortened synagogue services, dumped the use of meaningless Aramaic prayers, and debunked the myth that the Talmud was inspired. They made it possible for those Jews who were once again moving into the mainstream of the Gentile world to live comfortably with their Judaism. That reform Judaism was brought over to the United States at the turn of the century, and it soon established itself in that country as though native-born.

ORTHODOX JUDAISM

Orthodox Russian Jews, migrating to the United States (1880-1920), ran headlong into reform Judaism. The meeting of Russian and American Jew was a shock for both. The American, looking askance at the Russian, could hardly believe that such anachronisms could really exist. The Russians, looking with horror at American Jews, could hardly believe that apostasy could have reached such a height.

As so often happens in such cases, the children of the Russian immigrants soon felt differently from their parents. They felt the magnetic pull of the great, pulsating, exciting country to which they had come, and before long were looking through American eyes at their bearded, backward parents. The Russian Jews, faced with the rebellion of their children, were wise enough to make concessions. They modernized the outward forms of their faith without changing its essential nature. Their brand of Judaism became known as Orthodox Judaism.

CONSERVATIVE JUDAISM

One other form of Judaism has emerged in the United States known as Conservative Judaism. It is a mix of ritualistic orthodox Judaism and the modern reform movement. In Conservative Judaism some of the dietary laws have been relaxed. The three brands of Judaism coexist in the United States on more or less friendly terms.

JUDAISM'S MISSING LINK

The real answer to Judaism, of course, is the Lord Jesus Christ. The whole legalistic growth of Talmudism is the outcome of the Roman scattering of Israel. Faced with biblical commands con-

cerning the sacrifices, the Temple, and living on the land of Israel—
a law that would no longer work in the everyday world outside
Palestine—and determined to have nothing to do with Jesus, the
Jewish rabbis devised a new system of legalism to replace both
Temple and sacrificial systems. It kept the Jews Jewish, but it did
not draw them any nearer to Christ.

NOTE

1. Some of the writers who shaped the *Haskala* were Havim Bialik (1873-
   1934), Saul Tchernichovsky (1875-1943), Mendele Mocher Sforim
   (1836-1917), and Franz Rosenweig (1886-1929).

8

THE RELIGIOUS JEW: THE
PSEUDO-MESSIAHS

The rabbis believed that the Messiah would appear 3,700 years after the Creation. The Hebrew calendar, of course, is different from the Christian calendar.

The Jewish calendar was an extraordinarily complicated mechanism for recording the passing of time. Instead of fixing the length of a year either by adapting to a solar or lunar year, the Hebrew calendar combined both, along with certain embellishments, to make up a "soli-lunar" year. That created enormous complications, because solar years and lunar years have different numbers of days. One ancient scholar measured the solar year at $12\frac{7}{9}$ lunar months; roughly 365 days. Other scholars claimed that the Jewish year of twelve lunar months totalled between 353 and 355 days (some said it was exactly 354 days, 8 hours, and 876 parts). The lunar year was shorter than the solar year by about eleven days. At some point the difference had to be adjusted. Formulating methods for bringing the solar and lunar years into line was called intercalation ("pregnancy" in Hebrew). It developed into a top-secret science.[1]

The Hebrew calendar purports to date from the creation of the world. The year 3700 in the Hebrew calendar coincides with the first century A.D. Actually the rabbis were not far off. Christ did appear about the time He was expected.

THE TRUE MESSIAH

The Jews rejected Jesus as Messiah, as is recorded in the four gospels and the book of Acts. They persisted in their rejection even though large numbers of Jews, including many priests, believed in Him. That rejection, so far as the Jewish people are concerned, has been stubborn and unyielding ever since.

The Jews have invented the most astonishing tissue of fabrications to explain away Jesus of Nazareth. He was an Essene, they say, whose date and place of birth is uncertain and whose ministry was an embarassment to the Jews because it threatened to embroil them with the Romans. He was taken into protective custody by the Jews to protect Him from Himself. Under pressure, the Jews then surrendered Him to their Roman masters who crucified Him.

The story of His resurrection is made out to be a lie put about by His disciples. The story of Jesus, as found in the gospels, they say, cannot be trusted because individual gospels each give only part of the story, and the four accounts when put together contain numerous contradictions.[2] Christianity, they claim, was the invention of "an ugly little Jew" by the name of Paul, a man who had repeated hallucinations and who suffered from malaria and epileptic seizures.

The Jews have thus explained away the two greatest men who ever appeared in their history, Jesus of Narazeth and Saul of Tarsus. Such whitewashing of the facts (and that by reputable Jewish historians) reveals their a priori prejudice against the Lord Jesus.

For fifteen hundred years the name of Jesus was never mentioned in the ghetto. In early rabbinic literature He is sometimes referred to as "The Man" without mentioning His name. In all those fifteen hundred years not a line was written by a representative Jew about Jesus either in Hebrew or in any other language. The silence was complete. Occasionally an outsider from the establishment, such as Spinoza, had something to say about Jesus, but such men made no impression on the Jews.

Official Jewish silence about Jesus is the more marked because the Jews never hesitate to speak about Muhammed and Buddha, who are often mentioned and discussed even by the most pious Jews. No doubt the attitude of many in the Christian church down through the ages has done nothing to dispose Jews toward a serious consideration of Jesus as Messiah. With the dawn of the twentieth century Jews have been more open in discussing Jesus, but even so they go little farther than acknowledging Him to have been a great ethical teacher.

The Talmud contains some truly vicious attacks on the Lord Jesus. It teaches that He was an impostor, a wicked man, a sorcerer, and even an idolater, a *Masis-Umadiack* (a falsifying tempter), and a *Manzer* (a bastard). It says that He is in hell, and that His name should not be mentioned without saying *"Yimack-Shemoh-Wezrickroe"* (May His name be blotted out, and His memory). The New Testament is called *Avon Gilyon* ("margin of evil" or "blank page of sin"). In addition, the Talmud contains impure stories about Jesus. The precious name of Jesus (Yeshua), which means "Jehovah-Savior," has been changed to *Yeshu*, which is made up of the initial letters of the above curse. It means "Let his name and memory be blotted out." Tourists in Israel should listen carefully if they have a Jewish guide. He will often use the word "Yeshu" when referring to Jesus. The uninitiated think he is saying "Yeshua."

EARLY PSEUDO-MESSIAHS

With such a history of hatred toward Jesus, the true Messiah, it is not surprising that the Jews should have become open to the deceptions of a host of unscrupulous messianic quacks. Having rejected the true Messiah, they have become targets of false messiahs. And some of them have been strange characters, as even the Jews themselves confess.

THEUDAS

Ten years after the crucifixion of Jesus a pretender appeared by the name of Theudas. He raised an immediate and numerous following. The Roman procurator Cuspius Fadus made short work of him, cutting off his head and killing his disciples.

BAR KOCHBA

The next false messiah was the famous Bar Kochba (Simon bar Koziba). Bar Kochba was a born leader. He was enormously strong, possessed a magnetic personality, enjoyed life to the full, and had the ability to inspire his followers with fanatical devotion. His messianic claims, which were not based on a single shred of Scripture, were endorsed nevertheless by the rabbi Akiba, one of the great Jewish religious leaders of the day.

Akiba was so carried away by the messianic speculation of the time that he hailed Bar Kochba as the "Star out of Jacob" and assured the deluded people that Bar Kochba was the true Messiah, the son of David. Akiba's endorsement of the new messiah was all that was needed to sweep the Jews off their feet. Jews of every political and religious persuasion rushed to rally behind Bar Kochba's banner. Only Christian Jews refused to join the new mass movement.

This rebellion, which broke out in A.D. 132, took the Romans by surprise. The Jews defeated every force the Romans sent against them until, at length, the Roman Emperor Hadrian summoned Julius Severus from Britain and sent him to put down the revolt. The Jews defeated him, too. That did it! The tough and seasoned veteran decided on total war. He systematically destroyed everything in his path, slaughtering the civilian population as he went. For two years the carnage and devastation went on until Bar Kochba's forces were annihilated. The false messiah was slain, and his false prophet, Akiba, was seized and tortured to death. Jews were banished from Judea, and Palestine was put out of bounds for Jews.

SETTING NEW DATES

The Pharisees were disappointed. Their intellectuals had set the date of 3700 as the year for the coming of Christ. But Jesus had not been to their liking, Theudas had been a mere flash-in-the-pan, and Bar Kochba had let them down. Now what could they do?

They changed the date. The rabbis revised the creation calendar and refigured the date for the coming of Messiah. The new calculations set a date in the fifth century. One Jewish scholar, Hanasi, declared that the time would be exactly 365 years after the destruction of the Temple (A.D. 70); that is, in the year A.D. 435. Rabbi Hanina, another Jewish scholar, set the date for the year A.D. 470 instead. He wanted a round four hundred years after the destruction of the Temple for the maturing of his predictions. Sure enough, as the time approached so did a rash of false messiahs.

MOSES OF CRETE

The most promiment pseudo-messiah was Moses of Crete (c. 440-490). That pretender was able to convince the entire Jewish population of the island of his messianic claims. He would lead them to the promised land just as Moses the lawgiver had done, he declared. He would smite the Mediterranean as Moses had smitten the Red Sea, and the people would walk on dry land to

Palestine. On the appointed day the Jews assembled on a prom-
ontory jutting out into the sea and leaped boldly into the waters.
The waters refused to cooperate, and the majority were drowned
including Moses himself, who had neglected to learn how to swim.

ABU ISSA

The next messianic pretender was a tailor by the name of Abu
Issa of Isfahan. By this time Islam had overrun the East and the
meteoric rise of the prophet Muhammed from the ranks of the
simplest and poorest of the people excited Jewish expectations.
They now believed that the Messiah would be preceded by Elijah
and that when he did come he would have miraculous powers.
This time the world of the Gentiles seemed to be in step with the
world of the Jew, for Persia had collapsed and Rome had withdrawn from Asia. Anything could happen; the end of the world
was in sight.

The advent of this ignorant tailor with the imposing name Abu
Issa (Father of Jesus) fanned expectations (c. A.D. 700). Abu Issa
told his followers that Moses, Muhammad, and Jesus were all
prophets but he, himself, was the true Messiah. He would free the
Jews from the rule of the caliph, he promised. He would toss the
Muslims out of Palestine and lead the Jews back to the promised
land.

An army of 10,000 men was mustered, and the new messiah set
forth on his mission. The deluded masses believed fully in the
messiah's miraculous powers. He would draw a magic circle
around his soldiers, he promised, so that the Muslim soldiers would
not be able to harm them. The battle was joined and ended in
disaster. Abu Issa committed suicide, his followers fled, and another pretender was exposed.

SERENUS

Abu Issa was followed in the year 720 by Serenus, a messiah
somewhat lacking in originality for he, too, promised to lead his
followers to the promised land. The Jews had learned nothing by
past failures and came running to his standard and marched
blithely in his train. He was captured by Caliph Yazid II, where-
upon he recanted and assured the caliph that he had never meant
to incite rebellion. His only thought had been to embarrass the

Jews. The caliph handed him over to the Jews for punishment, and presumably he was put to death.

MORE PSEUDO-MESSIAHS

The twelfth century produced another crop of pseudo-messiahs, one of whom arose in Yemen in 1172.[3] He stands in sharp contrast with the cowardly Abu Issa, for when captured and brought before the king he boldly stated that, if he were to be beheaded, he would at once rise from the dead. He tempted providence too far. The ruler cut off his head and, of course, he did not rise from the dead. Perhaps he was just canny enough to ensure a speedy death rather than an agonizing one at the hands of the king's torturers.

ABRAHAM ABULFIA

Next came Abraham Abulfia (1240-1291), the son of a prominent family of Spanish Jews. At the age of eighteen he headed east to find the river Sambatyon, where the lost ten tribes were supposed to be. He began to hear voices. One such voice spoke to him when he was on a pilgrimage in Jerusalem, told him he was a prophet, and ordered him back to Spain to spread the news. He tried his hand at prophecy with such dismal results that the authorities expelled him from the country.

On his way to Rome again another voice spoke to him. This time he was told to go to Rome and convert Pope Nicholas III to Judaism. Convinced he was inspired, Abulfia set off on his ambitious mission. The shock proved too much for the pope, who died within the week when told what Abulfia wanted him to do. Abulfia himself, needless to say, ended up in a papal dungeon with the knowledge he was to burn at the stake. He must have been quite a talker, however, for he accomplished that feat rare in history of talking himself out of the clutches of Rome.

He showed up in Sicily next, and once more his "voice" spoke to him. One would have thought that by now he would have recognized it as the voice of a lying spirit, but he did not. This time the voice plainly told him he was the Messiah. Although he managed to attract a number of followers, Abulfia seems to have been the most innocuous of messiahs, for he crumpled under the ridicule and opposition of tougher-minded Jews, and, when excommunicated by the rabbis, he left Sicily and vanished into oblivion.

MOSES BOTAREL

Moses Botarel was yet another self-proclaimed messiah who managed to receive the endorsement of a prominent Jewish scholar. Hasdai Crescas, an opponent of Maimonides, supported his claim. To prove his messiahship, Moses Botarel challenged the Spanish king to throw him into a burning fiery furnace, just as Nebuchadnezzar had done to Meshach, Shadrach, and Abednego. History does not record what happened, but since he was never heard of again the Spanish king probably picked up the gauntlet Botarel threw down and had the poor fellow roasted to death.

ASHER-LEMMLIN

In 1502 Venice played host to the next pseudo-messiah. Asher-Lemmlin assured the Jewish community of Venice that he was Elijah, and that he had come to take them to the promised land in his chariot of fire. They must have been a very gullible crowd, for they believed him and prepared for the great day with prayer and fasting. Of course, the day dawned and nothing happened. It was the last straw for many of them. A considerable number reacted against Judaism altogether and were baptized into the Catholic church.

The popularity of pseudo-messiahs in the sixteenth and seventeenth centuries can probably be accounted for by the Cabbalistic teachings that had become popular among the Jews. The harshness and misery of life in the Jewish world made the Jews clutch at any straw, and their Cabbalistic beliefs predisposed many of them to accept at face value the wildest claims made by pretenders to the messianic throne.

DAVID REUBENI

One of the most colorful of the false messiahs of the time was David Reubeni (1490-1535). He was a swarthy, emaciated dwarf. He descended on the Jews from the East, speaking a brand of Hebrew that was almost unintelligible, and announced that he had been sent to speak for the lost tribe of Judah. His brother, the king of Khaibar, he said, had assembled an army of thousands of fierce Jewish warriors in the desert of Arabia behind the Turkish lines. The Jews were cautious this time and treated his claims with a wholesome skepticism.

In 1524 Reubeni went off to Rome, rode into the Vatican on a milk-white horse, created a minor sensation, and won an audience with Pope Clement VII. It was an opportune time for Reubeni, for Clement's world was in ruins. The Turks had taken Belgrade, and Malta and all of Europe cowered. Worse still, Protestantism was hammering at the very foundations of the Roman Catholic church. Reubeni seemed like an answer from heaven, for here was a man who claimed to have a considerable army behind the enemy's lines. The pope consulted his astrologers and discovered that the heavens smiled on a joint venture with the Jewish dwarf.[4] He gave the false prophet his papal blessing and sent him off to King John III of Portugal, a supposed expert on Khaibar, to solicit more practical aid in terms of guns and ships.

King John was impressed, so impressed indeed that he stopped persecuting Marranos and promised military aid to Reubeni. Just as he had taken Rome by storm, riding in triumph through its streets, hailed as the Messiah by men and women alike, so the new messiah now swept all before him in Portugal. Hysteria fell upon the nation. In numbers of communities fanatics fell into trances, saw visions, made prophetic statements, and drew attention to themselves for which they would afterward suffer.

Many Marranos threw off their pretended Christianity and hailed Reubeni as Messiah, and numbers of Christians, excited by the news of the coming of the Messiah, converted to Judaism. That was too much for King John and his priests. They decided it was high time Reubeni was dealt with. The brave messiah became alarmed, fled from Portugal, and abandoned his followers to a vengeful church.

SOLOMON MOLKO

But Reubeni had made one notable convert, Diego Pires (1500-1532) a high-born Marrano. At the time of Reubeni's advent, he was royal secretary in the high court of justice in Portugal. Diego Pires, an avid student of the Cabbala, was sure the time was ripe for the coming of the Messiah, and he was swept off his feet by the pretender. Pires sought an audience with him and was repulsed by the crafty dwarf. Pires was not surprised. After all, he was a Marrano and a hypocrite. No wonder the messiah had rejected him. He must throw off his cloak of Christianity, have himself circumcised, proudly proclaim himself a Jew, and adopt a Jewish name.

So Diego Pires became Solomon Molko, under which name he was soon to set up messiahship for himself. At first, however, he was content to be messiah's messenger. He had drawn too much attention to himself in Portugal, it seems, so he slipped out of the country and showed up in Palestine, where he created a wave of excitement among the rabbis. They listened in awe to the cultured Portugese Jew who spoke with such authority, who opened to them mysteries of which they knew nothing, and who made bold prophecies.

Success went to his head. He went to Italy and proclaimed himself messiah, preaching to vast crowds and finally arriving in Rome. In keeping with the best messianic traditions, Molko spent a month in beggar's rags, ministered to the poor, and visited the sick, the leprous, and the lame. His fame reached the gullible pope, who encouraged him, granting him immunity from the omnipresent and menacing Inquisition.

By this time the original pretender, Reubeni, was in Venice. The two messiahs decided to get together. Some of Molko's prophecies now seemed to be coming to pass, for there were floods in Rome, and a comet appeared which terrified the people. Portugal was shaken by an earthquake in January 1531, and Lisbon was severely damaged.

In 1532 Molko went to Rome again, joined forces with Reubeni, and set off with him to interview Emperor Charles V of the Holy Roman Empire. The time had come to offer him a firm alliance against the Turks. The pair of pseudo-messiahs read the cards wrongly, however, for Charles V was the last man to have dealings with Jewish messiahs. He had been crowned by the pope and was a rabid Catholic and a merciless tyrant. He kept the Inquisition busy throughout his domains day and night and scourged himself to the bone every Friday for the good of his soul. He cast jaundiced eyes on those Jewish messiahs.

Emperor Charles V of the Holy Roman Empire knew how to deal with Jews, messiahs or no. He tossed them into prison and summoned the Inquisition to make them talk. Molko refused to recant. He was the Messiah, he said. He would offer himself up as the redeemer of all mankind. The Inquisition obliged him by burning him at the stake. Reubeni's fate is less certain. He was carried off to Spain for some reason where he is supposed by some to have perished, presumably at the stake. Others say that he was able to escape.

SHABBATHAI ZEVI

A century later yet another pseudomessiah appeared. This time it was Shabbathai Zevi, born in Smyrna of Spanish immigrant parents in 1626. The world was once again ready for a messiah. The Thirty Years War and various natural disasters had ploughed up the fertile medieval soil. Jew and Gentile alike were ready for new superstitions and delusions.

Shabbathai was a handsome man with piercing eyes and a charismatic personality. He was married twice and divorced within the week by both wives for failing to consummate his marriage. He made the best of his enforced celibacy, however, by becoming an ascetic, performing the most vigorous penances, lacerating his flesh, and plunging into the icy sea in the dead of winter.

From earliest childhood Shabbathai had steeped himself in Cabbalistic mysticism, and, at an early age, showed signs of self-delusion. His asceticism brought him the reputation of being a holy man, and stories soon began to circulate that Shabbathai could perform miracles. With that the stage was set for him to become the next messiah.

In the year 1648, a year that was marked in Cabbalistic calculations as a year of miracles, Shabbathai announced himself as the Messiah to his Jewish compatriots by taking upon his lips the ineffable name of Jehovah, an action considered blasphemy by the Jews. That, together with his tirades against the Talmud, so shocked the Jewish community of Smyrna that they drove him out, but a prophet, after all, is not without honor save in his own country and among his own people.

Shabbathai was not to be daunted. He traveled throughout the Middle East preaching, praying, proclaiming himself the Messiah. The people flocked to him, rich and poor, scholar and fool, from India to England. At the height of his popularity over a million Jews are said to have believed in him, a third of the Jews of the world. In Salonika he had himself married to the Torah in a mystical ceremony that awed the Cabbalists but that so outraged the rabbis that they excommunicated him.

Driven out of Smyrna and Salonika, Shabbathai went to Egypt, swept Cairo off its feet, and triumphed everywhere. Then, tearing a page out of the history of Hosea, he married a harlot. The woman he chose was almost as colorful a character as he. The beautiful and vivacious Sarah came from Poland. Her parents had been slain by the Cossacks when she was a child of eight, and she had been raped. The unfortunate girl found refuge in a convent and was reared as a nun, but the drabness of that kind of life had no attractions for her. She fled the convent and became a prostitute in Amsterdam. There she fell under the spell of Shabbathian preachers and convinced herself that she was destined to be the messiah's bride. News of this reached the messiah himself. Despite his inability to consummate a marriage, Shabbathai lost no time in sending for Sarah. Their marriage attracted the attention of the world.

The messianic fever spread, and stories of Shabbathai's miracles were believed everywhere. He returned in triumph to Smyrna where he was greeted with hosannas: "Long live the messiah!" His fame spread throughout Europe, and members of some of Europe's greatest houses became his disciples. Samuel Pepys, the famous English socialite, jotted him down in his diary along with the other assorted items of interest he vacuumed up for posterity. He noted that there were Jews in London who were taking odds of ten to one that Shabbathai would be owned by the princes of the East as king of Jerusalem within two years.[5] In Amsterdam new prayer books were issued containing special prayers for Shabbathai.

In 1656 the self-deluded messiah headed for Constantinople, but it proved to be a wrong move. Disturbing rumors had preceded him that he had an army ready in Arabia to unleash against the sultan, but Shabbathai could not control the weather, and storms at sea made his voyage to Constantinople a hazard. It was a disheveled messiah who finally arrived, having been well nigh shipwrecked on the way. The sultan had been given sufficient time to decide upon his course of action against this unwanted Jewish messiah. As soon as Shabbathai arrived he was arrested.

But the sultan lost his nerve. He hesitated to put the popular Jew to death for fear he might make a martyr out of him. Instead, he imprisoned him in the fortress of Abydos, and there Shabbathai's star blazed forth. His followers flocked to him by the thousands, bringing him rich gifts so that he could live like a king.

Even his guards were seduced. Throughout the world, every Sabbath day, prayers were offered for Shabbathai.

The sultan took fresh counsel. Execution would only make Shabbathai a martyr, and imprisonment made him a hero. But exposure would render him harmless, reasoned the sultan. He therefore offered Shabbathai a choice between conversion to Islam or death. The sultan this time had the measure of his man. The latest messiah of the Jews chose Islam and changed his name to Muhammad Effendi. He was at once released from prison and appointed keeper of the royal door.

The conversion of Shabbathai to Islam shook his followers but did not destroy their faith. The messiah had stooped thus, they said, to reach and redeem the lowest of the low. A large number of his followers followed him into Islam. It soon turned out, however, that the new Muhammad Effendi could no more resist playing the messiah than could the old Shabbathai Zevi. The movement began to take fresh root, and this time the sultan imprisoned the messiah as a public nuisance. He remained in prison in Dulcigno in Albania until his death.

JACOB FRANK

Shabbathai's dubious mantle was picked up by a scoundrel, Jacob Frank (1726-1791). Frank was a traveling salesman from the Ukraine whose business took him to Turkey. While there he picked up the Shabbathai myth, studied the Cabbala, and evolved a new form of Shabbathaism. He decided that all messiahs were really incarnations one of another. David, Elijah, Jesus, Muhammad, and Shabbathai were simply one and the same person appearing in different ages in different forms. He himself would be the last and final messiah (c. 1740).

A Polish prophet named Leib Krysa heralded Frank's messianic claims, but this time there was a new satanic twist to the theology. Jacob Frank, it was revealed, was the second person of the trinity; a trinity comprising God the Father, Jacob Frank, and God the Holy Spirit. The Talmud was abolished, and redemption through sexual indulgence was proclaimed. Money poured in so that the messiah could live in a palace in a style fitting for so illustrious a being, and converts to the new cult cheered their lusty new messiah and joined in his orgies.

The Polish rabbis promptly excommunicated Frank and his followers and indignantly disassociated themselves from the adultery, incest, and licentiousness that formed the backbone of the movement. The Frankists appealed to the local Christian bishop for support, claiming their movement was being persecuted by the Jews because it exposed the Talmud. The Frankist attacks upon the Talmud delighted the Catholics, and in 1757 thousands of copies were publicly burned.

In 1759 Frank received a further revelation—he and his followers must convert to Christianity. The Frankists willingly proclaimed their belief in the Trinity, so the church received them warmly. Its ardor soon cooled when it found out just what the Frankists meant by the "Trinity." The church threw the messiah into prison and only refrained from burning him at the stake because his godfather was the king of Poland. They did keep him incarcerated for thirteen years, but then the Greek Orthodox Russians invaded Poland and the messiah was set free.

Jacob Frank the messiah, a free man once more, went to Austria where he set himself up in style. He was fawned upon by Viennese society and even found a patron in the Empress Maria Theresa. In the end he died of an apoplectic fit.

EVE FRANK

Jacob Frank had a daughter, a seductive temptress named Eve. She carried on the family specialty of duping the credulous. She adroitly combined immorality with religion, and her charisma was sufficient to keep her in the style to which she had been accustomed. With the passing of time the years robbed Eve of her bloom, and as her charms faded away so did her followers. She died in poverty in 1817, and with her the lingering ghost of Frankism vanished from the earth.

BAAL SHEM TOV

About the time that Jacob Frank was practicing his deceptions, another messiah was emerging in the same region of the Ukraine. Israel of Moldovia, better known as Baal Shem Tov (Master of the Good Name), was born of aged parents to whom, it was said, an angel had appeared to announce his coming. Shortly after his birth the child was orphaned.

Baal Shem Tov was poorly educated. As a boy he liked to roam the hills and commune with nature, and his contemporaries thought him lazy. His disciples later glossed over some of the less attractive details of his life. They depicted him as a man who slept during the day because he spent the long night hours poring over Cabbalistic literature and communing with God. His early manhood, they said, was spent in the wilderness performing miracles—he walked on the water as Jesus did, he caused a bush to burst into flames simply by looking at it (a greater than Moses was here), he exorcised evil spirits, healed the sick, made profligate women pure, spoke in parables. To the more critical, however, Baal Shem Tov was just a lazy lout.

He was twice married, first at the age of eighteen and then, after his wife's death, to the daughter of a wealthy man who disapproved of the marriage enough to disinherit his daughter. That did not deter Baal Shem Tov. He and his wife settled in the heart of the Carpathian mountains with all his worldly goods—a horse donated to him by his brother-in-law. There the budding messiah dug lime, which his wife hauled into town and sold.

When he was forty the same deceiving voice spoke to him that had spoken to other deluded messiahs. He was to announce to the world who he really was, throw off his present manner of life, and proclaim himself the messenger of God.

Since Baal Shem Tov had barely any education, he did not understand the hair-splitting niceties, the mental subtleties, the intricate arguments into which Talmudic Judaism had degenerated. They meant nothing to the average man and they meant nothing to him. He had no difficulty in writing them off as worthless.

Disciples gathered around him. He left no written scriptures behind him, so his teachings can be gathered only from the writings of his followers, who often embellished his ideas with their own. In essence the new messiah's teachings were pantheistic. God was to be approached not through Talmudic learning, but through prayer and faith. Never mind dull books! Sing and dance your way into God's grace. Never mind fasts and introspection. Don't wallow in misery. Clap your hands and be happy! Baal Shem Tov's gospel was one of experience, or ecstasy, not doctrine.

His original following was not large, but it was significant enough to attract the attention of the rabbis who excommunicated him. It was not until after Baal Shem Tov's death, when the movement he founded began to grow, that their real hostility began. When the master died in 1760 he had about 100,000 followers. The movement took such a hold that eventually it included about half the Jews of eastern Europe.

Baal Shem Tov seems to have been the most realistic and sane of all the Jewish pseudomessiahs. His success hinged upon the fact that his Hasidic-type movement offered the people an outlet for their emotions.

Baal Shem Tov's ideals degenerated after his death. Like all movements that decry doctrine and enthrone emotion, Hasidism sank swiftly into hysterical prayer and religious exhibitionism. His depreciation of learning bred contempt for scholarship.

In time a new breed of Hasidic rabbis took over the movement, the Zaddikim. Baal Shem Tov had taught, so they said, that holy men who achieved communion with God through faith, prayer, and mysticism should be regarded as prophets and venerated. In time the Zaddikim themselves were nearly worshiped.

Such have been the false messiahs of the Jews. There have been warrior messiahs like Bar Kochba, lunatics like Moses of Crete, fanatics like Abu Issa, cowards like Serenus, crackpots like Abulfia and Reubeni, turncoats like Shabbathai, sex maniacs like Jacob Frank, and ignorant enthusiasts like Baal Shem Tov. Colorful they might have been, Christlike they have never been. Not one of them fulfilled even the barest requirements of being the true Messiah—that He should be born in Bethlehem, of the tribe of Judah, of the family of David; that he should be virgin born, that He should be crucified and triumph over the tomb.

There is only one person in all of Hebrew history who qualifies to be Israel's Messiah. And His name is Jesus.

NOTES

1. D. Dayan, "The Hebrew Calendar—Catechism of Judaism," *Israel Magazine*, n.d., pp. 24-29.
2. Simon Greenleaf, American lawyer, educator, and royal professor of law at Harvard Law School, was in his day an acknowledged authority on jurisprudence on a par with Blackstone and Kent. He wrote a book that was used as a text in American law schools for a hundred years. After years of experience he also wrote a volume entitled *The Testimony of the Evangelists, Examined by the Rules of Evidence Administered in Courts of Justice,* reprint (Grand Rapids: Baker, 1965). In that book the renowned authority cross-examined Matthew, Mark, Luke, and John as he would have done in court and found them absolutely credible and reliable witnesses.

3. See Max Dimont, *Jews, God and History* (New York: New American Library, Signet, 1962), p. 278. See also Max Dimont, *The Indestructible Jews*, new rev. ed. (New York: New American Library, Signet, 1971), p. 199.
4. Dimont, *Jews, God and History*, p. 273.
5. Abram Leon Schar, *A History of the Jews* (New York: Random, Knopf, 1964), p. 243.

9

THE RELIGIOUS JEW: THE TRUE MESSIAH

Written deeply into the *Torah*, the *Neveeim*, and the *Kethuvim* (the Law, the Prophets, and the Writings), the three great divisions of the Hebrew Bible, is the confident expectation of a coming Messiah. He was to be the seed of the woman, the seed of Abraham, the seed of David. He was to be both a savior and a sovereign. The moral law depicted His perfect life; the sacrificial law pointed to His atoning death. In the Hebrew Scriptures He appears in direct prophecy, in picture and illustration, in type and shadow. News of His coming can be found everywhere in the Jewish Bible.

The many prophecies and foreshadowings of Him sometimes appear contradictory, for both the greatest of sufferings and the most spectacular glory are associated with Him. Some of the rabbis postulated *two* Messiahs as the only way to reconcile the differences—one Messiah to suffer and another one to reign. History has cleared up the difficulty. There was to be one Messiah but two comings—a coming to redeem and a later coming to reign.

Many books could be, and indeed have been, written to show how persistently those themes occur in the Tennach, the Jewish Bible and our "Old Testament." In this chapter we are going to give just a few examples. Let us go back, once more, to the beginning.

Cain and Abel

The first man to die on this planet was murdered, a martyr to the faith. His name was Abel, and he was killed by his brother, Cain, because Cain deeply resented his brother's religion (Genesis 4).

God had made it quite clear from the very beginning of the

Torah that He could be approached only on the ground of shed blood, only by sacrifice, by substitution, by the death of an innocent victim slain in the place of the sinner himself. Abel understood that. He brought a lamb, shed its blood, and stood accepted before God for his faith. Cain, however, decided he had a better way, a much more refined way to approach God. He worked and toiled and brought the fruit of the earth, the fruit of his labors, to God, and God refused to have anything to do with it. Abel's offering was accepted, Cain's was rejected. The Bible tells us why from beginning to end: "Without shedding of blood [there] is no remission [for sin]" (Hebrews 9:22).

ABRAHAM'S FAITH

Abraham was the founding father of the Hebrew race. He was born and raised a pagan in Ur of the Chaldees. When he reached the age of seventy-five God spoke to him, and, in obedience to the call of God, he journeyed westward toward the promised land. There God spoke to him again and told him of a coming seed. He believed. "Abraham believed God," we read, "and it was counted unto him for righteousness." He believed the promise concerning the "seed," a specialized expression in the Scriptures, a title for the coming Messiah. Faith in the coming of the Messiah is what constituted Abraham a righteous man. He was counted righteous, not because of his works and not because he received the sign of circumcision, which in any case was not given until some time after he became a believer. He was counted righteous because he believed God, and specifically because he believed the promise concerning the seed.

The high point in Abraham's life was reached on Mount Moriah (Genesis 22) where he showed what a magnificent believer he had become. His final surrender to God was when he was called upon to give up his son.

The altar was built, the wood was laid in order, the beloved son was stretched out upon the wood, the knife was raised in Abraham's hand, it was about to descend. Then God arrested Abraham and provided a substitute for Isaac, a ram, caught by its horns in a nearby bush. Abraham wept out his relief and called the place *Jehovah Jireh*. "The Lord will provide." Provide what? Why, the ultimate sacrifice, the perfect substitute. A greater Father than

Abraham would one day provide a great substitute for sin in the person of a greater Son than Isaac.

Throughout the entire Old Testament, in type and shadow, in psalm and prophecy, in ritual and ordinance God hammers home the same basic truth. One day He would send a seed, send a Savior, send His Son. That Messiah would come not just to reign but also to redeem; he would not be simply "the lion of the tribe of Judah," He would be "the lamb of God" sent to take away the sin of the world.

JOSEPH MIRRORS THE MESSIAH

Joseph's history as recorded by Moses seems deliberately designed to mirror the actual history of Jesus of Nazareth, the true Messiah of Israel. Joseph was the father's well-beloved son, set apart from all others by the unique position that was his, and sent from the presence of the father to seek his lost brethren, his kinsmen according to the flesh. They hated him, could not speak peaceably to him, and when they had him in their power they stripped him of his robe, dyed it in blood and flung it back at the father.

Joseph, like Jesus, was sold for the price of a slave, rejected by his brethren, rejected by the Gentiles. He was falsely accused, made to suffer for sins not his own, cast out, and put in the place of death. In the fullness of time he was brought forth from that place, exalted to the right hand of the king, and given a name that was above all other names, that at that name (*Zaphnath-paaneah*, "Savior of the world") every knee should bow. He was given a Gentile bride, and, in time, began a process of judgmental dealings with his brethren, the children of Israel, designed to bring them to the place of repentance for their former rejection of him. He put them in the fires of testing until they cried, "We are verily guilty concerning our brother." At last he told them plainly who he was, the scales fell from their eyes, and they knew him and were troubled. Finally he wiped away their tears and lifted them high, ministering to them and giving them positions of trust in the magnificent kingdom over which he ruled.

There are a score of points in which Joseph is a studied type of Jesus. The one story exactly parallels the other. The life of Joseph was a dress rehearsal, so to speak, for the life of Jesus, rejected by

Israel, betrayed into the hands of the Gentiles, cast out and crucified, dying for sins not His own, rising from the dead, sitting in
triumph at God's right hand, calling out a Gentile bride for Himself (the church) and, one day, so to deal with Israel as to bring
the nation to repentance—all that is clearly foreshadowed in the
story of Joseph.

THE SIGNIFICANCE OF THE OFFERINGS AND SACRIFICES

Consider the offerings as they were set forth in the early chapters of Leviticus. Can we miss the spiritual significance of the
burnt offering, the peace offering, the sin and the trespass offerings? Only if we fail to see in them a portrayal of the death of
Christ on the cross of Calvary.

For instance, the burnt offering and the sin offering were similar
in their ritual but different in their teaching. The burnt offering
was all for God. The offerer brought his ox, his lamb, or his pigeon.
He identified himself with the offering. He slew it, shed its blood,
and watched as it was burnt to ashes in the flames of the altar. It
typified what the sufferings of the Messiah meant to God. It spoke
of a perfect life being offered up in full and complete surrender to
Him.

The sin offering, on the other hand, was for man. The symbolic
actions were very much the same as with the burnt offering. The
priest examined the offering to make sure it was spotless, without
blemish, and perfect in every respect. The sinner then identified
himself with the offering and, with his own hands, shed its blood
as a confession of his personal guilt. Then the carcass of the slain
creature was carried outside the camp and burnt to ashes.

It took the two offerings to portray one glorious truth centered
in the sacrificial death of Christ at Calvary. In the sin offering, all
the *vileness* of the sinner was symbolically transferred to the substitute; in the burnt offering all the *virtue* of the substitute was
symbolically transferred to the sinner. In both cases the offerer
identified himself with the offering by laying his hands on the
sacrifice. In what more graphic way could God ever have taught
to Israel the truth of substitution? When we accept Jesus as Savior
and substitute by personally appropriating His death for us by
faith, all our vileness is removed from us and all His virtue, holi-
ness, and acceptability with God are transferred to us.

The Significance of the Passover

A similar truth is taught in the annual feasts that were so prominent in Israel's religious calendar, especially the feasts of Passover and Yom Kippur. "When I see the blood I will pass over you." That was the central message of the Passover. Israel, born in slavery and under the sentence of death, found in Moses a Kinsman-Redeemer. Moses showed his credentials by giving Israel's foes a mighty demonstration of divine power. But those miracles, great as they were, did not redeem Israel. It was the shed blood of the Passover lamb that redeemed. Each Hebrew father had to become an actor in the drama. He had to take and tether a lamb, watch it for four days, and make sure it was without blemish. Then he had to slay it and apply its blood to the lintel and the door-posts of his house, gather his family inside, and shelter behind the blood in simple faith. Nothing else would do. God had no other means of escape for men when the angel of judgment appeared. He still has no other escape. That Passover lamb was a picture of the Messiah. His blood was to be shed for sin; it alone can shelter the sinner in the hour of judgment.

The Significance of Yom Kippur

Yom Kippur teachers a similar truth. The word *atonement* simply means "to cover." The same Hebrew word used to describe the Day of Atonement is used to describe Noah's action when he *pitched* the ark within and without with pitch. Noah simply covered the ark with a substance that would come between him and the judgment waters of the Flood. The Day of Atonement taught the same truth, only on that day it was blood that became the saving, sealing agent whereby sin could be ritually covered for another year.

To prepare himself for his role, the Old Testament high priest first made sacrifice for his own sin. He then took the blood of his offering, together with incense, and went into the Holy of Holies in the Temple. He threw the incense on the live coals in the censer in his hand so that the thick, ascending cloud might hide him from the presence of God. The blood he took to the Mercy Seat upon the Ark where God sat enthroned between the cherubim. The blood alone made it possible for him to draw near.

The high priest then returned outside and took two goats, one

to be a sin offering for the people and the other to be a scapegoat
for their sins. It took two goats to symbolize the one great sacrificial act of the Messiah at Calvary. The blood of the goat that was
sacrificed was taken into the Holy of Holies by the high priest and
presented before the Mercy Seat. It was a token of Calvary, a reminder that temporary provision had been made for the sins of
the people. Sin could be covered for yet another year.

Once more the high priest retreated from the Holy of Holies to
take his stand before the gathered hosts of Israel. He now took
the scapegoat, placed his hands upon the little creature's head, and
began a recitation of all the sins of the people for the past year.
Symbolically he was now transferring the nation's sins to the substitute. The scapegoat was delivered then into the hands of "a fit
man" who led it away into the wilderness where, "in a land not
inhabited," it perished. Sin was covered, the ritual of atonement
was over for another year. The whole point of Yom Kippur as it
was celebrated in Bible times lay in the fact that sin was not
cleansed; it was only covered. The ritual had to be repeated year
after year. Each time it was performed it pointed forward to Calvary. Each Day of Atonement there was a fresh remembrance
made of sin.

Here is a man who is in debt. He goes to the bank to borrow
money, but his credit is worthless. A wealthy friend comes along
and agrees to endorse the note and become surety for his friend's
indebtedness. A note is drawn up and made out to fall due in a
year, at which time the debt will become due in full. At the end
of the year the debtor is unable to pay. Worse still, he has gone
even deeper into debt. The guarantor agrees to enlarge the note
and carry forward the debt in its new and bigger form for another
twelve months. This kind of thing goes on year after year until, at
last, the banker says: "We cannot continue like this. We are going
to demand payment now, in full. This indebtedness must be paid."
The guarantor assumes the liability and pays off the debt for his
friend.

That is the whole point of Yom Kippur. Sin was not cleansed
or canceled, but simply covered and carried forward for another
year. God could treat it thus because a guarantor had been found
in the person of His beloved Son, the Lord Jesus Christ the true
Messiah. Each year the ritual connected with Yom Kippur sym-
bolized the carrying forward of an accumulating debt. At Calvary,

the entire indebtedness was paid in full by the death of the Messiah. It is of great significance that as Jesus hung upon the cross the Temple veil was rent in two from the top to bottom, to declare to Israel that no longer would the veil stand between the people and God (Matthew 27:51). Sin's debt was paid. The Day of Atonement had fully come. There was no more need for sin to be "covered"; it was canceled.

EMPTY JUDAISM

Judaism today is a religion of sacrifice, but for nearly two thousand years, no sacrifice has been possible. On Passover and the Day of Atonement for many, many centuries no lamb has been slain and no sacrifice offered. It is a sacerdotal religion without a priesthood, a religion of a Temple without a Temple. Its altar fire is quenched, its ashes are scattered. Judaism without Christ is surely a religion without meaning and hope.

There is hardly a place in the Hebrew Bible that does not underline the truth that the Messiah was to die for sin. Psalm 22, Isaiah 53, and Psalm 69 clearly speak of Messiah (Jesus) and the cross. They are unmistakable prophecies that leap to life in the light of the sufferings and death of the Lord Jesus Christ.

THE RESURRECTION FORETOLD

The resurrection of Jesus Christ, a proven fact of history, was clearly predicted long before the event took place. Did not David prophesy that? He emphatically wrote: "Neither will thou suffer thine Holy One to see corruption" (Psalm 16:10). Surely Christ really is the Messiah and Savior of Israel. In the New Testament, Romans, Matthew, and Hebrews explore the Hebrew Bible to show how fully all its types and shadows were fulfilled in the person and work of Jesus.

The early church was made up entirely of Jews, all of whom were absolutely convinced that Jesus was the Messiah, the Redeemer of Israel, the fulfillment of Old Testament prophecy. It was not until about A.D. 41 that Gentiles began to be added to the church.

THE TESTIMONY OF ONE OF GAMALIEL'S DISCIPLES

The most influential Jew of the first century of the Christian era was Saul of Tarsus, who later became the apostle Paul. For years this man, a rabbi, a disciple of the renowned Gamaliel, was a bitter foe of Christianity. He became the accredited agent of the Sanhedrin in Jerusalem commissioned to persecute any Jews who belonged to the hated new sect.

Paul became so convinced that Jesus was indeed the true Messiah that he became the greatest exponent of the new faith. The Jews of his day turned on him bitterly and persecuted him in his turn. But he never lost his love for his countrymen. He wrote: "Brethren, my heart's desire and prayer to God for Israel is, that they might be saved. For I bear them record that they have a zeal of God, but not according to knowledge. For they being ignorant of God's righteousness, and going about to establish their own righteousness, have not submitted themselves unto the righteousness of God. For Christ is the end of the law for righteousness to every one that believeth. . . . For whosoever shall call upon the name of the Lord shall be saved" (Romans 10:1-13).

How does one become a "completed Jew" (or a completed Gentile, for that matter)? By calling on the name of the Lord Jesus Christ, the true Messiah. "Thou shalt call His name Jesus: for he shall save his people from their sins" (Matthew 1:21). "Neither is there salvation in any other: for there is none other name under heaven given among men, whereby we must be saved" (Acts 4:12).

10

THE PERSECUTED JEW

We have been analyzing the world of the Jew and looking particularly at some of the religious refuges in which he has sought to find a home down through the centuries. He has needed a home and hiding place. Throughout his long history, mostly dispersed among the Gentiles, two forces have been at work to destroy him—the counter forces of persecution and assimilation. In this chapter we are going to look at some of the fierce fires of persecution through which the Jewish people have had to pass in their tormented exile from the promised land. The latest of those, the one still fresh in the minds of our generation, is the Nazi holocaust.

Nazi Persecution and Genocide

Auschwitz and other death camps were Hitler's demented answer to the "Jewish question." He became chancellor of Germany in January 1933. A month later he engineered the Reichstag fire, decreed a state of emergency that was to last until his death, and set to work in earnest on the Jews.

Hitler had been preparing for this for years. In September 1935 the Nuremberg Laws were promulgated for the "protection of the blood," and repressive measures against Jews became common throughout Germany. It was a criminal offense for a Jew to marry a Gentile. A new word was coined and put into circulation to describe Germans who had relations with Jews—*Rassenschande,* "race shame." The Rassenschaender, the man guilty of race shame, was stigmatized as a criminal and subjected to the attentions of the Gestapo.

Julius Streicher became the Nazis' chief Jew-baiter with his vile paper *Der Stürmer.* Poems in filthy language, obscene cartoons, and parodied children's nursery rhymes all helped fill the pages. Streicher assured his readers that Jews had confessed to the execution of ritual murders as required, so he said, by the Talmud. He

111

told his audience that Jews forcibly tapped blood from their victims and used it as wine when celebrating the Passover, a feast that he assured the German people was kept annually to commemorate the murder of Christ. In Berlin *Der Stürmer* so inflamed the people that they readily gave popular support to the Nuremberg decrees.

First it was discrimination, then the ghettos and the concentration camps, and finally mass murder. In his opening statement for the prosecution at the Nuremberg trial, Justice Robert Jackson said, "History does not record a crime perpetrated against so many victims or ever carried out with such calculated cruelty."[1]

The Nazi aim was to make Europe *judenfrei*—free of Jews. Fifteen years after the end of World War II the results of their work was still evident (see fig. 10:1). For the Nazis to kill six mil-

POPULATION OF JEWS IN EUROPE BEFORE AND AFTER WORLD WAR II

Country	1933	1961
Poland	3,300,000	30,000
Germany	550,000	30,000
Austria	190,000	10,000
Hungary	400,000	80,000
Czechoslovakia	315,000	18,000
Rumania	850,000	180,000
Netherlands	150,000	23,000
Belgium	100,000	33,000
Yugoslavia	75,000	6,500
Greece	75,000	6,000
France	320,000	300,000
Italy	57,000	30,000
Total	6,382,000	746,500

Fig. 10.1[3]

lion Jews from 1939 to 1945, they had to kill on an average two people a minute, day and night, seven days a week, for six long years. It has been estimated that the Holocaust robbed the Jews of $55.5 billion in personal losses, community property such as stores, schools, and synagogues, and resettlement costs.[2]

HISTORICAL ANTI-SEMITISM

Were the Nazi Holocaust the sole outbreak of anti-Semitism in history it would be horror enough. But it is not. It was only the surfacing, in epidemic form, of a disease that has been endemic in human society ever since the Jews became a nation in the land of Egypt.

Six times in their history the Jews have been brought to the very verge of annihilation. First the Pharaohs attempted to exterminate them (1571-1491 B.C., Exodus 1:22), then the Assyrians tried their hand by deporting them (775 B.C., 2 Kings 17), next Nebuchadnezzar attacked, massacred, and deported them (588 B.C., 2 Kings 25). Haman instigated a purge of Jews throughout the Persian Empire (510 B.C., Esther 3), a purge that was averted only because of the bravery of Esther. It is still commemorated annually in the Jewish feast of Purim. The Jews were also nearly destroyed by Antiochus Epiphanes (170 B.C., Daniel 8:23-25), and finally by the Romans under Titus (A.D. 70) and Julius Severus.

Down through the ages, persecution of the Jews has been national policy in one country after another. Constantine outlawed them, cut off their ears, and dispersed them as vagabonds. Justinian excluded them from the provisions of his legal code, abolished their synagogues, deprived them of their civil rights, and forbade them to bequeath property (A.D. 529). The earliest legislation in France was an ordinance against Jews. Even Britain's famed *Magna Carta* (1215), a revolutionary political document and hailed as the forerunner of all statements of civil rights, legalized an act of injustice against Jews.

Stephen Langdon, Archbishop of Canterbury, in the days of King John, when the barons forced the signing of the *Magna Carta,* preached against the Jews and forbade Christians to sell them the very necessities of life. At one time every Jew in England, regardless of age or sex, was imprisoned, and all Jewish wealth was confiscated. At another time they were expelled from England and were not allowed to return for four hundred years.

There were more than 850,000 Jews in Spain in A.D. 1300. They were valuable members of society who made great contributions to the wealth, culture, and leadership of the country. But, as the detested Moors were driven out of Spain, persecution of Jews took root and flourished. Many Jews professed to become Christians in

the vain hope that they would be accepted and assimilated, but
then came the Inquisition, founded in 1478, to hunt them down,
torture them, and kill them. Not until the coming of Hitler did the
Jews suffer such widespread persecution as they did in Spain. The
decline and fall of the Spanish Empire can be dated from the time
that Spain expelled all its Jews.[4]

Every country at one time or another has turned its hand against
the Jews. In Europe Jew-baiting became almost a sport. Kings
would allow them to settle in their domains and accumulate
wealth, then they would confiscate their property and drive them
back out. On one occasion all Jews found on the shores of Lake
Geneva in Switzerland were burned alive (1348). At Strasbourg,
Germany on February 14, 1349, an entire Jewish community of
about 2,000 people was dragged to an immense funeral pyre and
thrown on the flames.

RELIGIOUS PREJUDICE AGAINST THE JEWS

Persecutions and horrors were inflicted on Jews throughout
Europe during the Dark Ages, but probably none was worse or
had such far-reaching results as those inflicted by the Crusades to
free the Holy Land. Pope Urban launched the first Crusade in
1095, and that expedition was followed by seven more. They were
futile. The Crusades themselves made havoc of the economy of
Europe, spread pillage and suffering everywhere, and made it a
point to commit atrocities against Jews.

Prejudice against Jews existed among Protestants as well.
Martin Luther, at the height of his struggle with Catholicism, advocated tolerance for Jews, and reminded Christians of their debt
to the Jews as the people who had given mankind both the Bible
and Christ. In 1523 he published a pamphlet entitled "That Jesus
Was Born a Jew." But when it became evident that the Jews were
not about to flock into the church, Luther turned upon them, and,
in his later outbursts, accused them of everything from ritual
murder to poisoning wells.[5]

All Christendom, Protestant and Catholic alike, helped herd the
Jews into ghettos where they could be properly segregated and
kept from contaminating Christian people with their unbelief. The
Roman church, however, was far more intolerant toward the Jews
than the Protestant church.

The Fourth Lateran Council introduced the Jewish Badge,

which Jews henceforth would have to wear, marking them off from the rest of mankind. The ghetto system was given special endorsement by Rome in 1555, and under Clement VIII (1592-1604) persecuting Jews became a fixed part of papal policy.

MODERN ANTI-SEMITISM

Modern anti-Semitism had its rise in Germany. It attained prominence in 1879 when Bismarck used it to discredit the Jewish leaders of the National-Liberation Group, which was calling for constitutional reform.

In France modern anti-Semitism surfaced in the Dreyfus case. Napoleon had liberated the Jews from the ghettos, and many were living in France in elegant upper-class society. The Dreyfus trial sounded the warning for all Jews, rich or poor. Captain Dreyfus was a French Jew who was falsely accused of treason. His trial set off new waves of anti-Semitic feeling throughout France. When Theodore Hertzl was in Paris he heard the words "Death to the Jews" echoing through the streets and decided that Europe was no place for the Jewish people. History proved him right, as the Holocaust showed.

ANTI-SEMITISM IN AMERICA

The United States has not been free from anti-Semitism. In America, anti-Jewish feeling tends to surface during times of economic depression. It reared its head, for instance, in the 1920s when Jews were accused of being the architects of America's economic woes. At that time it had its roots in rural America where the unemployed blamed the big cities, and especially New York, for their troubles. They equated the big cities with Jews. At the same time there were plenty of people in business quite ready to back anti-Semitism if it would eliminate Jewish competition in business. The idea took root that Jews controlled American finance.

The anti-Semitism of the 1930s was fired by Nazi propaganda that took root among Americans of German descent. Many Americans, unable to understand why the world's wealthiest country should be in the grip of such economic depression, fell for Hitler's propaganda. The Ku Klux Klan, with a membership of some four million, preached hatred for Jews along with hatred for Blacks and Catholics and added fuel to the flames.

Another source of anti-Semitism in America was the preaching of Father Charles E. Coughlin in the 1930s. He spread the word that the Jews had deliberately engineered the Depression in order to wipe out savings, create economic havoc, and pave the way for Communism.

In the end anti-Semitism, as a movement in the United States, faded away because the Depression came to an end. Its roots still remain.

RUSSIAN ANTI-SEMITISM

Hatred of the Jews is by no means dead with Nazism. In Russia it expresses itself in various forms of anti-Semitism. The very word *pogrom*, which denotes the massacre of a helpless people, is a Russian word that first passed into other languages after the devastation of the Jews in the Ukraine in 1903. There are about three and one half million Jews in Russia today, and they are the objects of persistent and unrelenting pressure and persecution.

Persecution of Jews in Russia is in keeping with a long standing Russian tradition. Czar Nicholas I (1825-1855) shut six million Russian Jews up in the "Pale of Settlement." Alexander III (1881-1894) continued the policy of anti-Semitism. Nicholas II came to the throne in 1894 and carried out the terrible massacres of 1903 and 1906. Had it not been for the generous immigration policy of the United States, millions more Russian Jews would have perished in the days of the Czars.

Between the two world wars the plight of the Jews in Russia attracted international attention. The entire Jewish population of the Russian Western War Zone (some million and a half) were forcibly evacuated into the interior of Russia—old men and infants, the sick, the dying, the insane—everybody, at twelve hours' notice.

Sir Harold Rumbold, the British Minister at Warsaw reported to the Foreign Office: "The massacres of Jews in the Ukraine can find, for thoroughness and extent, no parallel except in the massacres of Armenians." *Dawn* magazine reported in August 1924:

> Wholesale slaughter and burials alive, rape and torture, became not merely commonplace but the order of the day. There were pogroms that lasted a week; and in several cases the systematic and diabolic torture and outrage and carnage were continued for a month. In many populous Jewish communities there were no Jewish survivors left to bury the dead, and thousands of Jewish

wounded and killed were eaten by dogs and pigs; in others the Synagogues were turned into charnel houses by the pitiless butchery of those who sought refuge in them. If we add to the figures quoted above the number of those indirect victims who in consequence of the robbery and destruction that accompanied these massacres were swept away by famine, disease, exposure and all manner of privations—the dread total will be very near half a million human beings.[6]

STALIN AND THE JEWS

Josef Stalin never forgot that his greatest rival had been Leon Trotsky, a Jew (born Leon Bronstein). The ghost of Trotskyism always haunted Stalin's demented mind, and during his era no prominent Russian Jew was ever safe.

In early 1953, Stalin's secret police arrested nine "terrorist doctors," six of whom were Jewish, and charged them with plotting to murder Soviet leaders "on orders from abroad."

The full story has been told by Ludmila Lufanov, a former librarian, who left Russia and now lives in the United States. At one time she had worked in Moscow with top secret archives of the state. The "plot" by the Jewish doctors gave Stalin the weapon he needed to proceed against the Jews. The trial was given continuous front-page, sensational coverage in the controlled Soviet press.

Also in early 1953, Stalin read a statement in which he outlined to the assembled Politburo his plan for the extermination of all Russian Jews. The result of the trial of the doctors was a foregone conclusion. They would be publicly hanged in Moscow a few days later. That would be followed by three days of "spontaneous" rioting against the Jews. The government would then step in and separate the Jews from the Russian people and ship them all to Siberia. But two-thirds would never arrive. They would be killed along the way by the enraged Russian people. The third who did arrive would die swiftly in slave labor camps. The proposal was received in dead silence.

On March 5 Stalin was dead. He suffered a stroke and was removed from the earth. *Pravda* announced on April 3 that the nine doctors were declared not guilty and had been freed. Those responsible for using "impermissible means of investigation" had been arrested. There is sometmes a grim appropriateness about the timing of God.

RUSSIA AND THE JEWS TODAY

Soviet policy toward its vast Jewish population has been somewhat ambivalent since World War II. It has wavered between expulsion, persecution, and assimilation. At one time, shortly after the rebirth of the state of Israel, the Kremlin actually considered the wholesale expulsion of its three and one half million Jews and their forcible deportation to Israel. The idea was simply to swamp the fledgling state under the sheer weight of such numbers. The plan was shelved, however, because of Russia's budding friendship with the Arabs.

One alternative the Soviets have kept in mind has been the forcible assimilation of its Jewish population. That might well have been a possibility at one time since the majority of Jews in Russia who speak Yiddish are over fifty years of age. The rebirth of the state of Israel, however, infused new hope into Russia's Jews by giving them an identity. Thousands of them have shaken off their inertia and have begun to fight back deliberately, doing things to force the hand of their Soviet oppressors, things that they hope will draw the attention of the rest of the world to their plight. From time to time the United States makes a token gesture in response, but obviously intends to do nothing that might irritate the oil-rich Arabs or too greatly infuriate Russia's leaders. The rest of the world simply yawns.

THE ARABS DON THE MANTLE

Russian anti-Semitism makes Russia the natural ally of the militant Arab states, which have now become the world's most vocal enemies of the Jews. Nowhere in the world today is hatred of the Jew given more virulent and violent expression than in the Arab world. In addition to all-out war against Israel, the Arabs have used boycott, terrorism, and propaganda as weapons. They have launched massive worldwide propaganda campaigns against Israel, financed by limitless bankrolls of petro-dollars. Their propaganda uses slick Madison Avenue techniques and is backed by constant oil blackmail.[7]

The Arabs have made no attempt to disguise their ultimate objectives—the eradication of the state of Israel and the extermination of every Jew who lives there. A major pawn in the propaganda offensive is the existence of the refugee camps, which could cease to exist overnight if the eighteen Arab countries had any humanitarian regard for their inmates. So long as the camps remain, however, they can be used to support the myth of a Palestinian nation.

One thing the Arabs have done in their campaign is to revive the *Protocols*. *The Protocols of the Elders of Zion* have been around for a long time. Hitler used them as one of his sources when writing *Mein Kampf*. The *Protocols* are supposed to be a secret document drawn up by the first Zionist Congress. They are said to contain plans for the subversion of the world in the interests of Jewish hegemony over the planet.

Attempts have been made to discredit the *Protocols* as a forgery. It is claimed, for instance, that they were originally based on a pamphlet entitled *Dialogue Au Enfero entre Machiavel el Montesquieu, ou la Politique de Machiavel au XIX Siécle*. This work is a satire on the government of Napoleon III written by Maurice Joly, a Parisian lawyer. It is likewise claimed that the *Protocols* were published by the Tsarist secret police to justify the Ukrainian pogroms of 1905. The Nazis gave the *Protocols* tremendous circulation. They have been translated into all the major world languages and have been widely circulated around the world. The *Protocols* are a favorite weapon of anti-Semitic groups.

No weapon is overlooked by the Arabs in their frenzy of hatred for Israel. Recently the world was shocked when Dutch officials disclosed that oranges from Israel had been injected with mercury pellets. More sabotaged Israeli oranges showed up in West German towns. The mercury found in the fruit was the same kind used in thermometers. It is especially dangerous to young children. It was an all-time low in sabotage even in a world that has become hardened to acts of terrorism. The Arab Revolutionary Army boasted of being responsible for this "courageous" achievement. Sabotaging Israeli oranges would pose a particularly effective threat to Israel economically. The Israeli orange export trade amounts to over $170 million a year and it is one of Israel's important sources of foreign exchange. Some of the Arab States, however, alarmed by world revulsion at this tactic backed off and disassociated themselves from this particular way of waging war.

The Arabs are financing the reprinting of the *Protocols* and are spreading copies throughout the world through Arab propaganda offices and with the assistance of neo-Nazis. Along with the dissemination of the *Protocols* they are using blackmail, bribes, bigotry, class hatred, nationalism, Fascism, and even Communism, so long as it helps create a climate of anti-Zionism and anti-Semitism. As a result, there is beginning to emerge a multireligious, multinational block of anti-Semitically-inclined countries, held together chiefly by Arab money and communist aid. One of the chief targets of this propaganda thrust is the United States.

THE BURNING BUSH

Ever since Moses stood at the burning bush, Israel has had to contend with the hatred of the world. At the very time Moses took off his shoes before that blazing desert shrub and bowed his head in the presence of God, the Pharaoh in Egypt was pursuing a plan to exterminate the Jews in the ghettos of the Nile. The burning bush Moses saw that day contained a message and a promise. The bush burned with fire but was not consumed, for *God* was in the midst of it. Moses was taught that the nation he was about to emancipate from Egyptian slavery would ever find itself in the fire, but it would never be exterminated and it would never be assimilated. God would be in the midst of His people as He was in the burning bush.

God had a great future for Israel then, and He has a great future for Israel today. The Jew has stood by the tomb of every Empire that has ever persecuted him, and he will yet stand by the tomb of the nations and empires that persecute him now.

NOTES

1. Robert Jackson, cited in G. M. Gilbert, *Nuremberg Diary* (New York: New American Library, Signet, 1961), p. 40.
2. See M. Hirsch Goldberg, "Mindscape of a Jew," *The Times of Israel,* March 1974, pp. 59-60.
3. See A. L. Sachar, *A History of the Jews,* rev. ed. (New York: Random, Knopf, 1964), p. 426. See also Solomon Grazel, *A History of the Jews,* new ed. (Philadelphia: Jewish Publication Soc., 1968), p. 674.
4. Sachar, p. 215.
5. Martin Luther, *Concerning the Jews and Their Lies,* cited in Sachar, p. 229.
6. D. M. Panton, "The Jew God's Dial," *Dawn,* 15 August 1924, pp. 197-201.
7. See Jerome Bakst, "Arabvertising, The New Brand of Arab Propaganda," *The Times of Israel,* April 1975, pp. 15-27.

11

THE BRILLIANT JEW

No analysis of Jewish history during the long period of the Dispersion would be complete without at least a brief look at the impact the Jew has had on the culture of the countries in which he has made his home. Little more can be done in a single short chapter than introduce the subject. Anyone interested in a more complete study of the theme could begin, for instance, with the *Encyclopedia Judaica*. Suffice it to say here that the Jew manages not only to survive in alien cultures but to succeed. We shall begin this brief review with a page or two from the debt the British Empire owed to two Jews—Benjamin Disraeli and Chaim Weizmann.

BRITAIN AND THE SUEZ CANAL

One of the keys to Britain's success as a major world power was her control of the Suez Canal. The Canal had been built by France. Britain contributed nothing to it, had no part in its construction, and bought none of its original stock. But in 1875 news filtered out of Egypt that the bankrupt khedive, Ismail Pasha, was putting up his shares for sale. It was simple imperial common sense that any nation that controlled the canal could control the Middle East, India, and the Far East as well. It was in the best interests of both Britain and France to buy up the khedive's shares.

The news reached Lord Beaconsfield, the British Prime Minister, but Parliament was in recess. By Monday morning, and by the time the slow machinery of British democracy had creaked through all the pros and cons, haggled over the details, and counted up the cost it would be too late; the French would have snapped up the shares. Beaconsfield could not wait for all that. Deciding that a bold move was best, he called the bank of England, borrowed the great sum needed on his own signature and bought out the khedive. When Monday came he presented the government and

the furious French with one of history's great scoops. He had
bought the Suez and guaranteed the growth of the British Empire.
And who was Lord Beaconsfield? He is better known, perhaps, as
Benjamin Disraeli, a Jew.

A JEW SAVES THE BRITISH EMPIRE

Forty years later the empire had its back to the wall in a desperate struggle with Germany. Then news came that shocked the
War Office—there was no more cordite in the country for the
manufacture of gunpowder, and the war was as good as lost. Lord
Balfour, Prime Minister of Britain, turned to a brilliant young
chemist. Could he devise some sort of synthetic cordite? It would
have to be cheap and readily available. And it was needed in a
desperate hurry. The chemist was sure that he could, and came
up with a formula for making the needed chemical from horse
chestnuts—abundant everywhere in the British Isles. In so doing
he gave the British Empire a lease on life for another generation.
We have met this chemist before. He was Chaim Weizmann, a
Jew.

JOHN F. KENNEDY AND THE JEWS

Jews have a way of turning up, either singly or in great numbers, at all the important turning points of history. When John
Kennedy became President of the United States he did not surround himself with rabid Catholics as his Protestant opposition
feared. He chose quite a different team to help him run the nation.
At the Justice Department there was Myer Feldman; in charge of
the Internal Revenue Service was Mortimer Caplin; running the
Treasury Department was C. Douglas Dillon; functioning as
Kennedy's Administrative Assistant was Arthur Schlesinger, Jr.;
influencing foreign policy was Walter W. Rostow; the influential
Press Secretary was Pierre Salinger; appointed to the Supreme
Court of the United States by Kennedy was Arthur J. Goldberg.
What did those men have in common? They were Jews.

In all ages Jews have not only had the will to survive, they have
had the will to excel. They have provided the world with its
thinkers far out of proportion to their numbers. When we think of
physics we think of Albert Einstein, a German Jew; when we think

of Philosophy we think of Henri Bergson, a French Jew; when we think of psychology we think of Sigmund Freud, an Austrian Jew. Of the four men said to have most influenced the thinking of the twentieth century (Einstein, Freud, Marx, and Darwin) three were Jews.

Before the Second World War, only 3 percent of the population of Germany was made up of Jews, yet they held over one hundred chairs in the country's universities and they dominated the professions, industry, and the banks. On the eve of the Holocaust in Germany, although less than 2 or 3 percent of the population was Jewish, Jews made up 10 percent of the country's doctors, 16 percent of its lawyers, 10 percent of its dentists, and 17 percent of its bankers. They were predominant in real estate, in retailing, in the clothing industry, and in ownership of department stores. Hitler wrote in *Mein Kampf*, "Wherever I went I began to see Jews. . . . Gradually I began to hate them."[1]

JEWISH BRAINS AT WORK IN ISRAEL

When Chaim Weizmann was asked why he wanted to return the Jews to Palestine when the country was practically devoid of natural resources, he is said to have replied that brains were the only necessary resource. There is no doubt that the state of Israel has a superabundance of brain power. Jewish academic prowess has caused a minor crisis in the country. About 15 percent of Israel's working force is drawn from the academic community—a higher percentage than is found in the United States, Canada, Britain, or France. One Israeli survey projected that by the end of the decade no less than one-fifth of the entire Israeli labor force will be made up of people with university degrees.

The International Labour Organization has rated Israel at the top of the scale among industrially advanced or developing nations in terms of the number of university graduates in relation to total national manpower.[2]

The country is having trouble absorbing such a high percentage of superbly educated people into its work force. A committee of experts, appointed by the Ministry of Commerce and Industry, for instance, has recently had to study ways and means of coping with the increasing number of engineers in the country. It has suggested that the country map out new projects in numerous fields into which surplus engineers can be channeled, and that the government cope with the economic problems involved in creating these new jobs.

AARON OF LINCOLN

No matter where we look in history or in today's world the story is same. Jews somehow make their way to the top. In the Middle Ages they became the world's bankers. In England, for instance, there was Aaron of Lincoln (1125-1186), who in twenty years amassed a fortune of such magnitude that it was second only to that of the king. He built a system of financial agents all across the kingdom, and before long Henry II and many of his nobles and high churchmen, including the Archbishop of Canterbury, were in Lincoln's debt. So deeply did England become indebted to him that when he died the king simply took over all Aaron's assets. The total involved was so great that a special branch of the royal exchequer had to be set up (called the Exchequer of Aaron) to collect the outstanding debts that now, of course, fell due to the crown.

Such enormous sums were owed by the barons, in interest alone, that clause 10 of the *Magna Carta* restricted kings thereafter to collecting only the principle, not the interest, of expropriated Jewish wealth. It also led, in 1194, to the proclamation of the Ordinance of Jewry, which set up archives so that the King could be kept fully informed of the wealth of his Jewish subjects and thus could confiscate it as leisure.

The Jews, dispersed as they were throughout three continents and in as many civilizations, were nevertheless one people. They were held together by a common language, by religion, and by Talmudic law.

The Talmud contained a section dealing with commerce, contracts, the honoring of oaths, trade, damages—however, it is chapter upon chapter of ethical and legalistic discussions, judging money-handling in light of Mosaic and rabbinical commands. It was not familiar in the Middle Ages except to the Jews and to their rabbis, who were as familiar with that section of the Talmud as they were with the rest of it. Although the Talmud teaches basic financial common sense and business ethics, anyone who thinks it to be a master-key to modern financial success, big-time banking, or international money changing has assuredly never read one page of the Talmud. It was enough to serve as a primer on business wisdom, much like the biblical book of Proverbs today. In finance, "wisdom," versus foolishness, is the key.

By the tenth century the Jews had widespread commercial enterprises in Europe, North Africa, and the Middle East, with branches reaching as far as India and China. The rising middle class in Europe finally broke the Jewish monopoly, but that did not deter the Jews, who continued to increase their hold over international commerce and banking.

COURT JEWS IN EIGHTEENTH CENTURY EUROPE

In the seventeenth and eighteenth centuries Jewish financial genius was so fully recognized by European monarchs that they realized they could not get along without Jewish counselors at court. Thus emerged the "court Jew" entrusted with the financial affairs of the kingdom, authorized to raise loans, suggest taxes, control currency, and keep things solvent. The court Jews made it possible for kings to become independent of their barons and helped bring Europe into the modern age. The coming of the court Jew heralded the approach of capitalism as a means of creating wealth and of carrying on the business of the world.

THE JEWISH BANKER

In time the court Jew disappeared, and the banker took his place. Without the Jew the advance of banking would have been delayed for centuries and without banking great government enterprises and the wholesale expansion of industry would have been impossible. The banker made it possible for credit to be expanded and for international loans to be made.

Modern capitalism utilizes the stock market, and that had its origin in the Jewish practice of conducting business by means of securities and credit and of discounting bills of exchange. It was the Jewish house of Rothschild that made the stock market an international institution. In Germany, the stock exchange was Jewish right from the start. Of its first four presidents two were Jewish, and of its twenty-three members ten were Jews.

JEWS AND THE SPREAD OF RAILROADS

One of the things that helped shape the modern world was a total revolution in methods of communication and travel, and in that Jews took a leading role. Jews, for instance, made the European railroad system possible. In 1825 Nathan Meyer Rothschild, impressed by the success of the newly opened railroad in England, urged other members of the Rothschild clan to get involved in railroad construction. Before long Jews were financing railroads in all parts of continental Europe as well as in the United States, Mexico, and Brazil. In Russia a Jew, Samuel Salomowicz Poliakoff, played a vital part in constructing five of the country's major railroads. He was called "the Railroad King of Russia," and at the time of his death he owned no less than a quarter of the Russian railroad system.

JEWS IN THE ACADEMIC WORLD

Jews have been in the forefront of learning as well as finance. The fact that they were barred from European universities for centuries did not deter them. They were accepted in Islamic institutions, and in the ghettos they created their own systems of education. Their saturation with Talmudic ways of thought made abstract thinking and legal logic second nature to them. It also helped them develop phenomenal memories. Astronomy, geometry, languages, medicine, and sociology were all areas where they excelled.

When the doors of European universities finally opened to them they surged in and surpassed the majority of their Gentile fellow students. In Holland, then in Germany and Austria, ever increasing numbers of Jews became professors. So numerous were their appointments to high academic posts that Hitler found it easy to denounce, for instance, the Judaization (*Verjudung*) of the German universities. In Hungary, Sweden, Denmark, France, England, and the United States the story has been much the same.

COLUMBUS AND THE JEWS

The Jews have influenced the thinking of every age. Centuries before Columbus, for instance, Jews disproved the notion that the world was flat. In the Midrash (No. 13) it is stated that the world is shaped like a ball thrown from the hand. In the *Zohar* compiled by Moses de Leon, two hundred years before the time of Columbus, it is stated that the earth revolves like a ball and that, as a result, when it is day on one half of the world it is night on the other.

There is no doubt that Jews were much involved in Columbus's expedition to find the new world. Most of the maps of the age were drawn by Jewish cartographers. Jews compiled the astronomical tables used by navigators. The sea quadrant (often called "Jacob's Staff") was invented by Levi Ben Gershon, a Jew.

When the Spanish king hesitated to promote the expedition he was finally persuaded to do so by three Jews—Gabriel Sanchez, the chief treasurer of Aragon, Juan Cabero, the king's chamberlain, and Luis de Santangel, the treasurer of the royal household. De Santangel said that he would personally lend the necessary funds to Columbus when Ferdinand and Isabella balked at spending the money. A number of Jews were part of the expedition, including the ship's surgeon, Maestro Bernal, and Luis de Torres, a linguist.

THE JEWS AND ASTRONOMY

The science of astronomy is greatly in the debt of the Jews, who brought Arabic learning to the West. They translated and edited the great Arabic, Latin, and Spanish works, and the works of the great Greek astronomers. Sir William Herschel, a Jew, discovered the planet Uranus, the first planet to be discovered in modern times. For this achievement he was appointed Astronomer Royal of England. He went on to catalog hundreds of stars and thousands of nebulae. It was he who discovered the binary character of double stars and who determined the sun's motion in space. William Beer, a German Jew, was the first man to map the mountains of the moon. Fritz Cohn calculated the orbits of the planets. Albert Michelson, a Jew, determined the velocity of light. In fact, so accurate were his calculations that even with today's sophisticated instruments his figures have been shown to be only four kilometers a second off. Einstein on several occasions acknowledged his indebtedness to Michelson.

THE JEWS AND MEDICINE

The Jews have always excelled in medicine. During the Middle Ages, when Europe was hostile to the Jews, Jewish doctors flourished in Arab lands, and many of them were renowned. Scores of caliphs kept Jewish physicians on their staffs. One of the most famous Jewish physicians was Maimonides. He made extensive contributions to the medicine of his day as did his son, his grand-

son, and two of his great-grandsons. Kings and popes relied on
Jewish physicians. Emperor Frederick III employed a Jew, Jacob
Loans, as court physician. Popes Julius III, Clement VII, Paul III,
Sixtus V, and numerous others who occupied the throne of St.
Peter employed Jewish doctors.

The list of Jewish contributions to medicine is almost endless.
Cassimir Funk discovered vitamins; Abraham Jacobi, founder of
American pediatrics, invented the laryngoscope. O. M. Schloss
introduced the scratch method of studying allergies. Numerous
diseases are called after the Jews who identified them—Flexner B
dysentery (Simon Flexner), Buerger's disease (Leo Buerger),
dermatitis Schambergi (J. Frank Schamberg) and Libman's disease (Emanuel Libman), for instance.

There is not a branch of medicine in which Jews have not been
leaders and pioneers. Jonas Salk developed the vaccine that has
largely stamped out polio. Nobel Prize winner Selman Abraham
Waksman discovered the antibiotic streptomycin, now a common
weapon against a variety of diseases. The American Medical Association (formerly the National Medical Association) was founded
by a Jewish ophthalmologist, Isaac Hays. Joseph Goldberger laid
the foundation for the science of nutrition, Simon Baruch was the
first doctor to identify and successfully operate for appendicitis.
The procedure to identify syphilis was developed by August von
Wasserman, and Paul Erlich and another Jew discovered its cure.

JEWS IN MANY FIELDS

Finance, astronomy, medicine—those fields only begin to introduce the subject of the world's debt to the Jew. Only 3 percent of
the population of the United States is Jewish, yet Jews make up
80 percent of the country's professional comedians. Milton Berle,
George Burns, David Brenner, Sid Caesar, Joan Rivers, David
Steinberg, and Abe Burrows are all Jewish. The greatest stage
actress of all time, Sarah Bernhardt, was Jewish.

The Jews have been the world's foremost inventors. The micro-
phone, the gramophone, and the internal combustion engine all
originated in the mind of a Jew, Emile Berliner. The calculating
machine was invented by Abraham Stern. Herman Jones invented
synthetic rubber. Petroleum, the basic energy source of the modern world, owes its discovery and distillation to Abraham Schreiner.
Atomic research was largely the work of Jews, notably Michelson

and Einstein, closely followed by J. Robert Oppenheimer. Otto Lilenthal, a German Jew, made history's first successful attempts at glider flying, and his findings inspired the Wright brothers to go on and achieve fame. Marconi did not invent the radio; he simply exploited the work of a German Jew, Heinrich Hertz, who discovered the functions of radio waves. Alexander Graham Bell was not the first to invent the telephone; a German Jew, Johann Reis, was demonstrating a telephone in Europe years before Bell took out the patent on his.

The Jews have not been the world's only benefactors, researchers, inventors, and pioneers. The point is that, out of all proportion to their numbers, the Jews have put the world in their debt. Perhaps no book has done more to shape the destinies of mankind than has the Bible, and the Bible, needless to say, was given to the world by God through the Jews.

NOTES

1. Adolf Hitler, *Mein Kampf*, trans. Ralph Manheim (Boston: Houghton Mifflin, 1943), p. 56.
2. Josef Almogi, "Is Too Much Brainpower Too Much?" *Israel Magazine* 5, nos. 11, 12 (1973).

12

THE REPATRIATED JEW: THE ZIONIST CAUSE

A Significant Land Purchase

Sir Moses Montefiore, Queen Victoria's financial adviser was a Jew. When he visited Palestine over a hundred years ago he found that the only land a Jew could possess was land for a synagogue and land for a grave. Through the help of the British ambassador, Sir Moses purchased a plot of land outside the walls of Jerusalem. It was the first piece of property in Palestine for twelve hundred years purchased and owned by a Jew. Today the Jews hold the land of Israel in their hands, and, left alone by the superpowers, they could probably take it all from the Nile to the Euphrates.

Attempts to Annihilate the Jews

Again and again the Jews have been brought to the verge of annihilation, but they seem to have been as miraculously preserved for their land as their land has been for them.

The preservation of the Jew, contrary to the laws of history, was such a puzzle to Hegel, the German philosopher, that he exclaimed in exasperation, "The history of the Jew is a dark, troublesome enigma to me. I am not able to understand it. It does not fit into any of our categories."

Herzl's Dream

And now the Jew is returning home. Home for the Jew is Palestine. In 1903 the British government offered 6,000 square miles in British East Africa to the Jews to be an autonomous Jewish state within the British empire. The Zionists examined land also in Cyrenaica, west of Egypt. Other places were considered, but all were turned down. No other place would do, no place but Palestine. God had already signed His decree. "I will

131

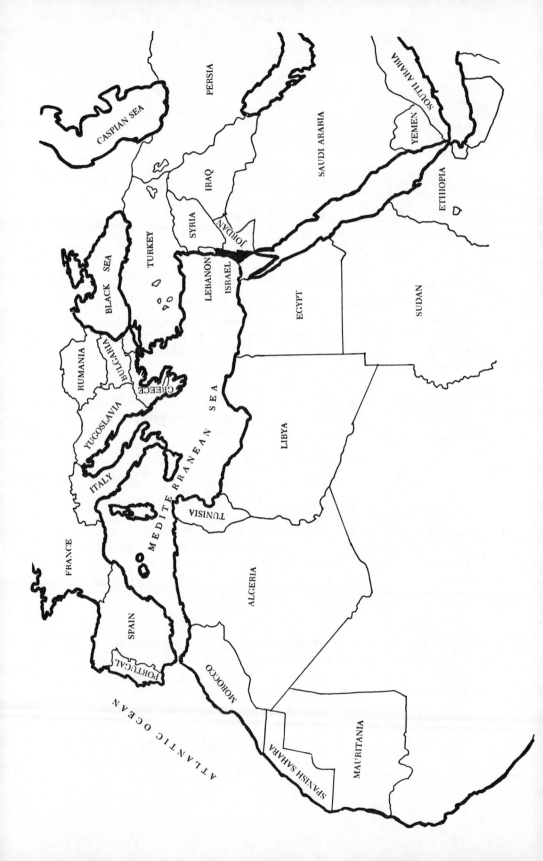

gather them out of all countries, whither I have driven them . . . and I will bring them again to *this* place" (Jeremiah 32:37, italics added).

The man who gave birth to Zionism was "an assimilated Jew" who knew little or nothing about Judaism until the Dreyfus trial in 1894 intensified anti-Semitism in Europe. Up until then Theodor Herzl's thoughts had been in quite a different direction. He wrote in the spring of 1895: "Two years ago I meant to solve the Jewish problem with the help of the Catholic Church, at least in Austria. I meant to go to the Pope and ask him to help us in the fight against anti-Semitism. 'If you do as I say, I shall make myself the leader of a huge movement aiming at voluntary and honest conversion to Christianity.'"[1]

The Dreyfus trial changed his mind. Instead of seeking the mass conversion of Jews to Romanism, Herzl created the World Zionist Organization. He announced to a startled and skeptical Jewish world, at the first World Zionist Congress in Basel, Switzerland, in 1897, that the Jewish state would become a fact in fifty years.

THE PROMISED LAND IN MANY HANDS

The actual land grant deeded to Abraham, to Isaac, and to Jacob stretches from the Nile to the Euphrates. "Unto thy seed have I given this land, from the river of Egypt unto the great river, the river Euphrates" (Genesis 15:18). According to Ezekiel 47:13-21 the promised land extends far beyond the boundaries ever possessed by Israel. It extends to Mount Cassius on the river Orontes as the northwest boundary and to Bir (Berothah) on the Upper Euphrates as the northeast boundary. The southwest boundary is the Nile, and the southeast boundary the Euphrates where it empties into the Persian Gulf. The western boundary is the Mediterranean, the eastern the Euphrates. From north to south the land stretches for about 600 miles. Roughly speaking, the Promised Land embraces about 300,000 square miles.

The Jews have never possessed more than a tithe of their country, even in the palmiest days of empire under David and Solomon. The land actually promised to Abraham is at least twelve times the size of the British Isles. The extreme length of the land in Bible times ran from between 140 to 150 miles. The average breadth varied between 40 to 80 miles. The land, as occupied by Israel, rarely exceeded 20,000 square miles.

The land itself has changed hands many times, but the title deeds in Israel's name are recorded and filed in heaven.

ISRAEL'S STRATEGIC LOCATION

As the meeting place of three continents, Israel is the most strategically placed country on earth. It stands astride the vital waterways of the Mediterranean, the Suez Canal, and the Red Sea. It has excited the imperial ambitions of every would-be world conqueror from the beginning of history. From Pharaohs reaching to the east to Russians reaching to the south the country has been a prize to be seized. Yet Israel itself is small. It can be crossed by car from east to west in an hour and a half. From Jerusalem to Tel Aviv is an hour's drive; from Jerusalem to Haifa is a mere ninety-five miles, to Jericho only twenty and to Bethlehem just five.

CHARACTERISTICS OF THE PROMISED LAND

The country has four chief rivers, none of them large. The Jordan flows through Israel for 157 miles, the Yarkon for 16 miles, the Kishon for 8 miles, and the Yarmuk for 5.

There are seven principal mountains of which the highest, Mount Hermon near Safed, has an elevation of 9,232 feet. Nearby Mount Canaan stands at 3,149 feet. Mount Herzl in Jerusalem stands at 2,741 feet, Tabor rears its head at 1,929 feet, and Carmel looks down at the Mediterranean from 1,791 feet.

The country has three climates. The coastal plain enjoys mild winters, with rainfall coming mostly between the months of November and March. In the mountains the winters are cool with rain and occasional snow falling in the same months as the coastal plain. The mountain regions enjoy warm, dry summers and refreshing, cool evenings. The desert areas and the Jordan Valley have mild winters and burning hot summers. Rainfall is uneven. There is usually enough in the north but never enough in the south, where every few years the land knows severe drought. Irrigation and desalination are essential to make the land yield its full potential. The flora is varied and abundant, and there are several new and great forests planted under the sponsorship of the Jewish National Fund.

This is the land that Theodor Herzl claimed should be given rightfully to the Jewish people. "There is a land without a people," he cried. "There is a people without a land. Give the land without a people to the people without a land."

THE BALFOUR DECLARATION

Chaim Weizmann, another ardent Zionist, was able to render a monumental and vital service to the British government during the First World War. The grateful administration pledged itself to establish a national home for the Jew in Palestine after the war.

Lord Balfour, encouraged by President Wilson of the United States, sent a letter to Lord Rothschild from the Foreign Office under date of November 2, 1917. It read:

> Dear Lord Rothschild—I have much pleasure in conveying to you, on behalf of His Majesty's Government, the following declaration of sympathy with Jewish Zionist aspirations, which has been submitted to, and approved by, the Cabinet.
>
> "His Majesty's Government views with favour the establishment in Palestine of a national home for the Jewish people, and will use its best endeavours to facilitate the achievement of this object, it being clearly understood that nothing shall be done which may prejudice the civil and religious rights of existing non-Jewish communities in Palestine, or the rights and political status enjoyed by Jews in any other country."
>
> I should be grateful if you would bring this declaration to the knowledge of the Zionist Federation.
>
> > Yours sincerely,
> > Arthur James Balfour[2]

A week later the *Jewish Chronicle* (November 9, 1917) made the following statement in its lead article:

> With one step the Jewish cause has made a great bound forward. The declaration of His Majesty's Government as to the future of Palestine in relation to the Jewish people marks a new epoch for our race. For the British Government, in accord—it is without doubt assumed—with the rest of the Allies, has declared itself in favour of the setting up in Palestine of a National Home for the Jewish people, and has undertaken to use its best endeavours to facilitate the achievement of that object. The Jew is at last coming to his rights. In place of being a wanderer in every clime, there is to be a home for him in his ancient land. The day of his exile is ended.

Zionism in the US

Zionism has had a checkered career in the United States. The issue caused early tension in the American Jewish community. Some Jews who had achieved affluence and influence rejected the whole idea of a national homeland for the Jew. Others believed Zionism was philosophically unsound. The movement took its earliest roots in America among the poor immigrants from eastern Europe. At the first Zionist Congress in Basel, Switzerland, there was only one American delegate.

Gradually some American Jewish intellectuals espoused the cause. Emissaries arrived from abroad. Pro-Zionist organizations were formed. Money began to flow in to alleviate the hardships of such Jews as had migrated to Palestine. Zionism became an increasingly important factor in the American Jewish community.

The leaders of the Zionist movement in America put this weight and influence behind negotiations in Britain, which led to the signing of the Balfour Declaration on November 2, 1917. Powerful forces in London opposed the whole idea, but it was President Wilson who helped tip the scales. He let Lord Balfour know that the US fully approved the measure.[3] And behind President Wilson, of course, was American Zionism.

The advent of Hitler aroused many Jews to the soundness of the Zionist cause. When war broke out in Europe, the United States became the bastion of Zionism. By the time Britain handed the Palestine problem over to the United Nations, Zionism in America had the full moral, political, and financial support of most American Jews. The warmth and goodwill of the American people lay with the Zionists, too.

American Jews have occupied themselves with lobbying for American support for Israel in the halls of Congress and with providing enormous sums of money, often sacrifically, to aid the state of Israel.

In 1917 the British began their drive to roll up the Turkish power in the area like a worn out carpet. An army under General Allenby marched from Egypt into Palestine, and on December 9 he captured Jerusalem without firing a shot. Next year the whole Turkish army was routed, and Palestine passed into the hands of the British.

If the Arabs wish to base their claim to Palestine on *tenure,* then obviously the country belongs to the Jews. From the days of Joshua onward, Jews have lived almost continually in the land. Palestine has never been an *independent* state except when it has been a Jewish state. The great majority of so-called Arab "Palestinians" actually came to the country as a result of Zionist enterprise and development, which in turn was a result of Jewish settlement. If the claim is based on *conquest,* then the country belonged last to Britain, and she, in cooperation with the League of Nations, envisioned it as a national home for the Jew.

THE THIRD JEWISH COMMONWEALTH

At an allied premier's conference at San Remo, April 24, 1920, the Western powers confirmed Britain's mandate. On July 24, 1922 the League of Nations Council confirmed the Palestine and Mesopotamian Mandate of Great Britain, thus validating by international decree the right of all Jews to go there and build a national home.

King George V of England applauded the Mandate: "I realize profoundly the solemnity of the trust involved in the government of a country which is sacred alike to Christian, Mohammedan, and Jew, and I shall watch with deep interest and warm sympathy the future progress and development of a State whose history has been of such tremendous import to the world."[4]

The Zionists hailed the beginning of "the Third Jewish Commonwealth." The British government, under Prime Minister David Lloyd George, appointed a Jew, Sir Herbert Samuel, to be the Civil Administrator of Palestine with direct responsibility to the British cabinet. Thus a Jew became ruler of Palestine for the first time since the days of the Maccabees.

When the British government expressed itself in favor of establishing a home for the Jew in Palestine, British Jewry met to publicly express its thanks. The *Times,* the leading newspaper of the day, actually stated, in reporting the meeting, that the return of the Jew to Palestine was a fulfillment of prophecy.

> The great meeting held to express the gratitude of British Jewry to His Majesty's Government for their recent declaration in fa-

vour of the establishment of a National Home for the Jewish people was more than a political demonstration. . . . Its outstanding features were the Old Testament spirit which pervaded it and the feeling that, in the somewhat incongruous setting of a London theatre, the approaching fulfillment of ancient prophecy was being celebrated with faith and fervour.[5]

BRITISH ADMINISTRATION OF PALESTINE

Sir Herbert Samuel's administration was a resounding success. He resigned in June 1925 and was succeeded by Field Marshall Lord Plumer, a capable administrator and a keen Christian deeply interested in Zionism. He in turn was followed by Sir John R. Chancellor. Chancellor suggested the establishment in Palestine of a twenty-eight-member legislative council made up of fourteen Arabs, seven Jews, and some officials and a president who had not previously been connected with Palestine to help solve some of the growing problems in running the country. Both Arabs and Jews rejected the idea. The British colonial secretary invited the leaders of both sides to London to discuss the whole matter, but by then the Arabs had decided on terrorism as a solution to the Jewish presence in Palestine. In 1938 Sir Harold MacMichael was appointed administrator with special instructions to deal with the Arab terrorists. In November 1944 Field-Marshal Viscount Gort became the British representative in the country.

JEWISH IMMIGRATION INTO PALESTINE

Between 1918 and 1948 the Jewish community in Palestine was reinforced by successive waves of immigrants. The initial response to the British Mandate was disappointing to the Zionists, for fewer than 8,000 Jews a year found their way back to the promised land. The hardy pioneers who did come, however, were for the most part ardent Zionists prepared to clear land, drain marshes, build roads, and work themselves to premature old age and hasty death.

Persecution of the Jews in Poland in the 1920s brought a new flood of immigrants into Palestine. Many of those Jews settled in Tel Aviv and started small factories and engaged in commerce. The depression forced some of them out of business, however, and some even left the country because of the hardships brought on at that time.

In the 1930s Jews began to migrate to Israel from Europe in

greater numbers because, by then, the strident voice of Adolf Hitler was making itself heard. Many Jews who came at that time would just as soon have been assimilated into other European communities, but things looked so ominous on the continent they chose Palestine instead. There was nowhere else to go.

Pressure was mounting on the British to curb the influx of Jews who were entering Palestine. The Arabs were protesting in violent acts of terrorism. By 1929 Arab intransigence had blossomed into outright acts of intimidation. By 1935 it had become open rebellion against Britain, largely financed by Mussolini and with Germany supplying arms. Then, as now, the oil reserves of the world were in Arab lands, and in order to placate the Arabs and keep her hands on Arab oil, Britain began to set immigration quotas and to restrict the movement of Jews into Palestine.

THE WHITE PAPER

On May 17, 1939 the British government passed what it called a White Paper, a document that practically stopped further immigration of Jews into Palestine except those included in a five-year quota of 75,000. That was an outright bid to appease the Arabs. The British position was made more difficult by the fact that Indian Muslims were listening to Arab propaganda and were determined to join in a holy war against Britain and the Jews. With war with Germany looming on the horizon, Britain could not afford trouble with the Middle East and India.

The undisputed leader of the Palestinian Arab community at that time was Aaj Amin al-Husseini, the Grand Mufti of Jerusalem, a bitter enemy of the British. He joined the Nazis and spent the war years in Berlin.

The White Paper broke the spirit of the Balfour Declaration. It put the brakes on Jewish immigration at the very time that hundreds of thousands of European Jews were being slated for mass extermination. One of the voices raised in the British Parliament against the White Paper was that of Winston Churchill.

During those years the Zionists were not idle. They created a shadow government in Palestine, determined to be ready to take over the country when the hour of freedom finally came. The Jewish Agency became the recognized body for liaison between world Jewry and the British government, the League of Nations, and the Jews in Palestine. The Zionists recruited an underground army, the *Hagana*, and went steadily ahead forging the educational systems and administrative bodies Israel would need when nationhood arrived.

With the outbreak of World War II, affairs in Palestine were forced into the background. The Jews fought on the side of the British with courage and desperation, and the Arabs intrigued with the Germans. The Nazi program of genocide put tremendous backbone into the valiant little Jewish brigade.

Britain Turns Against the Jews

After World War II it became evident to the Jews that the British were going to oppose large-scale immigration of Jewish refugees into Palestine. Sir Winston Churchill had been bundled out of office by a war-weary and ungrateful British public. A socialist party installed a government staffed by men who were not disposed to be friendly to the Jews. British warships were sent out into the Mediterranean to hunt down "illegal" Jewish immigrant ships trying to run the blockade. Jewish refugees from Hitler's death camps were taken off those vessels and interned on the island of Cyprus. A tiny quota of Jews was allowed to trickle into Palestine from the Cyprus camps each month. The situation could not last. Each time the British allowed a few Jews into the country the Arabs exploded with violence; each time the British intercepted an immigrant ship the Jews went on a rampage.

Jewish Guerrilla Warfare in Palestine

The Jewish answer to Britain's new policy was to take up arms against its former friend and ally. There were two chief anti-British organizations in the country operated by Jews. The *Irgun Zvai Leumi* (National Military Organization) was one. If we could experience the feeling of Jews who watched as their brother survivors from the holocaust were turned away homeless from Israel by the British occupation force, we could understand the Irgun. Hundreds of Jews drowned in Haifa Bay as they, having lived through the Nazi terror, sought to swim from boats through the British blockade to Israel's shores. The Irgun was led by Gurion once even labeled Begin a fascist.

The Irgun opposed the methods of the Jewish Agency, which sought independence from Britain through negotiation and compromise. It demanded that the British turn all of Palestine and

Judea over to Israel. Its motto was "Judea collapsed in fire and blood; Judea will rise in fire and blood." One of its acts of retaliation was to blow up the King David Hotel in Jerusalem, an episode that brought upon it the repugnance of the world. On another occasion the Irgun caught two British soldiers in reprisal for British acts against them. They tortured the soldiers to death, hung their corpses in an orange grove, and, for good measure, booby-trapped the bodies.

The other guerrilla organization was the Stern Gang, led by Abraham Stern, a cold-blooded fighter who left the Irgun because Begin's group declared a truce in the struggle with Britain upon the outbreak of World War II. The official name of the Stern Gang was "Fighters for the Freedom of Israel." The Stern Gang classified Britain as an enemy and the Mandate as "alien rule."

The logo of the Stern Gang was a map of Palestine and Jordan, across which was flung a fist holding a rifle. Underneath was the motto: "If I forget thee, O Jerusalem, may my right hand forget her cunning." When the Irgun, in 1944, again took up arms against Britain in Palestine, its members hesitated to join hands with the Stern Gang. Stern's methods and goals were too bloody even for them. The Stern Gang's acts of violence were not confined to Palestine. For instance, they murdered Lord Moyne in Cairo because they identified him with "sins against the Jewish people." Anyone, regardless of rank, who wore a British uniform was a target for the Stern Gang. They attacked British installations and made the railways a permanent target.

So fierce did the guerilla war against Britain become in Palestine toward the end that the British had to keep 100,000 troops in the country—one for about every half dozen Jews. Even so she could not keep the peace. By 1947 Britain was weary of the whole Palestine problem. She was receiving nothing but abuse from abroad and nothing but trouble in the country itself. At last she handed the Palestine issue over to the United Nations.

THE UNITED NATIONS AND PARTITION

After studying the problem, the United Nations recommended that the country be partitioned between Arab and Jew with Jerusalem to be held under international control. The Arabs were incensed. Their proposal to the United Nations was one they had maintained for thirty years. There should be a single Palestine,

they said, and it should be an Arab state. Jews would be allowed
to live there, but only as a minority. For good measure they further proposed that Palestine should be ruled by an Arab freedom-
fighter, one who had participated in Germany's massacre of the
Jews.

The partition resolution in the United Nations needed a two-
thirds majority in order to pass, and both Russia and the United
States would have to endorse it.

Now an old man, Chaim Weizmann came from a bed of sickness
to talk with President Truman. The thing that weighed on his
mind was not just US support for the partition proposal. He was
desperately anxious that the Negev be included in any new state
of Israel. He was able to persuade the American president. The
way was now clear for the fight on the UN floor.

It looked hopeless right from the start. The Jews needed twenty-
two votes just to offset the eleven members of the Arab-Muslim
bloc in the United Nations. As for Soviet-American cooperation,
the two countries had never voted together on anything. The
Arabs used every weapon available to them to persuade Britain,
France, and other countries to vote the Resolution down. France
had large holdings in North Africa. Britain had vast interests in
Jordan, Saudi Arabia, Egypt, Persia, Yemen, and Iraq, and, moreover, she was embittered over Jewish terrorism in Palestine.

The British ambassador to the United Nations, Sir Alexander
Cadogan, held himself coldly aloof from the whole debate. (His
sole contribution to the fierce debate over Partition was the addition of a comma to a report.) Having made known to the General
Assembly that Britain would not raise a finger to help any solution
that did not have complete Arab and Jewish support (something
he knew to be impossible), he sat back and waited the coming
vote. He was going to vote against partition in any case; it would
be one last way of paying back the Irgun and the Stern Gang for
the British blood they had shed.

The Soviet Union changed sides and supported the resolution
because the Kremlin strategists suddenly saw how much could be
gained by such a move. At that time the Arabs were pro-Nazi
and therefore anti-Communist and had little love for Russia.
Russia, wanting a toehold in the Middle East, saw Israel as a possible pawn. By supporting partition, Russia could reap propaganda benefits by posing as the great humanitarian, wrung by

Israel's sufferings, determined to befriend the Jew. She could drive a wedge between Britain and America, because if Russia voted for partition then America would be forced to do the same (to avoid alienating Israel), and that would help sour Anglo-American relations. So Russia cynically changed sides.

The vote on November 19, 1947, in the United Nations was tense. The Secretary General declared at the beginning: "We shall have a roll call of nations on the partition resolution; a two-thirds majority is needed for passage. Delegates will answer in one of three ways: for, against, or abstain." Then began the roll call of the nations.

The votes seesawed back and forth with the Jews slowly gaining ground. Some delegates were calm, others complacent. Some voted with voices choked with rage.

When *The United Kingdom of Great Britain* was called, the British Ambassador rose to his feet and looked around the assembly hall. At the last moment, with world opinion strongly on the side of the Jews, Britain gave up its determination to vent its spite on the terrorists. But it could not forget or forgive all it had suffered at their hands. Britain voted to abstain.

In the end, the Jewish victory was overwhelming. The Arabs collected only thirteen votes, eleven of which were from Arab or Muslim countries. One vote was coerced from the Greeks by pressure from Egypt. The thirteenth vote was that of Cuba, the only country on earth the Arabs had been able to persuade to believe that the Jews had no rights in Palestine.

A CHANGING CLIMATE

The Jews had won. The world had again decided that they must be given a national home in Palestine. The Arabs were enraged. With cries of "Perish Judea" on their lips, they left the hall to call for a *Jihud,* a holy war. What could not be won by bribes and threats and votes must be won by war.

In March 1948, faced with growing threats of war in the Middle East, the United States suddenly withdrew its support of partition. It looked as though the Arabs would win after all. The State Department in Washington repented of its partition policy only months after its adoption in the UN. Both political collapse and military defeat now seemed imminent for the Jews.

March 19, 1948, became known as "Black Friday." Warren

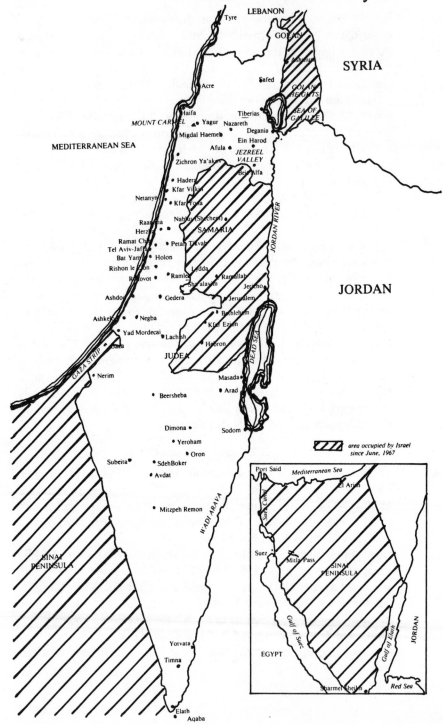

Austin, the US Ambassador to the United Nations, addressed the Security Council and advocated that all efforts to implement partition be suspended. It looked as though the Jewish state would be aborted.

On May 14, 1948, the British High Commissioner left Palestine. Before leaving, however, the British authorities in Palestine saw to it that most of their military installations were left in Arab hands. It was a spiteful act of betrayal, a final gesture of the British government's feelings toward the Jews. Many Christians believe that God has since stripped Britain of her empire because she betrayed her trust and broke her word to the Jewish people.

THE BIRTH OF A NATION

The same day that the British Commissioner left Palestine the General Zionist Council at Tel Aviv proclaimed, at four o'clock in the afternoon, the establishment of the state of Israel. David ben Gurion became its first prime minister, and Chaim Weizmann its first president. The *Declaration of the Establishment of the State of Israel* is a document of great interest to Christian people. It marks the rebirth of the state of Israel and heralds the dawn of tremendous coming prophetic events. It reads:

> Eretz-Israel was the birthplace of the Jewish people. Here their religious and political identity was shaped, here they first attained to Statehood, created cultural values of national and universal significance and gave to the world the eternal Book of Books.

> After being forcibly exiled from their land, the people kept faith with it throughout their dispersion and never ceased to pray and hope for their return to it and for the restoration in it of their political freedom. . . .

> In recent decades they returned in their masses . . . made the deserts bloom, revived the Hebrew language, built villages and towns, and created a thriving community . . . aspiring towards nationhood.

> In the year 5657, at the summons of the spiritual father of the Jewish State, Theodor Herzl, the first Zionist Congress convened and proclaimed the right of the Jewish people to national rebirth in its own country. . . .

> This right was recognized in the Balfour Declaration. . . .

> Survivors of the Nazi holocaust in Europe, as well as Jews from other parts of the world, continued to migrate to Eretz-Israel. . . . On the 29th November, 1947, the United Nations General Assembly passed a Resolution calling for the establishment of a Jewish State in Eretz-Israel. . . .
>
> Accordingly we, members of the People's Council, representatives of the Jewish community of Eretz-Israel and of the Zionist movement, are here assembled on the day of the termination of the British Mandate over Eretz-Israel and, by virtue of our national and historic right and on the strength of the Resolution of the United Nations General Assembly hereby declare the establishment of a Jewish state in Eretz-Israel, to be known as the State of Israel.
>
> We declare that, with effect from the moment of the termination of the Mandate, being tonight, the eve of the Sabbath, the 6th Iyar, 5708, until the establishment of the elected regular authorities of the State in accordance with the Constitution which will be adopted by the elected constituant assembly not later than 1st October 1948, the People's Council shall act as a Provisional Council of State, and its executive organ, the People's Administration shall be the Provisional Government of the Jewish State to be called Israel.
>
> The State of Israel will be open for Jewish immigration and for the ingathering of the exiles. . . .[6]

That historic and prophetically significant document was signed "on this Sabbath Eve, the 6th of Iyar, 5708 (14th May 1948) by David Ben Gurion and thirty-seven other signatories. From the standpoint of the prophetic Scriptures it was one of the most significant moments in history.

The United States had its moment with destiny, too. Even as the United Nations committee debate was being interrupted by Dr. Silver to announce the fact that Israel was now a sovereign state, President Truman was meeting in the White House with his Secretaries of State and Defense. Before them was a letter from Dr. Weizmann urging the United States to recognize Israel. Now came the announcement that the fledgling state was a fact. Israel's future hung in the balance as President Truman weighed the news.

At 5:16 P.M. the president made up his mind and announced

full American recognition of Israel. The news astounded the United Nations General Assembly. Even the US delegates were taken by surprise.

Thus the state of Israel was born.

NOTES

1. Abba Eban, *My People: The Story of the Jews* (New York: Random, 1968), p. 326. See also Max Dimont, *The Indestructible Jews*, new rev. ed. (New York: New American Library, Signet, 1971), p. 398; A. L. Sachar, *A History of the Jews*, rev. ed. (New York: Random, Knopf, 1964), p. 353.
2. Eban, p. 357.
3. Ibid., p. 351.
4. *Times* (London), 12 July 1920.
5. Ibid., 3 December 1917.
6. *Facts About Israel* (Jerusalem: Israel Ministry of Foreign Affairs, Information Division, n.d.), p. 42. Also quoted verbatim in Eban, *My People*.

13

THE REPATRIATED JEW: THE FLAG OF DAVID

THE NEW FLAG

With the announcement of the birth of the state of Israel, the flag of David was unfurled—the traditional shield emblem of David was chosen, two equilateral triangles in blue on a white background. One triangle points downward to the land, the other upward to God. To this was added the traditional two stripes of blue, commanded to be upon the dress of every Israelite. Those were to remind them to obey God's commands (Numbers 15:38-39).

It did not take the Arabs long to react. The reborn state was indeed very vulnerable. It had several thousand irregular troops in the makeshift army, the Hagana. It had less than one rifle for every five men and no artillery at all. The Israeli air force was made up of a few Piper Cubs. Its navy consisted of a handful of old tubs (including the famous *Exodus*) that had once run the British blockade and were tied to the Haifa breakwater. The Arabs outnumbered the Jews 40 to 1 in troops, 100 to 1 in population, 1,000 to 1 in military equipment, and 5,000 to 1 in land mass.

The discrepancy in numbers and armaments between fledgling Israel and her hawkish neighbors was so great that the Arabs and British military experts had no doubts at all about the outcome. The Arabs could capture Haifa by May 20 and Tel Aviv and Jerusalem by May 25. The exodus of the British left the Jews virtually defenseless. Their defense forces desperately needed total organization, yet they had to be flung instantly into a hopeless war.

THE WAR OF INDEPENDENCE

No sooner was the state of Israel proclaimed than the Palestinian guerillas, already operating in the country, were joined by the

149

regular armies of Egypt, Jordan, Syria, and Lebanon, and by a contingent from Saudi Arabia.

Many of the armies were British trained. The Jordanians, particularly, had a crack force, the Arab Legion, which Jordan thought could handle the Jews by itself. In Egypt, Azzam Pasha, Secretary-General of the Arab League, proclaimed Arab goals of Israeli extermination to the world. He said, "This will be a war of extermination and a momentous massacre which will be spoken of like the Mongolian massacres and the Crusades."

That 1948 war, the first of several the Jews had to fight, was known as the War of Independence. The world watched with astonishment as the Jews first stemmed the inrush of the Arab tide and then flung the armies of their foes back across the borders. The Syrian tanks were stopped at Degania; Kaukji, the Syrian guerilla leader, was repulsed at Sejari, and the Egyptians failed to take the Negba.

Meanwhile Israel was getting stronger; a couple of truces gave her the breathing spell she needed to organize, and arms were arriving. The tiny Israeli air force bombed the Egyptians when they broke the truce, and the little Israeli navy damaged two Egyptian warships off Gaza and sunk their flagship, the *Emir Farouk*. A wide corridor was cleared in the Negev. When the Syrians also broke the truce, three Israeli brigades launched a well-organized attack against Arab-held Galilee and took it in twenty-four hours. At the same time the Egyptians were cleared out of an area from the south of Jerusalem to Lachish. The Israeli forces raised a six-month old seige of Sodom at the southern end of the Dead Sea and began to move over a forgotten Roman road to clear the way to Sinai. Only Anglo-American intervention halted the Israeli advance.

The Arabs had been humiliated. Between February and July, 1949, Egypt, Lebanon, Jordan, and Syria signed armistice agreements with Israel. Israel now occupied about 8,000 square miles, but its borders were irregular and could never be regarded as permanent.

THE SINAI WAR

The Arabs refused to recognize Israel's existence. With Russian aid they began to rebuild their armed forces in preparation for a second attack. On the political front, at home and abroad, they worked incessantly for Israel's exclusion from the family of nations. On the economic level they boycotted Israel. On the propaganda front they began a systematic policy of poisoning the minds of men against Israel. Across their common frontiers with Israel they kept up a vicious campaign of terror and intimidation. At sea they tried to hinder the movement of Israeli ships by closing both the Suez and the Tiran Straits to Israel.

In 1956 the Sinai War broke out. Arab terrorists were infiltrating Israel. Then Egypt joined hands with Syria and began to develop military bases in Sinai with massive Russian aid. This time, however, Israel had two unexpected allies. France and Britain were alarmed at Egypt's seizure of the Suez Canal. The strategic implications involved in that movement were only too clear to nations that had vital interests in the East. They decided to intervene. Together with Israel they struck, hoping to liberate the Canal. Their effort was aborted by intense pressure brought against them by Russia and the United States. (It was a shortsighted policy on the part of the Americans. At that very time the Russians were in process of putting down, with ruthless determination, a rebellion in Hungary. Surely the United States should have put the heat on Russia, not on her own friends and allies.) The Israelis were able to gain a little more elbow room during the Sinai War, but that was offset by growing Russian influence with the Arabs.

AN UNEASY CALM

For the next ten years there was a deceptive calm in the Middle East. The United Nations sent an emergency force into Sinai to act as a buffer between Israel and Egypt, and Israel grew in population, economic strength, technical power, and international prestige. The Arabs watched with impotent rage. They found a spokesman in Egypt's president, Gamal Abdel Nasser, the man chiefly responsible for opening the Pandora's box by inviting the Russians into the Middle East. In a statement published jointly with President Araf of Iraq on May 25, 1965, he made clear that the Arabs had not lost sight of their goal. "The Arab national aim," he said, "is the elimination of Israel."

THE SIX-DAY WAR

Arab threats to destroy Israel were losing credibility, however, and the world began to regard such statements as mere rhetoric. Then a new government took over in Syria. The left-wing Ba'ath Party, which had the active backing of the Soviet Union, seized the country, and suddenly invectives against Israel reached new crescendos. Terrorist activity was stepped up, Syrian guns began to shell Israeli settlements at the foot of the Golan Heights, and fresh attempts were made to cut off the waters of the Jordan.

Along with that escalation in the north, Israel began to view with alarm new Egyptian moves in the south. The Egyptians moved the bulk of their army into Sinai, some 90,000 men and 900 tanks. Then Jordan, Iraq, and Syria mobilized and moved their men into position. The Western powers remained strangely silent. Then Egypt ordered the UN emergency force out of the buffer zone, and Israel was left to face her foes alone.

On June 5, 1967, the Six-Day War broke out, a war that astonished the world. Israel, deserted by all her friends, was determined to survive, and she had a surprise up her sleeve for the Arabs—Moshe Dyan. She had forgotten allies as well in the Jews of the Diaspora, who began to besiege Israeli embassies all over the world for passage to Israel. They wanted to help defend Zion. Funds began to pour in from the Jewish brotherhood abroad, and the Israelis were heartened.

It took them less than a week to settle accounts. Jordan was flung back across the river. The West Bank fell to the Jews. Syria lost the Golan Heights, Egypt lost the Gaza Strip, and Sinai and Jerusalem, with the Temple area, fell intact into Hebrew hands. With victorious Jewish armies reaching for Cairo and Damascus, the Arabs screamed for help, and once again the United States pressured Israel to force a halt.

The dismayed Arabs called for a summit conference. They convened in Khartoum in August 1967 to review the disaster that had befallen them, to solicit aid from Russia and the rich sheikdoms of the Gulf, and to plot further mischief against Israel. They restated the four basic principles of Arab policy: no peace with Israel, no negotiations with Israel, no recognition of Israel, and no cessation of efforts to restore the country of Israel to the Palestinians.

In the years that followed, Egypt did her best to force an Israeli withdrawal from the Suez and from Sinai. Jordan and the Palestinian terrorists kept up constant harassment of Israeli settlements.

Syria encouraged terrorists to use its territory as a base for clandestine operations against Israel. In this way desultory warfare was kept up. Russian arms continued to pour into the Middle East despite Egypt's squabble with the Soviet Union, and all Israel's offers to negotiate a permanent peace were ignored.

THE YOM KIPPUR WAR

Then came the Yom Kippur War on October 6, 1973. All across Israel transportation was halted, shops and businesses were closed. The Jews were observing Yom Kippur, the Day of Atonement.

Suddenly enormous masses of Egyptian and Syrian armor attacked. Between them, Syria and Egypt had no less than a million men in the field supported by 5,400 tanks, 980 planes, and 185 anti-aircraft batteries. The Israeli forces had been lulled into a false sense of security and had grown cocky and assured by their previous victories, especially those of the Six-Day War. Along both fronts they fell back, shocked and dismayed. The Israeli army was outnumbered this time twelve to one.

For three days Israel reeled under the weight of the offensive. The Arabs made substantial gains, especially in the Sinai. But the most immediate threat was from Syria, whose forces had been stiffened by the arrival of troops from Iraq, Jordan, Morocco, and other Arab states. The Israelis contented themselves at first with fighting a delaying action in Sinai while trying to cope with the menace from Syria. They were so successful that, by the end of the first week, Israeli guns were able to shell Damascus.

The main force of the Israeli army was then brought to bear on Egypt. Fierce engagements took place in the desert. The Egyptian armor was repulsed, and victorious Israeli units crossed the Suez Canal and took up positions to the rear of the Egyptian army. Cairo was now threatened by Jewish troops.

Again the superpowers intervened. Once more Israel was forced to give up some of her most important gains. Israel lost 2,500 men, of whom 25 percent were officers. The war itself brought Russia and the United States to the very brink of hostilities.

ISRAELI ASSESSMENTS

Israel learned some vital lessons from her wars with the Arabs. She learned that henceforth in any threatening situation she must strike first, and that when forced to fight she can rely only on herself. She needs to become industrially and militarily independent.

She learned, too, the power and potential of the Jews of the Diaspora. During the Yom Kippur War there was hardly a synagogue or Jewish community of any size in the US and Canada that did not have one or more native sons or daughters fighting. Those were the children of the thousands of Jewish families who went to Israel after the Six-Day War. Thus the war came home to American and Canadian Jews as never before. It brought into focus a vital issue. The weakest link in the Jewish fight for survival lies in the fact that ten of the world's thirteen million Jews live outside of Israel itself. Thoughtful Israelis are now saying that the Israeli Defense Forces (*Zahal*) should be expanded. It should become a true Jewish army, embracing not just Israelis but all Jews.

EGYPT AND ISRAEL MAKE PEACE

Another result of the Yom Kippur War was Egypt's reassessment of the value of continued war with Israel. In a courageous move Anwar Sadat of Egypt approached Israel's Menachem Begin to see if the two countries could resolve their differences with words rather than weapons. Negotiations led to the signing in April 1979 of a peace treaty between the two countries. Israel promised to withdrew from Sinai, and Egypt agreed to give Israel full national recognition. The treaty skirted the thorny question of how much autonomy the Israelis should give the Palestinians on the West Bank and in the Gaza Strip.

The Arab nations reacted predictably. Without Egypt the other Arab nations cannot hope to win a war with Israel. Since the treaty ignored the problem of Palestinian self-determination, the Arab world's response was bitter. Half a million Iraqis took to the streets in Baghdad, demonstrations were staged in Syria, bombs exploded in various places, and the Palestinian guerillas vowed war on Israel and the United States. Egypt was expelled from the Arab League and was promptly isolated diplomatically, politically, and economically by unanimous decision of the Arab world. Oil prices were hiked as part of standard Arab blackmail of the free world.

THE WEST BANK ISSUE

If there is one thing that will destroy all attempts by Israel and Egypt to bring about real peace in the Middle East, it is the question of the Israel-occupied West Bank of Palestine, seized from Jordan in the 1967 war.

The West Bank is the home of 650,000 Arabs. Israeli control of the area fills the Arabs with a sense of humiliation and resentment. Their feelings have been intensified by deliberate colonization of the area by the Jews, who have planted more than sixty Jewish settlements there since occupying it. They have done that in the face of continued Arab protests and repeated condemnation both by the United Nations and the United States. Jewish settlements in the area have been strategically planned so that they surround and isolate existing Arab centers of population. Begin has repeatedly referred to the West Bank as being "liberated" not "occupied," making it obvious that the Israelis regard the territory as rightfully and historically theirs. Zealous religious Jews call the West Bank "Samaria" and "Judea," bringing back its old biblical names. They vehemently affirm it belongs to Israel.

Frustrated and angry, the Arabs have stepped up terrorist activities against Israel, especially in the West Bank. Attacks have become more professional, better organized, obviously the work of experts.

The Israelis have responded in kind. Youthful Jewish settlers deliberately set out to terrorize Arab citizens in retaliation for Arab attacks upon Israelis. Militant organizations have surfaced among the Jews, adding a new dimension of tension to the area. One such group calls itself *Kach* ("Thus" in Hebrew), and it openly advocates violence to drive the Arabs out of the West Bank.

The Arabs have not been idle on the diplomatic front, either. In late July 1980, for instance, the UN General Assembly met in an emergency session to consider the plight of the Palestinian Arabs. The Arabs and their allies in the Third World forced a debate in order to bring pressure on Israel and alert the world to the seriousness of the situation. A resolution was introduced calling for a Palestinian sovereign state on the West Bank and for Israeli withdrawal from all territory occupied in the 1967 war. Previous emergency sessions of the UN have been called only to deal with fast-breaking crises such as the North Korean invasion of South Korea.

One major objective of the Arabs in the emergency session was to persuade the United Nations to assemble a military force to back the resolution. The UN vote was overwhelmingly in favor of the Arabs (112 to 7, with 24 abstentions), though the Arabs failed to get support for their plan to have a United Nations military force push Israel back to its pre-1967 boundaries. The resolution, it should be noted, made no mention of Israel's right to exist.

Israel refuses to be intimidated by either her foes or by her friends. Typical of her determination to survive was the bombing raid June 7, 1981 against Iraq's new nuclear reactor. Israel was convinced that Iraq, one of her most implacable enemies, would soon be in a position to make nuclear weapons. Israel decided on a preemptive strike against a country with which she is still officially at war. The strike was completely successful. Despite the momentary unification of the Arab world, and the pious protests of a number of world's capitals, many people seemed secretly relieved that the danger of nuclear blackmail in the volatile and energy-rich Middle East had temporarily been averted.

THE REVIVAL OF THE HEBREW TONGUE

Israel has been reborn. A million and a half Jews trekked back in the nation's first twenty-five years of statehood, coming from almost every country on earth. And when they came they took part in another modern miracle—they spoke Hebrew.

It was Eliezer Ben Yehuda (1858-1922) who first proposed to the Jews of the world that they should revive and speak the Hebrew tongue. The Jews considered him mad, and he was certainly an eccentric. He was a consumptive, recently married and taking his new bride by ship to Israel, when he made the big decision that henceforth he would speak only in Hebrew. He told his eleven children he had begotten them solely in order to speak Hebrew and disseminate it. He isolated them from other children, taught them Hebrew, and sent them into the streets to squabble with the neighbors' children—in Hebrew. Ben Yehuda's firstborn was the first child to be taught Hebrew as his native tongue since the days of the Romans.

Hebrew, as a language, is much older than the Hebrew people. It was a fully developed language long before the Jewish nation marched out of Egypt. At an early date a letter alphabet was invented, probably in southern Palestine, and became the source of the alphabets of later languages such as Phoenician, Hebrew, Greek, and Latin.

Hebrew was spoken by the Carthaginian general Hannibal when he camped his army before the walls of Rome. Hannibal's Hebrew, however, was only a Semitic dialect, not the Hebrew language as the world knows it today. The Hebrew of the Jews has influenced all the languages of Europe.

As the Jew made Palestine the holy land, so he has made Hebrew a holy language. Hebrew has never died in the sense that it has always been the language of the Hebrew mind and the Hebrew faith, but it did become a dead language in the workaday world. By the time of Christ, Greek, Latin, and Aramaic were the spoken languages of Palestine. As with Latin, the world passed by Hebrew even though it was studied by scholars for special purposes. Nobody speaks Latin today, and, for centuries, no one spoke Hebrew.

Ben Yehuda could clearly see the need for a revived, revitalized Hebrew tongue. A Jewish land without Hebrew would be what someone called a "linguistic Balkans"—Jews coming back from a hundred countries speaking a Babel of tongues. What should be the language of Israel? English? French? Why not Hebrew?

In the end Ben Yehuda lived to see scholars, teachers, philologists, and linguists assemble to coin new words from ancient Hebrew roots, to see the fig tree of the Hebrew language truly put forth its leaves, to see the League of Nations on September 23, 1922, officially recognize Hebrew as a spoken language of the world. Three months later, Ben Yehuda died.

Modern Hebrew is a virile language. The Hebrew of the Talmud and the old rabbis was a language of the intricate approaches and abstruse allusions of an essentially Eastern tongue. Modern Hebrew is concise, exact, full of action, and is essentially a Western tongue. The revisers of the Hebrew language stripped it of its cryptic phrases and substituted a more practical idiom. Almost every day new Hebrew words are being added to keep pace with the fast tempo of a modern, industrialized, Western-looking Jewish world.

Recently a Dutch inventor, Aad J. van der Toorn, began experimenting with Hebrew to see if it could be adapted to computers.

Machines that read writing are common enough in modern industrial nations. Banks and postoffices use them extensively. Van der Toorn found it fairly simple to get Hebrew data into a computer, but he faced a problem when it came to getting it back out again. Teletype machines could not reproduce Hebrew vowels (which are printed above or below the consonants) or the accents. Expanding the problem still further, the inventor recalled that Russian and Arabic script could not be handled by computers any more than Hebrew.

The solution seemed to be to design a new Hebrew script, one that could accommodate Arabic and Russian letters as well. He invented square-shaped letters made up of five basic lines, straight, horizontal, and vertical. He tried out the new shapes with Roman letters first and then applied the technique to Arabic and Hebrew letters.

He faced one seemingly unsolvable problem with Hebrew and Arabic. All Latin-based languages read from left to right; Hebrew and Arabic read from right to left. How could the two be reconciled to accommodate a computer? How could a teletype machine print backwards? He pondered the problem for months, and the answer, when it came, was deceptively simple. His experiments had been made using tapes. He suddenly saw that all he needed to do was print Latin-based letters with one direction for up and down, and then print the Hebrew and Arabic letters *upside down*. To read the Arabic and Hebrew he would only need to turn the tape around![1]

PROBLEMS OF IMMIGRATION

The Israelis regard immigration as their country's great mission. It is a fundamental principle of the state of Israel that any Jew, anywhere in the world, can migrate to Israel. The only exception is a Jew who has a criminal record or one who might endanger the health or the order of the state. Such migration has practically eliminated the existence of Jewish communities in Egypt, Libya, Iraq, and Yemen, countries in which Jews have resided for over two thousand years. The Nazi Holocaust frightened most of the surviving Jews of Poland, Hungary, and Romania into fleeing those lands.

One of Israel's biggest problems has been how to absorb culturally Jews from so many different backgrounds. About half of the immigrants into Israel have come from Muslim countries where they traditionally lived in poverty, raised large families, and subscribed to a traditional, authoritarian, and patriarchal form of society. About half of the immigrants have come from American and European cultures where basic attitudes are those of a modern, democratic, technical world. The state of Israel has used housing and education as a means of bringing the two together.

The early pioneers were idealists. They planned a society in which law would be replaced by spontaneous generosity. The microcosm of that society was the *kibbutz,* a rural or industrial community in which all the members share both the means of production and its results. Women work alongside men. Children sleep in their own separate children's houses. The first fact of life is equality. The kibbutz rests on the three principles of equality of work, practical democracy, and the abolition of private property. About 3.5 percent of the population in Israel today live in kibbutzim.

The *moshavim* were a later development. They resulted from dissatisfaction with the way the kibbutzim idea sometimes worked out in practice. The moshavim retained the kibbutz idea of national ownership of land, personal labor, and mutual aid, but much greater freedom was given to members to run their own lives and make their own decisions. Each member of a moshav is given the same initial means of production, but what he makes of it once he has it is up to him. So long as he works the land it is his to run, and he can plow his proceeds back into the land or spend them any way he wants.

RELIGION IN ISRAEL

Although a considerable number of Israelis consider themselves secular, or nonreligious, religion does play a powerful role in the country. Israel has about 6,000 synagogues scattered throughout the nation. Jewish dietary laws are enforced throughout the land and in the armed forces, as well as in the government and in public institutions. The Bible and the Talmud are part of the general school curriculum throughout Israel. Parents may have their children educated either in the state schools or in schools of their choice.

The constitution guarantees religious freedom for all in Israel, but the Ministry of Religious Affairs, which keeps a sharp eye on all such matters, is under sustained pressure from the rabbinate.

Supreme religious authority is vested in the Chief Rabbinate, made up of an Ashkenazi and a Sephardi rabbi and the supreme Rabbinical Council. The Rabbinate rules on the interpretation of all Jewish laws in matters that lie outside the jurisdiction of the rabbinical courts of which there are about eight in the country.

A close watch is kept on Jews who might be inclined to convert to Christianity. Christian missionaries who want to work among Jews are not particularly welcome in the country. Social and economic pressure is brought to bear upon any Jew who changes to another religion. It is not a sin in Israel for a Jew to be irreligious, but for him to become a Christian is unthinkable. Such a Jew is considered to have cut himself off from the national past of his people, and he is frequently treated as though he were actually dead.

The problem of Sabbath observance in Israel illustrates the inadequacy of religious Judaism. So long as Jews live in Gentile countries they have little problem. They can arrange to have a Gentile take over for them on the Sabbath if they are employed in one of the essential services, or they can seek some other kind of employment. But that type of evasion does not work in Israel. The Jews must operate all the vital services themselves—pumping stations, telephone and telegraph services, police and fire departments, the armed forces. When a Jew engaged in one of those services consults his rabbi as to what he should do when it is his turn to work on the Sabbath, the rabbi usually begs the question and tells him to get a different kind of a job. Who then is going to run the vital services?

When the state of Israel was organized in 1948 the government entrusted jurisdiction in religious matters to representatives of Orthodox Judaism, something that has since caused problems. The various religious parties band together to exert pressure for the passage of their kind of legislation. They exert an influence far in excess of their size. The kind of Judaism with which the Orthodox establishment is trying to shackle the entire nation is based on the sixteenth-century code found in the Shulcan Aruch. Most modern Jews consider it to be an archaic relic of the past, and they resent having it forced upon them. They consider it quite unsuitable to their daily life. The insensitivity of the Orthodox establishment to the needs and wishes of others is a constant source of friction.

SIGN OF THE FIG TREE

Israel has been reborn. The Jew sees in this a fulfillment of his national and religious aspirations over many a long age. The Christian sees in it an event of great prophetic significance. He is reminded that the Lord Jesus foretold that the fig tree (a well-established symbol for the state of Israel) would once more put forth its leaves prior to His return. Thus the rebirth of the state of Israel heralds the coming consummation of the age (Matthew 24:32-34).

Israel has been reborn. The repatriated Jew's feelings can best be summarized in the words of Israel's national anthem:

> So long as still within our breasts
> The Jewish heart beats true,
> So long as still toward the East
> To Zion looks the Jew,
> So long our hopes are not yet lost—
> Two thousand years we cherished them—
> To live in freedom in the Land
> Of Zion and Jerusalem.

NOTE

1. See "A New Shape for Hebrew: A Dutchman Did It," *Israel Magazine* 6, no. 12 (1974-75):61-65.

14

THE REPATRIATED JEW: THE PROMISED LAND

The land of Israel without the Jew was a land without a soul. With the rebirth of the state of Israel, the promised land experienced resurrection. Where once barren hills reared their forlorn heads against a rainless sky, forests, fields, and farms flourish. Where ruins littered the landscape, thriving cities now stand. Old Bible names live again—Jerusalem, Sodom, Gaza, Beersheba. What would the old pilgrim, who first journeyed into this land from far-off Ur of the Chaldees, think if he could see it now! He would surely stand astonished at the genius of his distant heirs, for never before has so much been accomplished by so few against such odds.

ISRAEL, A PARLIAMENTARY DEMOCRACY

Israel today is governed by a parliamentary democratic system patterned along British lines, in which the power of parliament (the *Knesset*) is supreme. Three principal political blocks vie for control of the legislative process with various small, splinter parties doing their best to make their voices heard.

The presidency of Israel is a ceremonial office only, as is the British monarchy. The first president of Israel was Chaim Weizmann. The position had been offered first to Albert Einstein. The thought had originally been that the presidency of Israel should go to the most famous Jew in the world, regardless of whether or not he was an Israeli. It was an attractive thought. Dr. Einstein declined the honor.

The president's ceremonial function is to name the Judiciary (the judges of the civil, rabbinical, and Muslim Sharia courts), and the appointments are for life to ensure complete independence from other branches of government.

Nominees for the civil courts are chosen by a commission in which the politicians, made up of ministers and members of the Knesset, are outnumbered by jurists who represent both the supreme court and the bar association. Nominees for the rabbinical and Sharia court judges are nominated by the religious authorities involved.

Israel's civil law is inherited largely from the British system, but is modified by the codes of other European countries and by the American code. When they were setting up the civil code, the Israeli legislators did their best to base legislation on the principles of justice laid down in the Torah, elaborated in the Talmud, and codified by Maimonides and other contributors to traditional Jewish law.

POLITICS IN ISRAEL

Israel has a multiparty system. The country is regarded as a single constituency, and voters do not choose between candidates but between slates of candidates. Seats in the Knesset are divided among the slates of candidates in proportion to the number of votes each slate receives. The system has fostered numerous splinter parties, but its redeeming feature lies in the fact that minority groups can obtain representation in the Knesset, something not really possible under the British and American systems.

The dominant party in Israel has been the moderate, socialist Israel Labor Party, which tends to command the majority of votes. Because of the system of proportionate representation, it usually fails to command a clear parliamentary majority and has to rely on coalitions with smaller groups. As a result the prime minister (the leader of the current dominant party in the Knesset) generally finds himself having to accept some ministers in his cabinet who are chosen by his coalition partners. The dominant party normally finds itself in a position in which it has to make concessions to minority groups. The demands of the National Religious Party have usually been the easiest to meet, so that party is generally included in the government where it can wield influence out of proportion to its size. Menachem Begin's *Likud* coalition, composed of the Herud party and its liberal allies, broke Labor's virtual control of the Israeli government.

THE KNESSET

The Knesset controls all legislation in Israel and, generally speaking, the courts cannot invalidate any law it passes. There is no capital punishment in Israel except for treason in time of war and for collaboration with enemies. Bills are generally introduced by the cabinet and presented to the Knesset by the minister chiefly concerned, but they may also be proposed by any member of the Knesset with the approval of the house or one of the Knesset committees. A bill is given three readings. After the first reading it is discussed in detail by the appropriate Knesset committee. At the second reading any amendments made are reviewed by the house, and at the third reading it is voted on.

LOCAL GOVERNMENT

Local affairs are run by democratically elected authorities. Israel is divided into municipalities and local regional councils concerned with education, culture, health, sanitation, social welfare, water, road repair, parks, and fire departments. The ministry of the interior supervises all local government, drafts the legislation that controls their activities, and supervises their powers of taxation and their bylaws.

THE CIVIL SERVICE

The Israeli civil service is headed by a commissioner who is directly responsible to the minister of finance. He is assisted by a civil service board.

THE JUDICIARY

Israeli courts enjoy complete independence under the constitution. In all the major towns there are magistrates courts to deal with minor matters such as ordinary disputes over money, minor criminal offences, and matters pertaining to land. Beyond the magistrates courts are the district courts made up of a judge (or in some cases three judges) but no jury, which try all matters outside the jurisdiction of the magistrates and which hear matters appealed from the magistrates courts. The supreme court, the highest in the land, has ten members and is located in Jerusalem. Its cases, heard by three or five judges, are cases appealed against

HOW ISRAEL IS GOVERNED

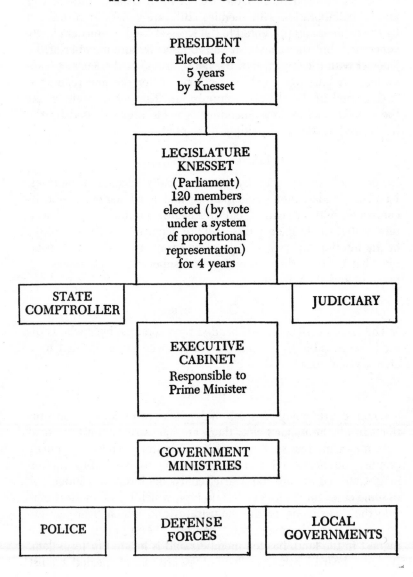

PRESIDENT
Elected for
5 years
by Knesset

LEGISLATURE
KNESSET
(Parliament)
120 members
elected (by vote
under a system
of proportional
representation)
for 4 years

STATE
COMPTROLLER

JUDICIARY

EXECUTIVE
CABINET
Responsible to
Prime Minister

GOVERNMENT
MINISTRIES

POLICE

DEFENSE
FORCES

LOCAL
GOVERNMENTS

the district courts and cases brought against the government by private citizens.

In addition to the secular courts, religious courts are found in every major community to rule on matters concerning personal status. Jewish and Christian courts have jurisdiction over matters relating to marriage, divorce, and alimony. Christian courts may also decide matters relating to wills.

THE ARMED FORCES

Israel is defended by its armed forces, which are kept strong by compulsory conscription. All men under twenty-nine and all women under twenty-six are called up for regular service of up to thirty months for men and twenty for women. Married and pregnant women and mothers are exempt from conscription. Exemption is also granted women on religious grounds, but in that case some form of national service is substituted. In Israel it is almost a stigma to be excluded from the armed forces.

A standing reserve makes it possible for Israel to swiftly mobilize whatever force is needed to meet aggression. All have to report annually for thirty-one days of consecutive training until they reach the age of forty, and thereafter must report annually for fourteen days of training until they reach the age of fifty-five. Everyone over the rank of private has to do an extra seven days' training a year.

The general staff, which controls all three armed services, is headed by a chief of staff who carries the rank of lieutenant-general. The general staff comprises the chiefs of the manpower, logistics, and intelligence services, together with the commanders of the air force and the navy, and the officers heading the various regional commands.

The army has all the usual corps—armored, artillery, signal, engineers, parachute, supply, ordnance, and medical, all of which are upgraded constantly to meet the increasing sophistication of the enemy. Commando and combat units take priority in Israel's army, backed by an efficient infantry. The word *Forward!* has been removed from all military vocabulary and replaced with the words *Follow me!* All officers must receive training as commandos or paratroops before they can lead regular troops. No assigned task is considered impossible until more than 50 percent of the task force is killed.

Israel's air force is one of the world's toughest. It trains all its own pilots and ground crews and maintains and produces spare parts for the most modern and sophisticated aircraft. It is equipped with the newest jets available.

The navy has arisen from a half dozen rusty old hulks, once used to smuggle immigrants into the country. When war with the Arabs first broke out, those ghost ships were manned by the very men who had once sailed them as smugglers. Israel now has a small but sophisticated navy, equipped with modern ships including submarines and able to fight in two theaters of war.

Israel's defense forces are supplemented by youth battalions— volunteers from fourteen to eighteen years of age recruited from secondary schools, youth organizations, and immigrant villages.

ISRAEL ENTERS THE NUCLEAR AGE

Israel entered the atomic age in 1953 when Prime Minister David Ben Gurion announced the actual formation of an atomic energy commission, to be headed by a scientist from the Weizmann Institute of Science. That commission is now chaired by the prime minister. Research is carried out at the Nahal Soreq Center and the Negev Nuclear Research Center. The main fields of research are nuclear physics and chemistry, solid state physics, reactor physics and engineering, metallurgy and electronics, radio biology, and nuclear medicine.

There is a growing conviction among most outside observers that Israel has secretly developed a nuclear weapon capacity. In a future war with the Arabs, should Israel find her back to the sea and total defeat imminent, she would doubtless use her atomic arsenal as a last, desperate measure. That would, of course, escalate Middle East confrontation overnight and possibly lead to a confrontation between the superpowers.

A German-built freighter, the *Scheersberg A*, left Antwerp on November 17, 1968, under the Liberian flag. It vanished, carrying 560 drums of "yellowcake", a crude concentrate of uranium. It was supposedly destined for Genoa, Italy, but it never arrived. On December 2 the ship turned up at the Turkish port of Iskenderun. Its cargo, 200 tons of uranium, worth $3.7 million, had vanished.

Investigators now believe that the disappearance of the *Scheersberg A* was part of an elaborate plot to disguise the secret purchase

of much-needed uranium by Israel for use in its French-built reactor at Dimona in the Negev. The West German government
is believed to have been involved. The story is that Germany
would look the other way at the secret purchase of uranium from
Germany, and that Bonn would receive in return access to Israel's
advanced uranium separation process—a process that can be used
to produce nuclear weapons. The Bonn government has refused
comment.[1]

POPULATION

The present population of Israel is about three million, of which
85 percent are Jews, 11 percent Muslims, and the balance Druzes,
Christians, and others. It is expected to reach four million before
the turn of the century. About 27 percent of Israel's Jews were
born in Europe and the Americas, about 25 percent were born in
Asia and Africa (mostly in Arab countries), and about 48 percent
are native-born Israels (generally known as *Sabras*). The population is mainly urban. About 85 percent of the people live in
about 100 towns and urban localities. In addition there are some
1,000 villages in Israel including the kibbutzim and the moshavim.
A large number of the settlements have been founded since Israel
became a state, most of them pioneered by immigrants. Jerusalem, the capital of Israel, is not the country's largest urban center.
That place is held by Tel Aviv, with Jerusalem ranking second and
the important seaport of Haifa ranking third.

EDUCATION

Education is the third largest item in Israel's national budget,
exceeded only by defense and housing. State education in Israel
is based, by law, on "the values of Jewish culture and the achieve-
ments of science; on love of the Homeland and devotion to the
State of Israel and the Jewish people; on training in agricultural
labor and handicrafts; on fulfillment of pioneering principles; on
the aspiration to a society built on liberty, equality, tolerance,
mutual aid and love of fellow-man."[2]

Education is free, compulsory between the ages of five and
fifteen, and financed partly by the state and partly by local authorities. Children can attend public or religious schools at the dis-
cretion of their parents. The language of instruction is Hebrew
in Jewish schools and Arabic in Arab schools; Arabic is an op-

tional language in Jewish schools, and Hebrew is taught in all Arab schools from the third grade. English is the leading foreign language taught, with French a popular second. One of the chief goals of the educational system is to eliminate the cultural gap that exists between Jews from diverse backgrounds. Special programs to achieve that goal are included in the curriculum as well as programs aimed at raising the educational level of boys and girls of Asian and African background.

The leading seat of higher learning in Israel is the Hebrew University in Jerusalem. The cornerstone for that university was laid on Mount Scopus in 1918, and the institution opened its doors in 1925. The Jordanians sealed off the site for nineteen years, so a new campus was opened in western Jerusalem. In 1968, when all of Jerusalem was back in Jewish hands, the foundation was laid for a new University City on Mount Scopus. Other leading universities in Israel are the Tel Aviv University, the University of Haifa, and the University of the Negev. The Bar-Ilan University near Tel Aviv trains Jewish scholars and professionals with a special emphasis on Jewish studies.

RESEARCH

The government of Israel places an unusually high emphasis on research and development. At first emphasis was placed primarily on agriculture and the production of consumer goods, but now a much wider range of research is promoted with government backing. The national council for research and development advises the government on national policy for applied research and technical development, and also initiates special projects such as research into water desalination. The Technion-Israel Institute of Technology in Haifa, the oldest institution of research and higher learning in Israel, trains engineers, scientists, technologists, architects, and physicians. The Israel Academy of Science and Humanities is another center that attracts some of the best scientists and scholars in the country.

THE ECONOMY

Israel's economy, marked by speedy and evident growth, has been stimulated by a steady rise in population, enlargement of capital investment, and growing productivity. The nation's vulnerable economic factor is its adverse balance of payments. Over the years Israel has been able to obtain capital from abroad in sufficient amounts to offset the deficit. As a result she has been able to accumulate considerable foreign currency reserves.

The sharp rise in import prices, particularly of fuel and oil products, coupled with heavy taxation necessary to pay for her wars (especially the Yom Kippur War) has given Israel a considerable amount of inflation. Israel has one unique economic asset in the Diaspora, the Jewish community abroad, which contributes generously to the state. Donations from abroad relieve the government of much of the financial burden for both social programs and the absorption of immigrants.

The bulk of Israel's imports is in the form of raw materials. Those come mainly from the Common Market and from the United States.

INDUSTRIALIZATION

Israel's industrial growth has been very rapid and has been achieved in the face of enormous handicaps such as the scarcity of raw materials and energy. Israel is rich in potash, copper, and phosphates, but has to import most of her other basic raw materials. The nearest natural market for Israeli products, of course, would be the neighboring Arab countries, but that market is closed because of the strict boycott against Israel maintained by the Arab states.

The local demand for manufactured goods gave the initial spur to the growth of Israel's industry, because a rapidly growing population, coupled with rising standards of living, provided domestic markets. Israel's factories, however, are small in comparison with those to be found in other developed countries.

Israel's most important industrial export is diamonds. She has a virtual monopoly in the type of stone in which she specializes. Almost her entire production is slated for export. Israel has one of the world's largest diamond polishing centers and the country is second only to Belgium as an international diamond center.

Much of Israel's industry is taken up with the food, beverage, and tobacco trades. Most of that output is consumed domestically. Textiles and clothing, first developed to provide employment for immigrants, are also vital industries.

Israel's largest single industrial enterprise is the Israel Aircraft Industries (I.A.I.) which, with its headquarters at Lod Airport, employs over 13,000 people. Many of its top engineers were recruited from the United States.

I.A.I. makes a twin turbo-prop commuter cargo plane with astonishing STOL (short takeoff and landing) capabilities. It can land and take off from almost any kind of terrain.

The amazing STOL of that plane makes it a good substitute for helicopters, and it has taken over many of their duties. It can maintain excellent maneuverability while flying at low speeds. It is ideal for military purposes since it can be used to drop men with great precision into a combat area. It can also be used in antisubmarine warfare. It is the first aircraft ever to be entirely designed and produced in Israel.

I.A.I. also produces the sophisticated Commodore jet, the Salvo, a jet fighter similar to the Mirage III only larger and with an excess of Mach 2 speed. It is powered by an improved version of the General Electric engine used in the Phantom jet.

OIL EXPLORATION

Israel's dependence on foreign oil has spurred exploration for that vital sinew of modern industry. Years ago geologist Herman Gunkel, professor at the Hebrew University, drew the attention of his friends to Genesis 19:28 which states that "the smoke of the country went up as the smoke of a furnace." The context tells of Abraham, the pilgrim patriarch, gazing down on the blazing ruins of Sodom. Professor Gunkel decided that natural gas would be found in the vicinity. It was. Natural gas was discovered by the shores of the Dead Sea near Rosh Zohar. Similar reasoning led businessman Xiol Foderman to prospect for oil in the same region. Israel's first oil wells were sunk there in November 1953. Oil is also being produced at Heletz and Kochav near Ashkelon. Offshore drilling for oil near Ashkelon is planned.

When Israel took over the Sinai she began developing the latent oil resources of that area. Magnetometric surveys, gravimetric surveys, and extensive seismic work and a network of bores were undertaken to pinpoint the most promising geological formations. Companies chosen by the ministry of defense were commissioned to carry on oil exploration in northern Sinai.[3] Inside Israel proper, oil exploration is carried on under the direction of the ministry of development. Israel hopes that sooner or later she will strike it rich in oil and become the Algeria of the eastern Mediterranean.

THE SEARCH FOR MINERALS

Most of Israel's mineral resources are in the Negev. One location is Makhtesh Hagadol. In this area, twenty miles long and twelve miles wide, a broad layer of iron ore has been found of a quality equal to that found in the Saar.

Years ago the famous biblical archaeologist, Rabbi Nelson Glueck, decided that 1 Kings 7:45-46 (where reference is made to Solomon's smelters) was the clue to mineral wealth in the country. The rabbi spent more than twenty years in Palestine exploring in the blistering heat of the Jordan Valley and the Negev. He became convinced that sooner or later he would prove the Bible right. In 1934 he found heaps of slag and the tumbledown walls and ruins of an ancient smelter a few miles south of the Dead Sea.

He had found Solomon's mines. Four summers later he found another site near the Gulf of Aqaba in the center of a geological rift where ancient furnaces had been designed to take advantage of the strong winds that blow down the rift. This time he had discovered the famed Ezion Geber, the Pittsburgh of Palestine. He had simply followed the clue in 1 Kings 9:26 which says: "Ezion Geber . . . is beside Eloth, on the shore of the Red Sea, in the land of Edom."

Other mineral assets in Israel include phosphates and copper. Valuable deposits of phosphate rock have been discovered and are being mined at Oron and Machtesh in the Negev. Copper reserves have been discovered in the Timna region about fifteen miles north of Eilat, near the site of Solomon's mines.

THE DEAD SEA'S WEALTH

Israel's greatest single mineral asset is the Dead Sea. As the Jordan flows south from the Sea of Galilee, hot springs and other tributaries empty their deposits of sulphur, potash, and other salts into it. The Jordan then pours its daily quota of 4,740,000 tons of water into the Dead Sea where it is trapped and can only escape by evaporation. Because of that evaporation the water of the Dead Sea contains about 24 percent solid matter, mostly various salts. The composition of the Dead Sea surface brine is given as 11.8 grams per quart of potassium chloride, 82.4 of sodium chloride, 142.4 of magnesium chloride, 33.0 of calcium chloride, 1.3 of calcium sulphates and 3.9 grams per quart of magnesium bromide.

Estimates of what the recoverable salts in the Dead Sea might be worth are varied. It is thought to contain some 1.3 billion tons of potash, 853 million tons of bromide, 11.9 billion tons of salt, 81 million tons of gypsum, 6 billion tons of calcium chloride, and 22 billion tons of magnesium chloride, with a total potential value in hundreds of billions of dollars.

The greatest single product from the Dead Sea is potash (potassium chloride) an important chemical fertilizer for which there is an enormous worldwide demand. When I was in Palestine toward the end of the British Mandate, potash was already a major item of export. The most impressive sight on the Haifa docks was the enormous mountains of potash piled up along the wharves awaiting shipment to the ends of the earth. The amount of chemical still stored in the Dead Sea is so vast that, at the present rate of extraction, the supply will last for centuries.

The Dead Sea has proved itself useful to Israel in another way. It has helped Israel solve its energy crisis. *Time* (25 February 1980) reported that water from the Dead Sea was being pumped into shallow, briny pools to create solar ponds. The salty water acts as a solar collector. It is linked to a heat-exchanging system and to a turbogenerator. The system is ingenious, economical, and harmless to the environment.

Israeli officials are planning a five-megawatt pond for the near future and eventually hope to build a network of such ponds around the Dead Sea. As much as one third of Israel's electrical needs could be filled in this way by the end of the century.

The system has sparked worldwide interest. In the United States the Southern California Edison company is planning to try similar experiments in the Imperial Valley.

AGRICULTURE

Agriculture is another important item in Israel's economy. Her farms produce three-quarters of the country's food—at least in terms of dollar value. Most of the nation's agricultural requirements are provided for by Israel's own farms except for such products as grains and animal fats, for which there is not sufficient well-watered land. In terms of gross national product and in terms of overall employment the contribution of agriculture is small, but it represents a tremendous achievement just the same.

After all, the early settlers were not men of farming stock, neither was the land inviting. It had been raped by the Turks and turned into a stone-strewn desert, barren of life, destitute of population, ripped clean of trees, and left a virtual wilderness. Today, Israel's agriculture is highly mechanized, efficient, and spectacular.

The early pioneers laid the foundations for the agricultural miracle in Israel. Those dauntless individuals had to drain swamps, anchor dunes by planting suitable vegetation, enrich the soil, find new sources of water, and then solve the problem of bringing it to arable lands. Large tracts of former wasteland have now been brought under the plow, soil erosion has been halted, millions of trees have been planted, and the land lives again.

Most of the land in Israel is owned by the state or the Jewish National Fund. It is not sold, but is leased under government supervision. The land miracle of Israel has been achieved by a series of pragmatic measures such as cooperative use of costly farm implements, widespread national irrigation, and cooperative marketing techniques.

LOOKING FOR WATER

It is interesting how frequently the Bible has played a role in the development of modern Israel. The Israelis have been rediscovering and reopening Abraham's wells in Beersheba, following clues found in Genesis. Abraham herded vast flocks and herds in what is now the Negev desert. Archaeologists, following that clue, found that even in the smallest gullies there were traces of ancient dikes, some of them only a foot or two high. Those were all interwoven into a complex drainage system. The Israelis reopened that system in May 1952 and found that it provided irrigation efficient enough to bring broad, lush acres of pasturage back to the area.

Exploring further, the Israelis discovered cisterns dug out of limestone, each positioned so as to take advantage of the natural run-off in the area. They reopened those ancient cisterns. Now there are many similar ones spread out over a wide area, each capable of holding thousands of gallons of water. Today more than fifty new agricultural settlements in Israel are positioned on sites where, centuries ago, Jews once lived and farmed. Almost every one of those sites sits alongside an ancient well or spring.

FOOD PRODUCTION

One of the sights that greets the visitor to Israel today is the extensive citrus groves. Jaffa oranges and grapefruit are world famous. Packing is done in modern, mechanized factories under the control of the citrus marketing board.

In addition to citrus, Israel produces olives, bananas, wheat, barley, oats, hay, cotton, tobacco, sugar beets, and vegetables. Her farms raise chickens, cattle, eggs, milk, and dairy products; and new crops are constantly being introduced. Cotton, for example, first sown in 1953, now meets all the domestic demand. Fishing in the Mediterranean, the Red Sea, the Atlantic, the Sea of Galilee, and in artificial ponds supplies most of the demand of the local market.

NEW FORESTS

Large scale afforestation in Israel embraces over 125,000 acres of land, of which 110,000 have been planted since 1948. There are also about 150,000 acres of natural forest and forest preserves. The Bible taught the Israelis what kind of trees to plant and where. Dr. Joseph Weitz of Keren Kayemet Le Israel, who planned and developed Israel's afforestation discovered, for instance, that Abraham planted tamarisk trees as a protection against sandstorms. He followed Abraham's lead. The tamarisk, a species of desert shrub with narrow leaves and masses of minute flowers, was found to be one of the few trees that would thrive in the south where the annual rainfall is less than six inches.

Afforestation became a means to penetrate new areas, particularly the mountains. In Israel today there flourish a number of impressive forests. There is the great Balfour Forest above Emek, the Menashe Forests near Mishmar Hamek, the beautiful wooded mountains along the road to Jerusalem, and the great Herzl Forest. One significant forest, the Forest of the Martyrs, contains six million trees to honor the Jews who died in the Nazi holocaust. More than a hundred million trees now beautify the land of Israel. Forestry experts are looking ahead to another 250 million.

Someone has defined Israel as a country where every tree has a birth certificate. Years ago the Israeli government hit upon the idea of a "Plant a Tree in Israel" program—much to the delight of the tourists. Over the years many tourists have become actively interested in Israel's need for trees. More trees mean more oxygen, more moisture in the soil, more organic matter in the surface, more raw materials for factories and farms. A tourist in Israel can now purchase a sapling from the government tourist office or from the Jewish National Fund and can plant it in a spot prepared for the purpose. After the planting ceremony the visitor receives a certificate as a souvenir. The certificate reads: "I planted a tree with my own hands." Those planting large numbers of trees receive their certificate in gold or silver. David Ben Gurion said, "He who plants a tree plants a future."

Making Deserts Bloom

Typical of Israel's determination to make the deserts blossom like the rose was the planting of date palms in the forbidding Araba desert. The Araba Depression contains not a single drop of water in the 110 miles between the Sea and the Gulf. Rainfall is usually nonexistent, and when it does come it descends with passionate violence producing freak floods and sweeping all before it. The Jews decided that since the Arabs grew dates in the desert they might as well do so too. They set about the task with such determination that today date palms dot the Araba.

The Jews decided on a variety of date palm that flourished only in Iraq on the Persian Gulf. But how to get seedlings—that was the problem. All date-producing countries jealously guard their seedlings. To hope that Iraq, an Arab country, would allow Israel to have some of its precious date seedlings was to hope for the impossible. The Israelis, however, managed to trick the Iraqis into shipping some of their well-guarded plants, supposedly to Italy. In actual fact the shipment was meant for Israel. Now Iraqi dates are grown in the Araba.

With courage, resourcefulness, and determination the Jews have taken a firm hold on the land of their fathers and have restored it to much of its pristine glory. They have given it back its soul.

Notes

1. "Uranium: The Israeli Connection," *Time*, 30 May 1977, pp. 32-34.
2. *Facts About Israel* (Jerusalem: Israel Ministry of Foreign Affairs, Information Division, n.d.), p. 149.
3. Under the terms of the 1979 treaty with Egypt the Sinai oil wells were returned to Egypt.

15

THE REPATRIATED JEW: THE CHOSEN CITY

Draw a circle on a map with a radius of 900 miles and with Jerusalem as its center, and you will encompass almost all of the Middle East. Athens, Istanbul, Antioch, Beirut, Damascus, Baghdad, Alexandria, Cairo, and Mecca will all lie within the magic circle. Western civilization is an offshoot of the things that were revealed, understood, and enacted in those ten cities and their hinterlands.

The ancient world was not very large. From Jerusalem to Egypt was about 300 miles; from Jerusalem to Assyria or to Babylon was 700 miles; to Persia was about 1,000 miles, to Greece was 800 miles, and to Rome about 1,500 miles. Jerusalem occupies a position in the center of the world. It was like that in Bible times; it is like that today. We read: "Thus saith the Lord GOD, This is Jerusalem: I have set it in the midst of the nations and countries that are round about her" (Ezekiel 5:5).

JERUSALEM IN THE BIBLE

Jerusalem is named in the Bible upward of 800 times. There are 465 verses in the Old Testament and 24 verses in the New that speak of the future of Jerusalem. That, of course, does not include the hundreds of verses that speak of events connected with the city that have already passed into history. We do not know whether Washington or Paris or London or Tokyo has a future, but we know that Jerusalem has. It is the only city on earth upon which God has been pleased to set His name. He calls it "a city of Truth" (Zechariah 8:3), "the city of Righteousness" (Isaiah 1:26), "the throne of the LORD" (Jeremiah 3:17), and "my City" (Isaiah 45:13).

TOPOGRAPHY OF JERUSALEM

Jerusalem crowns the crest of the central uplands ridge of Palestine at one of its highest points. The tableland on which it is enthroned was isolated in olden times by deep ravines. Continual wars, constant rebuilding, and countless changes have resulted in a gradual lowering of the heights and a partial filling of the valleys, so that Jerusalem today sits on five main hills—Mount Moriah, Mount Zion, Mount Ophel, Mount Scopus, and Mount Olivet. It was well situated to resist the attacks of its foes, being protected on the west by mountains, on the south by deserts, and on the east by the Jordan rift.

A BENJAMITE CITY

When Joshua divided the promised land among the tribes, Jerusalem fell to Benjamin, but since it stood on Judah's border and its great citadel, captured by David, commanded a portion of the territory of both tribes, David made the city the capital of the united kingdom. After the division of the kingdom in the days of Rehoboam it remained as the capital of the Southern Kingdom of Judah and Benjamin.

THE OLD CITY TODAY

Visitors to Jerusalem today are impressed by the great walls that surround the Old City. This enclosed city is all there was of Jerusalem a hundred years ago. It was a maze of alleys covering about 180 acres that contained about 24,000 people and 300 sacred sites. Since the Old City sits on the backs of mountains its streets ascend and descend in a series of steps and platforms, intersected by narrow, intricate lanes, many of them roofed over like so many arcades. The proud, imposing walls frown down upon the busy life of the Old City from their towering 38-foot height. Once a person enters through one of the gates that pierce the walls he is imprisoned within splendid ramparts of stone, and his feet hasten him back to Bible times. The pungent odor of frying sesame oil fills the air. The rattle of dice and the cries of vendors can be heard. Fresh-squeezed orange juice or a miniature crown of thorns can be purchased.

JERUSALEM: A JEWISH CAPITAL BUT MORE

Jerusalem was the capital of the Jewish nation from 1,000 B.C. to

586 B.C., and again from 516 B.C. to A.D. 70. It has been ruled by numerous foreign powers, but only for the Jews has it ever been a national capital. The walled area is roughly a square with a perimeter of barely two and one half miles, but for Muslim, Christian, and Jew alike it is the center of the world. There Christ was crucified, there stood Solomon's great Temple, there was the throne of David. To that spot came the Assyrians, the Babylonians, the Persians, and the Greeks. There came Pompey and Herod and Saladin and Lord Allenby, and thousands of others who make up the "Who's Who" of history.

Today Jerusalem is the home of some 300,000 people. There is the seat of the president of Israel, the Knesset, the supreme court, the Hebrew University, the Israel Museum; there the government meets, and there sits the Chief Rabbinate. The Wailing Wall, the holiest spot for the Jews, is in Jerusalem, as well as the Church of the Holy Sepulcher, the most sacred spot for Catholics; the Garden Tomb, the place of holy memories for many Christians; and the mosque of El-Aksa on the Temple Mount, one of Islam's holiest shrines.

Why the nations should have fought so over Jerusalem is a mystery. It is almost devoid of water and is rich only in limestone. It is located neither on the banks of a great river nor astride a major arterial highway. It is not, and never has been, of any economic importance.

THE CITY OF "PEACE"

The name *Jerusalem* means "City of Peace," though it has known little or nothing of peace in its 3,000 years and more of history. David wrested it from the Jebusites, the Babylonians snatched it from the Jews, Alexander marched his men through its streets, and the Seleucids and Ptolemies made it a battleground. The Romans trod it under foot for 666 years (from the battle of Actium 31 B.C. to the Saracen conquest in A.D. 636).

In 1099 the Crusaders clanked in and out of its gates. The Saracens held the city until the Ottoman Turks took it over in 1517. Then came Lord Allenby in 1917 to wrest the city from the Turks. With the end of the British Mandate, Jerusalem became a city divided against itself (1948-1967) and more or less paralyzed as Arabs and Jews faced each other with loaded guns across barbed-wire entanglements. The Six-Day War put Jerusalem into

Jewish hands as Israeli forces marched through its streets and planted the Star of David on the Temple site before the Mosque of Omar. Whatever else they may be forced to surrender, the Jews are determined never to give up Jerusalem. When the eloquent Abba Eban was asked, "Will Israel give up Jerusalem?" he retorted: "Will England give up London? Will France give up Paris?"

The city of peace! Historians vary when counting up the number of times Jerusalem has been besieged. One places the number as high as thirty-four times. Some of the sieges have been the most terrible in all the history of mankind.

THE ASSYRIAN SIEGE OF JERUSALEM

The siege of Jerusalem by the Assyrians that took place in the days of Sennacherib was the subject of various prophecies of Isaiah. Two years before the event he addressed the city under its poetic name of Ariel ("Lion of God") and promised deliverance in the coming time of trial. The prophecies were reiterated when the dreadful Assyrian hordes were swarming over Judah (Isaiah 30:19; 31:4-5), and they were fulfilled when the angel of the Lord smote the great host.

THE BABYLONIAN CONQUEST OF JERUSALEM

The destruction of Jerusalem by Nebuchadnezzar was likewise the subject of extensive Old Testament prophecy. Indeed, apart from prophecies relating to the two comings of Christ, there is probably no event so thoroughly foretold in the Old Testament. The first prophecy of Jerusalem's coming doom was made by a woman (2 Kings 22:16-17; 2 Chronicles 34:24) in the days of King Josiah. Isaiah predicted the Babylonian disaster even though, in his day, the event lay some 150 years in the future (Isaiah 4:3-5; 10:11-12, 32; 22:9-11).

Jeremiah was even more insistent. He lived to see his prophecies literally fulfilled and wept over their fulfillment in the tear-drenched book of Lamentations. Among other things, Jeremiah foretold Nebuchadnezzar's plundering of the Temple (27:18-20), something the Jews thought impossible, for the Temple had become a fetish with them. He foretold that the Babylon invasion would be progressive in character (34:22) and in various periods

(35:17, 38:2, 17-23), and he foretold that the resulting captivity would last for seventy years (25:9-11; see also Daniel 9:1-2).

Ezekiel also foretold Jerusalem's capture by the Babylonians. He himself had been carried away to Babylon in one of Nebuchadnezzar's earlier invasions. The Jews remaining in Jerusalem thought themselves heaven's favorites since they had escaped the fate that had overtaken their brethren, but Ezekiel prophesied differently. (See the sign-parable of the tile, 4:1-17; the sign of the sharp knife, 5:1-17.) Many of his prophecies were play-acted to add force to what he had to say. In all there are about two hundred verses in the Old Testament dealing with the fall of Jerusalem to the Babylonians.

The Talmud paints in some of the details. It tells how the followers of Nebuchadnezzar massacred the inhabitants of Jerusalem, the priests and the people, old and young, women, and children who were attending school, even babes in the cradle, until the feast of blood at last shocked even the leader of the hostile heathen, who ordered a stay of this wholesale murder. It tells how all the vessels of gold and silver were removed from the Temple and sent by ships to Babylon, after which the Temple was set on fire.

It tells how the High Priest donned his robe and ephod, saying, "Now that the Temple is destroyed, no priest is needed to officiate," and how he threw himself into the flames and was consumed. It tells how when the other priests witnessed this they took their harps and musical instruments and followed the High Priest into the fire. It tells how those of the people whom the soldiers had not killed were bound in chains, burdened with the spoils of the victors, and carried into captivity.

ANTIOCHUS AND JERUSALEM

The book of Daniel makes prophetic reference to three events connected with Jerusalem, two of which have already been fulfilled. Those two both have to do with the horrible atrocities committed by Antiochus Epiphanes. The third has to do with the destruction of Jerusalem by the Romans in A.D. 70 and the coming invasion of Israel by the Antichrist.

Antiochus was determined to add Egypt to his domain, and when his efforts in that direction failed he took out his spite on Jerusalem. Daniel 8:11-14 actually foretold the length of time the

Syrian menace would last—"two thousand and three hundred days; then shall the sanctuary be cleansed." Antiochus Epiphanes began to reign in 175 B.C. and was slain in 161 B.C. His power over Jerusalem was broken on December 25, 165 B.C., on which date the Temple was cleansed and the Hebrew festival known as Hanukkah was inaugurated. The 2,300-day period ended with that event.

The prophecy in Daniel 11:30-32 dealt with the same period but focused on the defilement of the Temple. Antiochus fulfilled Daniel's words when he set up a statue of the Olympian Zeus in the Temple, sacrificed a sow to it, and commanded the Jews to drink a broth made from swine's flesh. Those who refused were subjected to the most horrible atrocities.

THE ROMANS AND JERUSALEM

The prophecy in Daniel 9:26 referred to another destruction of Jerusalem, one that was fulfilled by the Roman general Titus. The Romans are referred to in this prophecy as "the people of the prince that shall come." The Lord Jesus elaborated on this prophecy in Luke 19:41-44 and in Luke 21:6, 20-24. Later in the Olivet Discourse He referred to a much more remote destruction of Jerusalem yet to take place (Luke 21:6; Matthew 24:2; Mark 13:2).

The Lord's prophecies concerning the Roman siege and destruction of Jerusalem warned that Jerusalem would be besieged; during the siege the enemy would seal off Jerusalem by building a bulwark around it so that escape would be impossible; the inhabitants, including little children, would be massacred; the demolition of the city would be total, and it would be handed over to Gentile domination "until the times of the Gentiles be fulfilled."

Jerusalem, considered impregnable by its defenders, was protected by an outer wall, known as the third wall, inside which was a second wall and inside which again, close to the Temple, was yet another wall. The outer wall had ninety protective towers, spaced about two hundred cubits apart. The middle wall had nineteen towers. The innermost and oldest wall had sixty towers, one of which was 105 feet high.

THE ROMAN SIEGE

When the siege began, Jerusalem was crowded to capacity.

Titus estimated that there were 600,000 visitors in Jerusalem for Passover at the time Roman operations against it commenced.

The Roman army appeared before the city in all its fearsome might. It was led by Vespasian, a general idolized by his troops and later to become emperor of Rome, the first decent emperor in half a century. Vespasian's elevation to the throne of the world took place before the siege of Jerusalem was over. He left the completion of the conquest to his son, Titus.

Jerusalem was defended by the Jerusalem Zealots headed by Eliezer Ben Simon, by the Galilean Zealots under John of Gischala, and by some Idumeans led by Simon Ben Kathla. Famine and senseless civil war among the defending factions did as much as the Romans, if not more, to bring about Jerusalem's fall. The Romans callously crucified any Jews they caught trying to flee the doomed city, in order to terrorize the defenders. As many as five hundred at a time were hung up before the eyes of the horrified beholders, the bodies of the victims being nailed on their crosses in all manner of ludicrous positions, until at last there was no more space to crucify the captives and no more wood for crosses.

The dreadful siege lasted five months. The Jewish historian Josephus has given us a full account of the war. His account can be taken and laid alongside the prophecies of the Lord Jesus and can be made to show how exactly the Lord's words were fulfilled.

The third wall fell in May, A.D. 70. In June the massive tower of Antonia was taken. On that fateful August 10, a torch was set to the Temple. It was the anniversary of the destruction of Solomon's Temple by the Babylonians. Titus, seeing the flames begin to spread, was moved with pity that such a magnificent building should be reduced to rubble. He gave orders to his troops to extinguish the flames, but it was in vain. A greater than he had long since foretold its total destruction.

One by one the various parts of the glorious structure tumbled into the flames, and then the ruins were ransacked by the Romans in a search for the treasure and gold that gleamed on every hand. The Roman army moved into the precincts of the former Temple, planted their eagles, and offered sacrifices to their pagan gods.

The siege continued until on September 7 the Romans took the final wall and rushed through the stricken city, slaying and destroying as they went. The number of prisoners, estimated at

97,000, overwhelmed even the Romans. The tallest and strongest were set aside to enhance the triumphal march of Titus through the streets of Rome. The old, the weak, the infirm were slaughtered, and the rest of the captives were sent off to various parts of the Empire to labor in the mines or to fight in arenas for the amusement of the people. It is believed that more than a million people died in that siege.

JERUSALEM LIVES AGAIN

In modern times Jerusalem's heart began to beat again when General Allenby, on December 9, 1917, took the city from the Turks. That was the first day of the Feast of Hannukkah (the 24th of Chisleu) and the anniversary, remarkably enough, of the freeing of Jerusalem centuries before by Judas Maccabaeus and of the rededication of the Temple. Allenby took the city without firing a shot.

A devout, practicing Christian, Allenby abhorred the thought of shedding blood in the very city that had once known the tread of the Lord Jesus, and he had no desire, either, to damage the city's walls. He brought up his troops determined to free the city but wondering how it could be done peaceably. Meanwhile, the rumor of Allenby's approach ran through the Turkish garrison. In Turkish, Allenby's name was rendered "Allah Bey," which means "the Prophet of God." The Turks were seized with superstitious dread, were convinced that God was against them, and fled leaving Jerusalem undefended.

General Allenby approached the city, dismounted from his horse, and walked bareheaded into the city. When asked afterward why he chose such a means of entry he remarked diffidently, "It seemed to me the obvious and natural thing to do. The only alternative to entering on foot by the Jaffa Gate was to enter on horseback through the enormous hole in the wall made especially to permit the German Kaiser to make what he regarded as a triumphant and spectacular entry into Jerusalem. That was a procedure I naturally shrank from repeating."[1]

THE UNITED NATIONS "INTERNATIONALIZES" JERUSALEM

Zechariah 12:3 warns that Jerusalem will always be "a burdensome stone" for all peoples. Britain found Jerusalem to be just that during the years of the Mandate. The United Nations has fared no better in trying to settle the fate of the city. Soon after the establishment of the state of Israel the UN decided to internationalize Jerusalem. That decision was enthusiastically supported by Pope Pius XII in an encyclical issued on April 15, 1949, and it was vigorously opposed by Arabs and Jews alike. The United Nations has not been able to enforce its own decree. Ignoring world opinion, the Jews declared Jerusalem the capital of Israel, and in 1967 put an end to an intolerable situation by taking the city, unifying it, and transferring to it the various government offices that still remained at Tel Aviv.

The Israeli Knesset, in August 1980, passed a provocative bill affirming the unification of Jerusalem. The gesture was largely symbolic since West Jerusalem has been Israel's capital for some thirty years and eastern Jerusalem has been in Israeli hands since the 1967 war. Premier Begin announced his intention of moving his offices to East Jerusalem to show his support for the bill.

The move naturally infuriated the Arabs. Yasser Arafat, the leader of the terrorist Palestine Liberation Organization, at once called for a summit of Arab heads of state to deal with the issue. Several Arab oil-producing countries backed him up and threatened to sever diplomatic relations with and cut off oil from countries that do business with the Israelis in any part of Jerusalem. In response, nations that maintained embassies in Jerusalem decided it would be prudent to move to Tel Aviv. Begin's was a hollow victory.

PLANNING PROBLEMS

Even the initial unification of Jerusalem in 1967 brought the Jews countless problems. How does a city provide roads, parks, and services in an area sacred to three incompatible faiths? A highrise apartment or a superhighway could upset a delicately balanced equation. City planners took a long-range look at Jerusalem and saw its population growing from 400,000 by 1985 to 550,000 by 2010. They pictured a tall, dense city with many seven-story buildings (buildings higher than that would create defense problems).

They planned to ring the city with parks both for recreation and to check urban sprawl. The Old City would remain a bazaar, ringed by a park, with adjacent buildings kept to one or two stories. New roads would have to be built, but some of them would run underground so as not to upset the balance.

The best laid plans sometimes go awry, and those for Jerusalem were no exception. Developers rushed in. A four-lane highway was pushed through the new Valley of the Cross, through a monastery, and through a spot that had been a park for 1,600 years. Skyscrapers began to raise their heads much higher than the architects had planned. Jerusalem was on the way to becoming another city built to the dictates of industry rather than to the desires of the people. The public, however, became aroused, and committees have been formed to force a halt to the exploitation of Jerusalem.

JERUSALEM TO BE TRODDEN DOWN OF THE GENTILES

Jesus said that Jerusalem would be "trodden down of the Gentiles until the 'times of the Gentiles' were fulfilled" (Luke 21:24). The significant "times" began with Nebuchadnezzar, to whom God gave Gentile world dominion. They will not end until Christ comes to crush the Beast, the Devil's messiah, at the battle of Armageddon, and set up His own millennial Kingdom.

When the Jews took Jerusalem from the Arabs many people thought the times of the Gentiles were over, but that is not so. Jerusalem is to revert back to Gentile control, and the Jews really only hold it under sufferance. The Arabs will never rest until they again have the city. Russia will try to take it from the Jews (Ezekiel 38-39) and will fail. The Beast, however, will succeed and will do so by using guile (Daniel 8:25).

A NEW TEMPLE

Both Testaments envision a new Temple being built in Jerusalem, presumably on the ancient Temple site, which is presently crowned by a Muslim shrine. References to that Temple are found in Matthew 24:15, Mark 13:14, and 2 Thessalonians 2:3-4. That coming Temple is to be desecrated by the Beast.

Years ago, when he was still commander of the Irgun, Menachem Begin declared that among Jewish objectives in Palestine was the rebuilding of the Temple. "The third Temple, as outlined by Ezekiel, will assuredly be rebuilt in our own generation" he declared. Others have said the same thing. There is a Talmudic seminary in Jerusalem, we are told, where the rites of animal sacrifices are being studied in the hope that the Temple will be rebuilt on its ancient site.

Soon after the Jews liberated Jerusalem in 1967, *Time* magazine carried an article entitled "Judaism—Should the Temple be Rebuilt?"[2] It made reference to Maimonides, who argued in his Code of Jewish Law that every generation of Jews was obliged to rebuild the Temple if its site was ever retaken.

One problem the article discussed was the fact that Jewish law requires that only Cohens (priests) who are descended from Aaron could be allowed to officiate in a rebuilt Temple. But so many Jews have taken the name of Cohen that tracing authentic genealogies would be something of a nightmare. Then, too, a rebuilt Temple would call for a resumption of animal sacrifices, something that would be repulsive to many modern Jews.

The greatest obstacle is the fact that the Temple site is presently occupied by the Mosque El-Aksa and by the structure known as the Dome of the Rock, sacred to Islam as the spot where Muhammad is supposed to have ascended into heaven. The Jews would not want to share the Temple site with those shrines, and any attempt to demolish them would assuredly lead to the fiercest holy war the Muslims have ever launched.

The *Time* article quoted historian Israel Eldad who said, "We are at the stage where David was when he liberated Jerusalem. From that time until the construction of the Temple by Solomon, only one generation passed. So it will be with us." Asked about the Muslim shrines, Eldad shrugged. "It is of course an open question," he said. "Who knows? Perhaps there will be an earthquake."

At present two radically different groups in Israel would like to see the Temple rebuilt. The extreme nationalists would like it because it would be a symbol of Israel's triumph over the Arabs, and it would be a focal point for Jewish religious culture. The Orthodox Jews would like to have the Temple rebuilt for purely religious reasons. Most Jews around the world are noncommital.

HISTORY TO REPEAT ITSELF

The fact that Jerusalem is today in Jewish hands, if not actually a sign, is certainly a matter of great interest. History has a habit of repeating itself. The last time the Jews held Jerusalem as an independent city Jesus came, as the prophets had foretold. Then the Romans came and took it from them. Now the Jews hold Jerusalem again. Shortly, we suspect, another and final "Roman Prince" (the Beast) will come and will take the city from them, and when that happens the ultimate coming of Christ will not be far behind.

Notes

1. *Sydney Morning Herald,* 26 January 1926.
2. "Judaism—Should the Temple Be Rebuilt?" *Time,* 30 June 1967.

16

THE FUTURE JEW

The Jews have begun to return to the promised land. They have transformed the country, fought off their foes, and dug in to stay, and they have created a small but virile and highly industrialized nation in the most strategic area of the world. Around them surges the Arab sea, and all over the world anti-Semitism is endemic still. Most nations have their quotas of Jews, and none feel really comfortable with them. There is a hate fringe in even the most tolerant of lands. The Jews are always going to find themselves eyed and loathed and envied, for in many cases their very wealth and success make them conspicuous, and their habit of exerting pressure to get what they want is not lost on their foes.

From time to time slumbering anti-Semitism awakes and roars like some incarnate fiend from the pit of hell, and when that happens blood flows—Jewish blood. The horror camps of the Nazis are not the end. Russian and Arab anti-Semitism is not the end. The Bible speaks with authority on what is yet to come. It warns that "the time of Jacob's trouble" will come and that all that has happened so far will prove to be just so many dress rehearsals for the horrors ahead.

EXIT OF THE CHURCH

The next item on God's prophetic program is the rapture of the church (1 Thessalonians 4:13-18). The church was injected suddenly, startlingly, and supernaturally into human history on the day of Pentecost. It will be taken back out of history in the same way, miraculously and mysteriously, at the rapture.

Before the coming of the church God spoke to men through the people of Israel. The Jews gave us the Scriptures, and the Son of God came into the world as a Jew. From Abraham to Christ, when God had something to say to man, He said it through a Jew. When the church has gone He will once more bring Israel back onto the stage and speak to men through Jewish lips (Revelation 7).

RESULTING CHAOS

A number of important things will happen once God has taken out the church, things that are the subject of numerous prophecies both in the Old Testament and in the New. First there is to be a time of worldwide upheaval and chaos. The anti-God and anti-Christian ideologies, which are already making such strident noises on earth, will triumph everywhere as men heed the lies and deceptions being preached. There will come a time of world war followed by natural disasters and national calamities. There will be earthquakes, famines, and pestilence, and the present ruling order will be shaken to its foundations (Matthew 24:1-44; Revelation 6).

THE COMING WORLD DICTATOR

There will come into the hearts of men a longing for a leader, no matter what his nationality, no matter who he is or what he is, so long as he can bring some kind of order out of chaos, some kind of peace to a shaken, frightened world. The Bible assures us that such a leader will come. He will be handsome, brilliant, charming, powerful, cunning, the Devil's messiah.

Though he is variously known in the Scriptures as the Beast, the man of sin, the son of perdition, the lawless one, the willful king (Daniel 11:36; 2 Thessalonians 2:3-8 (NASB);* Revelation 13:1; 17:8), he will seem to men to be the answer to all their problems. He will be ably supported and promoted by a colleague known as the False Prophet (Revelation 13). Those two men will dazzle the world. They will be deeply initiated in the occult arts, they will have strange powers, they will be able to perform genuine miracles and will do so many strange and startling things that men will be convinced that the gods have come down to earth (2 Thessalonians 2:9; Revelation 13:13-15).

The Beast (sometimes called "the Antichrist") will probably rise to power in one of the countries of Europe that borders on the Mediterranean. He is called "the beast out of the sea." In Daniel 7 he is called "the little horn" because when he first takes over

*New American Standard Bible.

one of the European countries he will only have a little power, but
that power will rapidly grow.

He will overthrow three nations of Europe, and he will become
the acknowledged head of a ten-nation European confederacy.
Within that European community the Beast's power will be supreme. What Napoleon and Mussolini and Hitler all failed to
achieve, that remarkable individual will do—he will revive the
Roman Empire and unify western Europe under himself. Overnight, as it were, Europe will become a power to be reckoned with
in human affairs.

THE IMPORTANCE OF ROME

The Beast will need a capital city, and what more appropriate
capital for a revived Roman Empire than Rome itself? (See Revelation 17:9.) For Rome not only formed Europe, she has lingered
on in history. Her law, her administration, her imperialism all lie
at the roots of European judicial, social, political, and military
systems.

A MARRIAGE OF CONVENIENCE

In a coming day the Beast and a world religion will join forces
at least for a while. The Beast and that church, also called "the
harlot" or "Babylon," will make a mutual assistance pact (Revelation 17); each will agree to help the other to world power. The
church will want to use the Beast to gain power and prestige in
the world; the Beast will use the church to bring all the West to
his feet. It will be a marriage of convenience, each partner knowing full well what the other is up to and each hoping to come out
on top.

Eventually the Beast will turn over the church to his con-
federates to be destroyed (Revelation 17). The Beast will then
stand without a rival in the West. All its enormous economic, industrial, and military potential will be his. Like Alexander of old
he will look for new worlds to conquer. A new era of peace and
progress will descend upon the western nations.

THE WESTERN DICTATOR SUPPORTS ISRAEL

With the West united, and with the church no longer so essential to his plans, the Beast will need a new center. He will choose

Jerusalem, and the Jews will thus be forced back into focus, to remain there for the rest of time. The Beast will make a seven-year pact with Israel (Daniel 9:27), significantly called by God "an agreement with hell" (Isaiah 28:15, 18). The Jews will sign it because it will seem to give them all that they have fought for so long—absolute security, the right to rebuild their Temple, and both protection against Russia to the north and the Arab states round about. Many Jews will hail the Beast as Messiah. He will be the last false messiah they will ever enthrone.

The Beast will guarantee Israel's frontiers against all attacks, he will warn off Russia, and he will serve notice to the Arabs that he is not going to permit intransigence of any sort from them. The Temple will rise again in Jerusalem under the Beast's sponsorship because he knows exactly what he intends to do with that Temple once it is finished.

RUSSIA ATTACKS ISRAEL

Ezekiel 38-39 tells us what will happen next.[1] The Beast's friendliness to Israel will not be real. He will simply be using Israel as a pawn in his game. It would seem that when the Beast first comes to power in the West, Russia will dominate areas he wants to control himself.

The Mediterranean must become again a Roman lake. The countries of eastern Europe presently under Russian domination must come back to Rome. The Middle East, to the banks of the Euphrates, all belonged to Rome in olden times, and the Beast will want it all back. He will really want the world. The Beast, tutored by Satan, will know exactly what will happen once Russia, in a desperate throw of the dice, risks everything for a total victory over Israel.

The Arabs, infuriated by developments in Israel and careless of the consequences, will call for a Holy War, and Russia will support it with all the resources at her disposal. She will strike for a swift, stunning victory in the Middle East, one that will annihilate Israel, give Russia a stranglehold on the whole area, and enable her to counterbalance the power of the Beast in the West and of China in the East.

THE RUSSIAN DEBACLE IN THE MIDDLE EAST

According to Ezekiel 38 and 39, Russia will launch a massive, efficient, and sophisticated attack against Israel. All her military resources, together with those of the allies, will be totally committed. The Russian armies will penetrate deep into Israel, rolling up the country like a carpet before them. The Beast will demand an explanation, but apparently will not do much to intervene. He will have no worries about the outcome. It will have already been revealed to him that when Russia attacks Israel it will be the end for her. The Russian forces will penetrate deeply into Israel, and then disaster will overtake her armies

The account in Ezekiel suggests that rebellion will break out in the Soviet forces (38:18-22). Probably the satellite countries, long forcibly incorporated into the Russian Empire, will turn their weapons against their hated Russian masters. Then some kind of holocaust coupled with a series of natural disasters will overtake the Russians on the mountains of Israel.

The Russian armed forces will be decimated, the destruction reaching back across all her supply lines deep into the hinterland of Russia itself. Five-sixths of the enormous invading force will be annihilated. A stunned world will listen to the news. Russia will no longer exist as a world power. Her manpower will have been decimated, and her war equipment will litter Israel from end to end, providing the Israelis with fuel for years to come. The very homeland of Russia will have been ravaged by the judgment of God.

THE WESTERN DICTATOR BECOMES WORLD DICTATOR

The world will be stunned, but not so the Beast, who has envisioned all this. Before the rest of the world will have time to recover and assess the implications of that vast geopolitical vacuum in the world, the Beast will act. We can imagine his armed forces pouring into Russia westward across Alaska and over the Bering Straits, northward across the Caucasian Mountains, eastward along the main truck lines and arterial highways used by Napoleon and Hitler, pouring in from all points of the compass. At the same time the Beast's forces will mop up the Arab states of the Middle East and take over the vast spheres of Russian influence in Africa and the Indian Ocean. The Beast will now control not only the western hemisphere but all of Africa and Eurasia as well.

The next move will follow naturally. He will issue an ultimatum to the powers of the Far East, to China and Japan, India and the

islands of the Pacific. "Join, or else!" The Apocalypse tells us
what the reply will be: "Who can make war with the Beast?"
(Revelation 13:4). The prophet Daniel clearly foresaw the revival of the Roman Empire at the end of the age, and John expanded the vision to include the whole world. The final Gentile
empire is to be a world empire, sponsored by Satan, controlled by
the Beast, and pacified by the False Prophet. The world is to lie
in the lap of the devil's "Christ" (Revelation 13:8).

THE NEW CRISIS FOR ISRAEL

Jerusalem will now have served its turn in the Beast's political
plans, and likewise the Jew. Jerusalem and the Jews will have
been very useful pawns, just as the world church will have been
in its day. The Jews will now be a nuisance to the Beast, who in
reality has detested them from the very beginning. He will seize
their rebuilt Temple as the first move in his plan to have himself
worshiped as God.

The Beast's seven-year pact with Israel will, by now, have run
half its course, and the world will be halfway through Daniel's
prophetic seventieth and final "week" (Daniel 9:20-27). The
Beast will break his agreement with the Jews, will rip off his jovial
mask, and inaugurate the Great Tribulation (Matthew 24:21). It
will be a time of persecution such as the world has never known
before, a persecution aimed primarily at the Jews but embracing
also all God-fearers left on earth, and all who show the slightest
desire to dissent from the policies of the Beast.

In Jerusalem, the False Prophet will set up an image of the
Beast (called "the abomination of desolation") in the Temple and
will comand all men everywhere to worship the Beast, his image,
and the devil himself (Revelation 13:4, 15). At the same time a
new economic world-system based on Beast worship will be announced. All people on the planet will be required to receive the
Beast's secret mark imprinted on their flesh. Without that mark
no one will be able to transact business of any kind anywhere on
earth. Trends in this direction are already evident.

Computers are becoming increasingly sophisticated and are
taking over more and more of the financial and business affairs of
the world. To refuse to receive the Beast's mark and to befriend
the ostracized and outlawed Jews of the world will be fatal. All

such will be slaughtered in the outbreak of persecution that will inundate the globe. The great reign of terror will have come.

Satan will have achieved his objective. The world will be ruled by him through his messiah, the Beast. Men everywhere will wear the Beast's mark, will worship at his shrine, will bend to his will. What C. S. Lewis calls "That Hideous Strength" will hold mankind in its iron grip. Dissidents will be hunted down and tortured to death. The horror camps of the Nazis will be revived, only they will be a thousand times more horrible than even Heinrich Himmler could make them. The plight of the Jews in particular will be desperate, but, with the tenacity and the stubborness with which they have fought for survival for centuries, they will fight back.

JERUSALEM COMES BACK INTO FOCUS

Jerusalem will come back into focus. Various prophecies suggest that the Jews will control much of the city as events march toward their close. The Beast, of course, will not want to bomb Jerusalem because its Temple will be the point from which he shows his blasphemous contempt for God. Contingents from all nations will be recruited to seize Jerusalem and ravish Israel (Zechariah 12:2, 9; 14:2).

The Beast's days, however, will be numbered. The sandglass of seven years, which began when first he signed his pact with Israel, will have almost run its course. God will begin a series of judgments, under the vials (Revelation 16:1-10), that will greatly weaken the Beast's power and influence and will effectively break his stranglehold on the world. Magnificent Babylon will go up in flames, swept away in a single hour, and the economic system centered there will collapse, bringing financial ruin to the nations. The inability of the Beast, for all his supernatural powers, to ward off the dreadful plagues that will now fall upon the world will further disillusion mankind, and the eastern portion of his Empire will break away.

ARMAGEDDON

Led no doubt by China, the eastern nations will march westward as "the kings of the east" (Revelation 16:12-16), to wrest the rule of the world away from the Beast once and for all. The armies of the world will be drawn to Megiddo for the final confrontation between East and West. The struggle for the control of Jerusalem will still be going on, apparently, but that will be only a minor matter now. The real issues are to be decided on the plain of Esdraelon where armies have fought almost since time began.

The famous battle of Armageddon will begin, it would seem, as a confrontation between East and West. But then the unexpected will happen. The heavens will split asunder, and the Lord Jesus will descend from the sky, backed by the armed might of heaven. The end will have come at last (Matthew 24:30; Revelation 19:11-16). Armageddon will end as a confrontation between earth and heaven. The "battle" is hardly a battle at all, for the Lord will simply put forth His power, and the armies of earth, suddenly united to face that new threat, will be swept away. The Beast and False Prophet are to be hurled headlong into the lake of fire (Revelation 19:20) and the devil is to be locked up in the abyss (Revelation 20:1-3).

HIM WHOM THEY PIERCED

Israel will be saved! The eyes of the Jews will be opened at last, they will "look on him whom they pierced" (Zechariah 12:10-11), and they will mourn. Jesus will be owned at last as the Messiah, Savior, and Lord. Israel will be a nation "born in a day" (Isaiah 66:7-9).

The judgment of the nations will then take place in the Valley of Jehoshaphat. Men will be judged according to their treatment of the Jewish people (Joel 3:2, 12; Matthew 25:31-46). The Valley of Jehoshaphat is the name of a valley that runs between Jerusalem and the Mount of Olives. In Jesus' day it was known as the Kidron Valley. The Lord's throne of glory will be set up in sight of the dark valley through which he passed on His way to Gethsemane. It was in this valley that good King Jehoshaphat overthrew the united enemies of Israel.

The Lord's throne will be on Olivet. The converted Jews will be called to stand by His side, the Gentiles will be massed before Him in the valley. There will not be many left, for the appalling judgments of the Apocalypse will have greatly depleted the population of the globe.

The criteria of judgment will be each man's treatment of the Jew during the Great Tribulation. Those who pass the test will be made to stand on the King's right hand; those who fail (presum-

ably all who have the mark of the Beast) will be made to stand on
His left, near Tophet, the valley of the sons of Hinnom, the place
where the ancient refuse fires burned, the place that gave its
name to Gehenna. Those will be sent to a lost eternity. The re-
mainder will form the nucleus of the world's population as the
millennial Kingdom of Christ begins.

THE MILLENNIAL KINGDOM

The Old Testament speaks in glowing terms of the Millennium.
The desert will blossom like the rose (Isaiah 35:1), the wolf will
lie down with the lamb (Isaiah 65:25), men will learn war no
more (Psalm 46:9; Isaiah 2:4), the curse will be removed from the
earth (Romans 8:18-21), and a man will be a youth at a hundred
years of age (Isaiah 65:20). Jerusalem will be the world's capital
(Isaiah 66:10-13, 18). The twelve apostles will sit on twelve
thrones judging the twelve tribes of Israel (Matthew 19:28). The
throne of David will be set up in Jerusalem (Isaiah 9:7; Luke
1:32).

A new Temple will be built (Ezekiel 40-43), and the offerings
and sacrifices will be restored, not as propitiatory but as commem-
orative symbols (Ezekiel 46:1-24). The earth will yield its bounty
with such prodigality that the plowman will overtake the reaper
(Amos 9:13) and all men will enjoy prosperity and peace (Joel
3:18; Zechariah 3:10).

Over the earthly Jerusalem will hover the New Jerusalem, the
celestial city from whence all rule will stem (Revelation 21:10).
Justice will be swift and sure (Isaiah 9:7). Jesus will reign over
the nations of the earth with a firm hand (Psalm 2:9), and the
Jews will be the administrators of the Kingdom.

The years will roll by, and the population of the planet will mul-
tiply again. Millions will be born into a world that has forgotten
the curse. But, as in all other ages, children born during the
Golden Age will still be children of Adam, born in sin and needing
to be saved. No doubt many will enter into eternal life through
Jesus Christ the Lord, but many will not respond to the means of
grace available to them. As children today can grow up in the
home of believing parents and yet be "gospel hardened" so, during
the Millennium, many will grow up to be "glory hardened." Dissidents will not dare to raise their voices openly, however, so rigid
will be the enforcement of the laws of the Kingdom. Judgment

will be so swift and sure they will render "feigned obedience" (Psalm 18:44; 66:3, NASB). Eventually they will begin to congregate at the extremities of the earth, as far as possible from the central glory in Jerusalem.

THE LAST REBELLION

Then Satan will be released from the abyss. Millions will flock to his standard, rejoicing in the new "liberties" he promises and confident of a speedy victory over the "Oppressor" in Jerusalem. The final march on the millennial capital will begin (Revelation 20:7-9). The redeemed will be removed from the scene, and God will ignite the planet (2 Peter 3:10-13). That will be God's last answer. Old things will finally and forever pass away, and God will make a new heaven and a new earth wherein righteousness alone will be known. The wicked dead will be summoned before the great white throne to be banished to a lost eternity, there to reap forever the due reward of their deeds (Revelation 20:11-15). The redeemed will enter into an eternity of bliss (Revelation 22:14-17).

This whole, tremendous sequence of events awaits but one thing—the rapture of the true spiritual Christian church. Every sign indicates that that event is near. It is a matter of great interest to us today that as the church age and the Jewish age overlapped at the beginning of the Christian era for about forty years—until the destruction of the Temple, so now again, at this other end of the church age, Israel has been reborn as a nation and once more Israel and the church are running along side by side. It cannot last for long.

ISRAEL IS GOD'S CLOCK

The nation of Israel is God's clock, a clock that has been stopped for many centuries but that suddenly has begun to tick again. It is ticking away today the last minutes of the day of grace. At any moment it might strike the hour, and the church will be gone. The age of judgment—"the day of the Lord"— will begin.

Jew and Gentile alike all need to take a fresh look at Jesus. Today God offers us salvation through Him. Tomorrow it may be too late; the amnesty may be withdrawn and the day of judgment begun.

NOTE

1. For a discussion of just where this event takes place in the Apocalypse, see John Phillips, *Exploring Revelation* (Chicago: Moody, 1974).

EPILOGUE

ISRAEL

What nation will you find, whose annals prove
   So rich an interest in Almighty love?

Where will you find a race like theirs, endow'd
   With all that man e'er wish'd or heaven bestow'd?
They, and they only, amongst all mankind,
   Received the transcript of the eternal mind;
Were trusted with His own engraven laws,
   And constituted guardians of His cause;
Theirs were the prophets, theirs the priestly call,
   And theirs by birth the Saviour of us all.

But grace abused brings forth the foulest deeds,
   As richest soil the most luxuriant weeds.
Cursed of the golden calves, their father's sin,
   They set up self, that idol god within;
View'd a Deliverer with disdain and hate,
   Who left them still a tributary state;
Seized fast His hand, held out to set them free
   From a worse yoke, and nail'd it to the tree:
There was the consummation and the crown,
   The flower of Israel's infamy full blown;
Thence date their sad declension, and their fall,
   Their woes not yet repeal'd, thence date them all.

William Cowper

APPENDIX:
HISTORICAL TIME CHART

Note: Biblical dating follows that of Whitcomb and Boyer. Some dates are uncertain. There is also some overlap, especially in the case of the judges and the kings.

B.C.

2090	*Abraham called by God*
2067	*Isaac born*
2007	*Jacob born*
1992	*Abraham dies*
1944	*Isaac dies*
1877	*Jacob arrives in Egypt*
1860	*Jacob dies in Egypt*
1806	*Joseph dies in Egypt*
1730	Hyksos invasion of Egypt; Hebrews bondage begins.
1728	Hammurabi of Sumer born
1570 (c.)	Hyksos expelled from Egypt; Amose I founds 18th dynasty
1548	Amenhotep I becomes pharaoh of Egypt
	Hebrew midwives ordered to destroy all Hebrew male children
1528	Thutmose I becomes pharaoh
	All newborn Hebrew males are to be cast into the Nile
1525	*Moses born*
1510	Thutmose II becomes pharaoh
1504	Hatshepsut becomes pharaoh
1487	*Moses flees Egypt*
1483	Thutmose III becomes pharaoh
	The great oppression of the Hebrews begins
1450	Amenhotep II becomes pharaoh
1447	*The Exodus begins*
1446	*The Tabernacle constructed*
1423	Thutmose IV becomes pharaoh
1410	Amenhotep III becomes pharaoh

B.C.

1407	*Moses dies; Joshua conquers Canaan*
1400	*Conquest of Canaan completed*
1377	Akhnaton becomes pharaoh; inaugurates monotheistic reforms
1375	*Othniel becomes judge*
1319	*Ehud becomes judge*
1318	Rameses I founds the 19th dynasty in Egypt
1240	*Deborah and Barak judge Israel*
1194	*Gideon becomes judge*
1167	*Eli born*
1155	*Abimelech usurps power in Israel*
1152	*Tola becomes judge*
1131	*Jair becomes judge*
1109	*Eli becomes priest*
1105 (c.)	*Samuel born*
1089	*Jephthah becomes judge*
1083	*Ibzan becomes judge*
1071	*Elon becomes judge*
	Samson becomes judge
1069	*Samuel begins to minister*
1066	*Abdon becomes judge*
1043	*Saul becomes king*
1011	*Saul and Jonathan slain*
	David becomes king of Judah
1004	*David becomes king over all Israel*
971	*Solomon ascends the throne*
966	*Solomon begins to build the Temple in Jerusalem*
945	Sheshhonk (Shishak) becomes pharaoh of Egypt
931	*Rehoboam becomes king of Israel and Judah*
	Jeroboam rebels; sets up a rival kingdom in the north
913	*Abijam becomes king of Judah*
911	*Asa becomes king of Judah*
910	*Nadab becomes king of Israel*
909	*Baasha becomes king of Israel*
890 (c.)	Benhadad becomes king of Syria
886	*Elah becomes king of Israel*
	Zimri becomes king of Israel
885	*Tibni becomes king of Israel*

B.C.

883	Ashurbanipal II becomes king of Assyria
880	*Omri becomes king of Israel*
874	*Ahab becomes king of Israel*
873	*Jehoshaphat becomes king of Judah*
859	Shalmaneser III becomes king of Assyria
858 (c.)	*Elijah begins to prophesy*
853	*Ahaziah becomes king of Israel*
	Jehoram becomes king of Judah
852	*Joram becomes king of Israel*
	Elisha begins to prophesy
841	*Jehu becomes king of Israel*
	Ahaziah becomes king of Judah
	Athaliah seizes the throne of Judah
	Hazael becomes king of Syria
835	*Joash becomes king of Judah*
830 (c.)	*Joel prophecies*
814	*Jehoahaz becomes king of Israel*
801	Benhadad II becomes king of Syria
798	*Jehoash becomes king of Israel*
796	*Amaziah becomes king of Judah*
790	*Uzziah becomes co-regent of Judah*
783	Shalmaneser IV becomes king of Assyria
783 (c.)	*Jonah begins his ministry*
782	*Jeroboam II becomes king of Israel*
776	Olympic games begun in Greece
767	*Uzziah becomes full king of Judah*
764	*Amos begins to prophesy*
755 (c.)	*Hosea begins to prophesy*
753	Rome founded
	Zechariah becomes king of Israel
752	*Shallum becomes king of Israel*
	Menahem becomes king of Israel
745	Tiglath-pileser III becomes king of Assyria
742	*Pekahiah becomes king of Israel*
740	*Pekah becomes king of Israel*
739	*Uzziah dies; Isaiah begins to prophesy*
	Jotham becomes king of Judah
736 (c.)	*Micah begins to prophesy*

B.C.

735   *Ahaz becomes king of Judah*
732   *Hoshea becomes king of Israel*
727   Shalmaneser IV becomes king of Assyria
722   Sargon II becomes king of Assyria
       Samaria falls; the ten tribes go into captivity
715   *Hezekiah becomes king of Judah*
705   Sennacherib becomes king of Assyria
701   *Judah invaded by the Assyrians*
686   *Manasseh becomes king of Judah*
681   Esarhaddon becomes king of Assyria
669   Ashurbanipal becomes king of Assyria
660 (c.) Zoroaster born
648 *(c.) Nahum predicts the fall of Nineveh*
642   *Amon becomes king of Judah*
640   *Josiah becomes king of Judah*
634 *(c.) Zephaniah begins to prophesy*
627   *Jeremiah begins to prophesy*
626   Nabopolasser becomes king of Babylon
622   *Revival in Judah*
619   *Habakkuk begins to prophesy*
612   Nineveh falls
609   Neco II becomes pharaoh of Egypt
       Jehoahaz becomes king of Judah
       Jehoiakim becomes king of Judah
605   Nebuchadnezzar becomes king of Babylon
       The Babylonians invade Judah
       Daniel begins to prophesy
597   *Jehoachin becomes king of Judah*
       Zedekiah becomes king of Judah
593   *Ezekiel begins to prophesy*
586   *The Babylonians destroy Jerusalem and the Temple*
       The Jews deported to Babylon
       Gedaliah becomes governor of Jerusalem
       The rabbis preempt the priests as the chief custodians
           of divine truth
563 (c.) Buddhism founded by Siddhartha
553   Belshazzar becomes regent in Babylon
550   Cyrus becomes king of Persia
       The temple of Artemis erected at Ephesus

B.C.

550 (c.) Confucius begins to teach
539   Babylon falls to the Medes and Persians
         Darius the Mede rules in Babylon
538   *Zerubbabel and Joshua lead a small party of Jewish
         repatriates back to Palestine*
536   *The Temple started in Jerusalem*
530   Cambyses becomes king of Persia
521   Smerdis becomes king of Persia
         Darius I Hystapses becomes king of Persia
520   *Zechariah begins to prophesy*
         Haggai begins to prophesy
         Construction of the Jerusalem Temple resumed
516   *The Temple completed*
509   The Roman Republic founded
486   Xerxes becomes king of Persia
484 (c.) Herodotus the historian born
480   The Greeks defeat Xerxes at Salamis
479   The Greeks defeat Xerxes at Thermopalye
478   *Esther becomes queen of Persia and later saves the Jews
         of the empire from extermination*
473   *The Feast of Purim started*
469   Socrates born
464   Artaxerxes Longimanus becomes king of Persia
458   *Ezra takes a small contingent of Jews back to Palestine*
447   The building of the Parthenon commenced
445   *Nehemiah takes a small contingent of Jews back to
         Palestine*
443 (c.) *Nehemiah and Ezra read the Scriptures to the Jews and
         help them understand them; the first delicate roots of
         the Midrash begin to sprout; the Sopherim (Scribes)
         flourish*
436 (c.) Malachi begins to prophesy
423   Darius II becomes king of Persia
404   Artaxerxes II becomes king of Persia
400   *The Midrash begins to develop*
399   Socrates condemned to death
359   Artaxerxes III becomes king of Persia
         Philip becomes king of Macedonia
342   Epicurius teaches his philosophy

B.C.

336   Darius III Codomannus becomes king of Persia
       Alexander the Great becomes king of Greece
335   Aristotle teaches at Athens
333   The Battle of Issus fought; Alexander defeats the Persians
       Alexander takes Egypt
332   Alexander destroys Tyre
331   Alexander seizes Babylon
330   Darius III of Persia slain
329   Alexander marries Roxana in a symbolic gesture of unit-
          ing East and West
327   Alexander invades India
323   Alexander claims to be the son of Zeus
       Alexander dies
       Alexander's empire divided between his four chief
          generals
       Ptolemy I Soter takes Egypt
320   *Ptolemy I seizes Palestine*
311   Seleucus I Nicator takes Babylon
300   Rome becomes a major world power in the western
          Mediterranean
       Seleucus I adds Syira to his realm
285   Ptolemy II Philadelphius becomes king of Egypt
       Between 285 and 130 the Septuagint translated
280   Antiochus I Soter becomes king of Syria
276   The first Syro-Egyptian war begins
275   Ptolemy of Egypt invades Syria
274 (c.) Hinduism codified in India
264   Rome's first Punic war against Carthage begins
261   Antiochus II Theos (the God) becomes king of Syria
260   The second Syro-Egyptian war begins
252   Antiochus II marries Bernice, daughter of Ptolemy II
250   The Parthian kingdom founded
246   Seleucus II Callinicus becomes king of Syria
       Ptolemy III Euergetes becomes king of Egypt
       The third Syro-Egyptian war begins
245   Ptolemy invades Syria
240   Seleucus invades Egypt

B.C.

223	Antiochus III (the Great) becomes king of Syria
221	Ptolemy IV Philopater becomes king of Egypt
	The fourth Syro-Egyptian war begins
219	Antiochus the Great invades Egypt
218	Rome's second Punic war against Carthage begins
217	Hannibal invades Italy
	Ptolemy IV invades Syria; Battle of Raphia
215	Rome's first Macedonian war begins
206	Rome drives Carthage out of Spain
203	Ptolemy V (Epiphanes) becomes king of Egypt
201	The fifth Syro-Egyptian war begins
	Carthage surrenders to Rome
200	Rome's second Macedonian war begins
200 (c.)	*The Mishna begins to appear among the Jews*
193	Ptolemy V marries Cleopatra, daughter of Antiochus III
190	Antiochus III defeated by Romans at Magnesia
187	Seleucus IV Philopator becomes king of Syria
181	Ptolemy VI Philomater becomes king of Egypt
175	Antiochus IV Epiphanes becomes king of Syria
171	Ptolemy VII becomes co-regent of Egypt with Ptolemy VI
	Rome's third Macedonian war begins
	Mithridates I begins the conquest of Babylonia and Media, adding those countries to Elam, Persia, and Bactra to form the Parthian Empire
169	*Antiochus Epiphanes captures Jerusalem*
168	The Romans interfere in Antiochus's war with Egypt and prevent his capturing Alexandria
	Antiochus pollutes the Temple in Jerusalem and suspends the sacrifices of the Jews
166	*Matthias leads the Jews in revolt against Antiochus Epiphanes*
165	*The Jerusalem Temple repaired and cleansed*
164	Antiochus Epiphanes dies
154	*The Jews in Egypt build a temple at Leontopolis*
149	Rome's third Punic war against Carthage begins
	Rome's fourth Macedonian war begins
146	The Romans destroy Carthage

B.C.

135   *John Hyrcanus becomes high priest in Jerusalem*
133   Rome begins to expand her empire eastward
130 (c.) The Pharisees begin to emerge as a sect
124   Mithridates II (the Great) conquers Scythia, adds it to
       the Parthian Empire, and makes a treaty with Rome
120   *Hyrcanus repudiates the Pharisees and declares himself*
       a Sadducee
106   Cicero born
88   Rome's first Mithridatic war begins
83   Rome's second Mithridatic war begins
74   Rome's third Mithridatic war begins
64   *Pompey captures Jerusalem; leaves the Maccabean high*
       priest Hyrcanus in power with Antipater as civil adviser
60   The first Triumvirate at Rome (Caesar, Crassus, and
       Pompey)
59   Julius Caesar becomes proconsul; Pompey marries Julia,
       daughter of Caesar
58   Caesar conquers Gaul
54   Caesar invades Britain
49   Caesar crosses the Rubicon
48   Pompey slain in Egypt
       Caesar makes Cleopatra queen of Egypt
44   Caesar becomes dictator of Rome for life
       Caesar assassinated
43   The second Triumvirate at Rome (Anthony, Lepidus,
       and Octavian)
40   *Herod appointed king*
37   *Herod captures Jerusalem*
31   Battle of Actium, Anthony slain, Octavian becomes mas-
       ter of the Roman world, the final triumph of Empire
30   Egypt becomes a Roman province
30 (c.) Shammai flourished
       Hillel flourished
       Philo of Alexandria flourished
27   Octavian assumed the title of Augustus
20   *Herod begins to rebuild the Jerusalem Temple*
4   *THE BIRTH OF JESUS*

A.D.

14	Augustus dies
	Tiberius becomes Roman emperor
26	*Jesus begins to teach; He characterizes rabbinic teaching (the Mishna) as "vain tradition"*
30	*Jesus crucified and raised from the dead*
	Pentecost; the Christian church is born
37	Caligula becomes Roman emperor
40	Gentiles are added to the church with the conversion of Cornelius
41	Claudius becomes Roman emperor
	Antioch becomes the new center of church activity
43	*Theudas claims to be Messiah and is executed*
54	Nero becomes Roman emperor
59	The apostle Paul is imprisoned at Caesarea
60	Paul appears before Agrippa
61	Paul a prisoner at Rome
66	*The Jews of Judea revolt against Rome*
68	Paul martyred at Rome
69	Jerusalem beseiged by the Romans
	Jochanan ben Zakkai seeks an audience with Vespasian
	Vespasian becomes Roman emperor
70	*Jerusalem falls; the Temple burned; the Jews deported*
73	*The last stand of the Jewish rebels at Masada*
79	Titus becomes Roman emperor
81	Domitian becomes Roman emperor
96	Nerva becomes Roman emperor
98	Trajan becomes Roman emperor
113	Rome goes to war with Parthia
116	*A further Jewish revolt against Rome is suppressed with great severity*
117	Hadrian becomes Roman emperor
132	*Bar Kochba claims to be Messiah and leads a revolt against Rome*
135	*Judea depopulated and the Jews denationalized by the Romans*
138	Antoninus Pius becomes Roman emperor
150	Tertullian born

A.D.

161   Marcus Aurelius becomes Roman emperor; Stoicism
       triumphs

180   Commodus becomes Roman emperor

182   Origen born

190 (c.) *The Jews in Parthia (Babylonia) granted self rule and are
       thereafter ruled by Exilarchs*

193   Pertinex becomes Roman emperor
       Septimus Severus becomes Roman emperor

200   Cyprian born

211   Caracalla becomes Roman emperor

212   By the Edict of Caracalla all free inhabitants of the em-
       pire are granted Roman citizenship

215   Clement of Alexandria born

218   Elagabalus becomes Roman emperor

220 (c.) *Judah Hanasi and his disciples codify the Mishna; the
       decisions and opinions of 148 Tannas from the time of
       Hillel to the time of Judah Hanasi grouped into six
       major categories*

222   Severus Alexander becomes Roman emperor

227   The new Persian (Sassanid) Empire founded; there is a
       revival of Zoroastrianism
       *Abba Arika and Mar Samuel open academies in Baby-
       lonia and found a new exegetical system called Ge-
       mara; the Amoras begin to flourish; the Mishna be-
       comes virtually the Bible of the Jews*

235   Severus Alexander murdered; the end of civil govern-
       ment in Rome and the beginning of military anarchy

240   The Franks first appear in Europe

284   Diocletian becomes Roman emperor; the empire is di-
       vided into east and west for administrative purposes

303   Diocletian persecutes the Christians with great severity

306   Constantine becomes Roman emperor

312   The Battle of Milvian Bridge; Constantine embraces
       Christianity

313   Edict of Milan; Christianity declared a legal religion in
       the Roman empire

324   Constantine reunites the empire

A.D.

325 The first Ecumenical Council of the Church convened by Constantine at Nice to settle the Arian heresy

330 Constantinople dedicated as capital of Roman Empire

340 Jerome born

350 *The Palestinian Gemara is linked to Hanasi's Mishna*

361 Julian the Apostate becomes Roman emperor
Julian promises the Jews to rebuild Jerusalem for them

364 Valentinianus becomes Roman emperor and defends the west against the barbarians
Valens chosen by Valentinianus to be coemperor in the east

371 *Rab Ashi becomes Chancellor of the Sura Academy; he reconciles all the Gemaras with Hanasi's Mishna; the Talmud is born*

375 Gatianus becomes emperor of the east, and Valentinian becomes emperor of the west

376 The Visigoths cross the Danube

379 Theodosius the Great becomes emperor in the east

395 Arcadius becomes emperor in the east; Honorius becomes emperor in the west; the Roman Empire is permanently partitioned
The Palestinian Talmud is finished

401 Pope Innocent I claims the pope to be the custodian of the apostolic tradition and to have universal jurisdiction over the church

407 The Romans evacuate Britain

408 The Huns under Attila ravage the Roman Empire and extort tribute

409 Alaric invades Italy

410 Alaric sacks Rome; Patrick arrives in Ireland

422 (c.) Pope Celestine adopts the theory of the supremacy of the popes of Rome

435 *The year for the coming of the Messiah according to the calculations of Hanasi; Moses of Crete appears about this time*

440 Leo the Great becomes the first real Pope

452 Attila invades Italy but turns back when faced by Pope Leo I

A.D.

455   The Vandals sack Rome

476   The Roman Empire of the west ends

490 (c.) *Rabina II publishes the Talmud as one standard text for*
            the first time

491   Anastasius I becomes Emperor of the east; wars with
            Persia

496   Clovis king of the Franks is converted to Christianity

500 (c.) *The Talmud closed by Mar Jose*
            The Saborim begin to flourish

527   Justinian becomes emperor

529   Benedict founds the first monastery

535   Justinian begins the reconquest of Italy

570   Muhammad born

589   Chosroes II becomes the last famous Sassanid king; the
            neo-Persian Empire reaches its greatest extent and
            faces its worst downfall

590   Gregory the Great becomes pope and makes the papacy
            supreme

610   Heraclius I becomes emperor; the empire becomes dis-
            tinctly Byzantine in character

614   Chosru invades Palestine, sacks Jerusalem, slaughters
            thousands of Christians, burns most churches, and
            carries off the "true cross" as a trophy

622   Muhammad flees Mecca; the Muslim era begins

630   Muhammad takes Mecca

632   Muhammad dies
            The Caliphate established

634   Caliph Omar establishes the primacy of Arabia in the
            Muslim world

635   The Muslims conquer Syria, Palestine, and Mesopotamia
            The Muslims take Iraq

642   The Muslims complete their conquest of Egypt
            The Muslims take Persia and incorporate the Sassanid
            Empire into the Caliphate

664   The Saracens attack Afghanistan and India

673   The Muslims blockade Constantinople

689   *The Saboras, heading the two leading Talmudic acad-*
            emies at Sura and Pumbaditha, assume the title Gaon.

A.D.

700 (c.) Abu Issa claims to be the Messiah

711   The Muslims complete their conquest of North Africa and invade Spain; Moorish rule in Spain begins

717   Leo III becomes emperor and takes a stand against the worship of idols and the spread of monasticism; he is opposed by Pope Gregory II

720   Serenus claims to be the Messiah

756   Pepin, king of the Franks, endorses the papal claim that the papacy is the legitimate heir of the Roman Empire in Italy

Omayyad Dynasty of Cordoba comes to power in Spain

760 (c.) Aran Ben David begins the Karaite revolt against Talmudism

762   Baghdad founded

771   Charlemagne becomes king of France

773   Charlemagne invades Italy and becomes king of the Lombards

776   Hindu scientific works are translated into Arabic

777   Charlemagne invades Spain

786   Haran Al Rashid (the caliph of *The Arabian Nights*) makes Baghdad the major city of Islam; a compilation of Greek manuscripts is made to preserve classical Greek learning

787   The Council of Nicea orders the church to worship images

800   Charlemagne crowned emperor of the west by Pope Leo III at Rome on Christmas Day

The Arabs take Madagascar and Zanzibar and begin to raid the interior of Africa for slaves

813   Mamun the Great becomes caliph; he sets up a House of Knowledge in Baghdad where scholarly translations are made of Greek, Syriac, and Sanskrit works of literature, philosophy, and science; a comprehensive work on gynecology, obstetrics, and ophthalmic surgery is produced; Hindu numerals and methods of calculation are introduced into the Muslim world

843   The Treaty of Verdun is signed in Europe. The Carolingian kingdom is divided into three states—the fu-

A.D.

ture nations of France, Italy, and Germany; Charles
the Bald founds the Carolingian Dynasty in France

850 Feudalism begins to flourish in Europe

852 A Christian uprising in Spain is quelled by the Muslims

856 The Vikings invade Britain

870 *The* Book of Formation *published in Italy; it gives Cabbalism a surge of popularity, especially in Spain*

871 Alfred the Great reigns in Britain

900 (c.) *Saadiah Gaon launches a counterattack against Karaism
The Jews have widespread commercial enterprises in all
parts of the world*

910 Garcia, king of Leon, begins to expand his domain, to
become known as Castile

912 Amayyad rule in Spain begins to reach its peak; Cordoba
becomes the intellectual capital of Europe

960 *The Karaite revolt ("Jewish Protestantism") reaches its
peak and influences every phase of Jewish society*

962 The Holy Roman Empire founded by Otto I of Germany

969 The Fatimite caliphate established in Egypt

987 Hugh Capet founds the Capet Dynasty in France

1000 End of the world expected throughout Christendom
Leif Ericson discovers America
Jews begin to arrive in England

1042 Edward the Confessor is king of England and begins to
build Westminster Abbey

1054 The Eastern Orthodox church breaks with Rome

1055 The Seljuk Turks conquer Baghdad

1065 Alfonso VI of Leon begins the reconquest of Spanish
lands held by the Moors;
*Rashi becomes rabbi of the Jewish community at Troyes
and Europeanizes the Talmud*

1066 The Normans land in Britain

1073 Pope Gregory VII asserts the Roman Catholic church to
be without error, the pope to be supreme and above
all law and entitled to the homage of all princes

1085 Toledo captured from the Moors

1088 *Alfasi flees Morocco for Spain and undertakes the first
major codification of the Talmud*

A.D.

1096	The first crusade is preached by Peter the Hermit
1099	Jerusalem is captured by the crusaders
1105	*A new school of commentators emerges to write a series of Talmudic commentaries known as the Tosaphot; the Talmud is finally closed, and the Torah is completely set aside as the prime source of authority among the Jews*
1126	Height of Muslim learning reached in Spain
1147	The second crusade is preached by Bernard of Clairvaux and is led by Conrad III of Germany and Louis VII of France
1150	The University of Paris founded
1152	Frederick I (Barbarossa) becomes king of Germany and aims to restore the glories of the Roman Empire
1158	*Maimonides begins his writings; his crowning achievement is the* Mishna Torah, *a codification in fourteen books of all biblical and rabbinical law*
1160 (c.)	*Aaron of Lincoln becomes England's chief financier*
1163	Foundations laid of Notre Dame de Paris
1168	Oxford University founded
1171	Saladin emerges as supreme ruler in Egypt and Syria
1172	*A false messiah surfaces among the Jews of Yemen*
1187	Saladin captures Jerusalem
1189	The third crusade begins, led by Barbarossa of Germany, Richard I (The Lionheart) of England, and Philip II of France; the crusades reach their peak
1194	*The Ordinance of Jewry proclaimed in England to keep track of Jewish wealth for the crown*
1202	The fourth crusade begins, led by Venetian Doge Enrico Dandolo
1204	Philip II makes France the leading European power
	The crusaders take Constantinople and sack it with horrible atrocities
1208	Albigensians and Waldensians revolt in France against the corruption of the church
1209	The Franciscan Order founded
	Cambridge University founded
1215	*Magna Charta* signed in England by King John

A.D.

1218   The Mongols conquer Persia
        The fifth crusade begins, led by Pelasius, a papal legate,
            against the muslims in Egypt; it fails
1219   The Mamelukes make Palestine an Egyptian province
1223   Mongols appear in Europe
1226   Louis IX (St. Louis) become king of France and brings
            to flower the golden age of Medieval France
1228   The sixth crusade begins, led by Frederick II; it results
            in the Sultan of Egypt's restoring Nazareth, Jerusalem,
            and Bethlehem to the Christians
        The Mongols ravage Mesopotamia and Armenia
1233   The Inquisition founded by Pope Gregory IX; the Do-
            minican friars given orders to root out the Albigensians
            in France
1248   The seventh crusade begins, led by Louis IX of France
1250 (c.) *The* Zohar *appears in Spain and becomes the foremost*
            book of the Cabbalists
        The Mamelukes begin to rule in Egypt; they check the
            Mongol advances
1270   The eighth crusade begins; Tunis is attacked; Louis IX
            dies of the plague
1271   Marco Polo leaves for China
1281   *Abraham Abulfia arrives in Rome as Messiah*
1288   Osman I, leader of the Ottoman Turks, founds the Otto-
            man Dynasty
1290   *Edward I expels all Jews from England*
1300   Pope Boniface VIII proclaims the Great Jubilee; it marks
            the zenith of papal magnificence and greed
1300 (c.) Jacob ben Asher combines French, German, and Spanish
            learning into European Talmudism
        The Karaite revolt begins to recede until it all but van-
            ishes from Jewish life
        The Renaissance begins in Europe, heralding the end of
            the Dark Ages
1305   Chaos in Italy forces Pope Clement V to leave Rome for
            Avignon
1326   The Ottoman Turks begin invading eastern Europe
1328   Philip VI (of Valois) founds the Valois Dynasty in
            France

A.D.

1337	The Hundred Years War breaks out when Edward II of England lays claim to the French crown
1346	English victory at Crécy proves the power of the English longbow
1347	The Black Death breaks out in Constantinople, ravages Europe for twenty years, and kills three-quarters of the population of Asia and Europe
1376 (c.)	John Wycliffe translates the Bible into English
1378	Rome and France begin to fight for the control of the papacy
1391	Ottoman Turks begin conquest of Byzantine lands
1415	The battle of Agincourt makes England a major European power
	Portugal begins exploring the African coast
1415 (c.)	*Hasdai Crescas, a Spanish Jew, lends credence to the claim of Moses Botarel to be the Messiah*
1415	John Huss burned at the stake
1431	Joan of Arc burned at the stake by the English
	The Medicis begin their domination of Florence, which becomes the center of the Italian Renaissance
1450	The Vatican Library begun by Pope Nicholas V
1452	Leonardo da Vinci born
1456	The Gutenberg Bible printed in Germany
1462	Ivan the Great becomes the first national sovereign of Russia
1469	Ferdinand of Aragon marries Isabella of Castile, uniting Spain
	Machiavelli born
1473	Pope Sixtus IV builds the Sistine Chapel
1478	The Spanish Inquisition set up
1488	Bartholemew Dias rounds the Cape of Good Hope and opens a sea route to the East
1492	Ferdinand and Isabella drive the Moors from Spain
	Spain drives out its Jewish population
	Christopher Columbus sails for the New World
	Jews who refuse to become Catholics driven from Portugal
1497	John Cabot explores the coast of North America
	Vasco da Gama sails for India

A.D.

1500   Portugal discovers Brazil
1502   *Asher-Lemmlin convinces the Jews of Venice he is the*
          Messiah
1508   Michelangelo paints the ceiling of the Sistine Chapel
1509   Henry VIII becomes king of England
1513   Vasco de Balboa discovers the Pacific
1516   The Ottoman Turks rule Palestine
1517   Martin Luther begins the Protestant Reformation
1519   Zwingli begins the Reformation in Switzerland
          Cortes lands in Mexico
          Magellan circumnavigates the Globe
1520   Seleiman I (the Magnificent) begins his reign and marks
          the golden age of Turkish culture
          Pope Leo X denounces Luther as a heretic
1521   Luther excommunicated by the Pope
          Henry VIII earns the papal title "Defender of the Faith"
          for writing against the Reformers
1523   Alvarado conquers Guatemala and Salvador for Spain
          David Reubeni rides into Rome as Messiah
1529   *Solomon Molko appears at Rome as Messiah*
1530   Portugal begins to colonize Brazil
1532   *Reubeni and Molko join forces as joint Messiahs*
          Pizarro pursues the conquest of Peru
1534   Henry VIII breaks with the papacy; the "Act of Su-
          premacy" proclaims him head of the church in Eng-
          land; the English Protestant Reformation begins
          Ignatius Loyola founds the Society of Jesus and launches
          the counterreformation
1541   Calvin heads a theocratic state in Geneva
1553   Bloody Queen Mary ascends the English throne
1555   *The papacy endorses the ghetto system for Jews*
1556   Philip II of Spain begins to reign; the Hapsburg Dynasty
          reaches its zenith
1558   Elizabeth becomes Queen of England; the golden age of
          English literature begins
1562   The slave trade with the Americas begins
          The Hugenots massacred in France

A.D.

1565   St. Augustine settled in Florida
Joseph Caro publishes the Shulcan Aruch *to give instant answers from the Talmud for all exigencies of ghetto life; he is carried away by Solomon Molko's claims to be the Messiah*

1566   William of Orange frees the Netherlands from Spanish domination

1587   John Knox preaches in Scotland

1588   The Bourbon Dynasty founded in France
The Spanish Armada sunk

1590   The microscope invented

1595   The Dutch begin to colonize the East Indies
Under Pope Clement VIII persecution of Jews becomes a fixed part of papal policy

1600   *The Court Jew emerges in Europe as the banker and moneylender of the rulers of the Continent*

1603   James VI of Scotland becomes James I of England and founds the house of Stewart

1607   Jamestown settled

1608   The Jesuits colonize Paraguay
The telescope invented

1609   Kepler unlocks the secrets of astronomy

1611   The King James Version of the Bible published

1613   The Romanov Dynasty comes to power in Russia

1618   The Thirty Years War breaks out in Europe, the final violent confrontation between Catholics and Protestants

1620   The Pilgrims arrive at Plymouth, Massachusetts

1621   *The first Jews arrive in the Americas*

1632   Galileo confirms Copernicus and is forced to recant this as heresy by Pope Urban VIII

1640   The Puritans revolt in England

1642   Pascal invents the adding machine
New Zealand discovered

1643   Louis XIV reigns as "the sun king" in France, bringing the doctrine of the divine right of kings to a new peak

1648   *Shabbathai-Zevi proclaims himself Messiah*

1649   Oliver Cromwell establishes a republic in England

A.D.

1654	*The first Jews arrive in New Amsterdam*
1659	Spain ceases to be a power in Europe
1660	The monarchy restored in England
1665	The Great Plague ravages in London
1666	The Great Fire destroys London
1672	Joliet explores the Mississippi
1675	Sir Christopher Wren begins to rebuild St. Paul's
1682	Peter the Great reigns in Russia and begins to westernize the country
	The French rule in North America from Quebec to New Orleans
1684	Newton publishes his theories on motion and gravitation
1688	William Dampier lands in Australia
1689	William and Mary begin to reign in England
1694	The Bank of England founded
1714	George I founds the House of Hanover in England
1715	The Age of Reason begins; philosophy flourishes in Europe
1721	Russia becomes a European power
	Revolts in Paraguay against Spanish rule begin the wars of independence throughout Latin America
1736	*Baal Shem Tov (the Besht) begins his ministry and founds the Hasidic movement*
1738	John Wesley begins preaching in England
1740 (c.)	*Jacob Frank assumes the mantle of Messiah in southern Poland*
1740	Frederick the Great becomes king of Prussia and makes Prussia the leading military power in Europe
1750	The Industrial Revolution begins in England
1754	England and France go to war in North America
1757	Lord Clive establishes British rule in India
1759	General Wolfe defeats the French in Quebec
1760	George III becomes king of England
	Baal Shem Tov dies; Hasidism embraces 100,000 converts and continues to spread until it embraces half the Jews of eastern Europe
1762	Catherine the Great becomes queen in Russia; *proclaims Russia out of bounds to all Jews*

A.D.

1769	James Watt invents the steam engine
1770	Captain Cook claims Australia for Britain
1770 (c.)	*The Vilna Gaon leads the Jews of eastern Europe in a crusade against Hasidism; its leaders in Vilna are forced to do public penance*
	Mayer Amschel Rothschild founds the family fortunes in banking and finance in Germany
1774	Louis XVI and Marie Antoinette begin their reign in France
1775	The American Revolution begins
1776	The American Declaration of Independence signed
	Gibbon begins to write *The Decline and Fall of the Roman Empire*
1783	The British surrender at Yorktown
	Moses Mendelssohn translates the Pentateuch into German; its influence is enormous and gives impetus to the Haskela (the Enlightenment)
1786	Britain begins her domination of Malaysia
1788	The Constitution of the United States ratified;
	Britain establishes penal colonies in Australia
1789	George Washington becomes President of the United States
	The French Revolution breaks out with the storming of the Bastille; Louis XVI and Marie Antoinette beheaded
1791	*Catherine II takes over Poland and inherits a million Jews; the Pale of Settlement is begun to confine Jews to a limited area*
1796	*The death of the Vilna Gaon spurs his followers to continue the fight against Hasidism*
	Reform Judaism sends out its first shoots in Amsterdam
1799	Napoleon seizes control of France
1800	Socialist philosophy begins to take root in Europe
1803	Britain takes possession of Tasmania
	The United States purchases the Louisiana Territory
1804	Napoleon becomes emperor
1806	Cape Town in South Africa becomes a British possession
1807	*Napoleon reconvenes the Sanhedrin*
	Britain outlaws the slave trade

A.D.

1810	Mexican War of Independence begins
1811	Paraguay and Venezuela become independent
1812	The United States and Britain go to war over the question of the neutrality of the seas; nationalist feelings strong in the US
1812	Napoleon invades Russia
1815	Napoleon defeated at Waterloo
	After Waterloo, Czar Alexander I turns against Russian Jews
1816	Argentina becomes independent
1818	Chile becomes independent
1819	Bolivar leads Greater Columbia toward independence
1820	Railroads introduced into England
1821	Mexico becomes independent
1822	Brazil and Peru become independent
1823	The United States adopts the Monroe Doctrine for the western hemisphere
1825	Bolivia becomes independent
	Two million east European Jews begin to arrive in the United States of America
1830	Greece becomes independent of Turkey
	Jews become increasingly active in European underground and revolutionary movements
1835	The Boers begin the Great Trek in South Africa to get away from British rule
1837	Victoria becomes Queen of England
1840	New Zealand becomes a British possession
1841	David Livingstone sails for Africa
1843	The British annex Natal
1844	Samuel Morse sends the first telegraphic message
1845	*Czar Nicholas I ("the Russian Haman") prosecutes his anti-Semitic measures with increasing ferocity; the Pale of Settlement narrowed; he proposes to rid Russia of all Jews*
	Engels publishes his observations on the state of the working classes in England
1846	Mexico and the United States go to war
1847	*Lionel Rothschild elected to the British Parliament and is*

A.D.

        refused his seat because he would not pledge to support Christianity

1848   Marx and Engels publish *The Communist Manifesto,* and revolutions break out in various parts of Europe

1849   *Jews begin to enter the United States in greater numbers*

1854   The Crimea War breaks out

1855   Alexander II becomes Czar of Russia and attempts to modernize the country and free the serfs

1857   The great Sepoy Mutiny breaks out in India

1859   De Lesseps begins to build the Suez Canal

        Garibaldi and others begin the unification of Italy

        Charles Darwin publishes *The Origin Of Species*

1861   The kingdom of Italy comes into being

        The American Civil War breaks out

1862   The Emancipation Proclamation ends slavery in the United States

1862   Otto von Bismarck becomes Chancellor of Germany and creates the German Empire

1864   Karl Marx organizes the first Internationale in London

1865   The American Civil War ends

1866   The first transatlantic cable laid

1867   Nobel invents dynamite

        Karl Marx publishes Das Kapital

        Austro-Hungarian Empire founded

        Canada becomes a Confederation

        The United States buys Alaska from Russia

1868   Feudalism abolished in Japan and rapid modernization of the country begins

1869   *Sir Moses Montefiore encourages Jews to begin agricultural colonization in Palestine; the first colony is founded and is called "The Hope of Israel."*

1870   The Vatican proclaims the dogma of papal infallibility

        Lenin born

1871   The Third Republic is born in France

        Czar Alexander II of Russia follows the steps of his predecessors and turns against the Jews

        William I becomes the German Kaiser

1875   *Benjamin Disraeli buys up the controlling shares in the Suez Canal for Britain*

A.D.

1876   Belgium annexes the Congo
1878   *Jews begin to become an overall majority in the mixed
        population of Jerusalem and some move beyond the
        walls to establish new homes in the western suburbs
        under the patronage of Sir Moses Montefiore*
        The Zulus revolt and wage a savage war against the
        British
        The Ottoman Empire dismembered by Russia, Britain,
        and Austro-Hungary
1879   *Bismarck uses anti-Semitism to discredit his political foes
        in Germany*
1880   *Some two million Russian and Polish Jews begin arriving
        in the United States*
1881   *Czar Alexander III continues the Russian policy of per-
        secuting Jews*
1882   *Baron Edmond de Rothschild puts his weight behind
        new Jewish colonies in Palestine*
1885   *Baron Nathan Rothschild becomes the first Jew ever ad-
        mitted to the English House of Lords*
1887   France combines Vietnam and Cambodia into Indochina
1888   Burma annexed by Britain
1889   Cecil Rhodes monopolizes the diamond mining industry
        of South Africa
        Japan adopts a modern constitution
        Brazil becomes a republic
1891   Britain annexes Nyasaland and fights the slave trade
1892   Oman annexed by Britain
1894   Sultan Abdu I-Hamid II begins the massacre of Armen-
        ians
1894   *The Dreyfus Affair breaks out in France; it changes the
        mind of Theodor Herzl about seeking the wholesale con-
        version of Jews to Roman Catholicism*
        Japan becomes an imperial power
        *Nicholas II becomes the last Czar of Russia and inaug-
        urates the two worst decades in the bloody history of
        Russian persecution of Jews*
1895   X-rays discovered
        Wireless invented by Marconi

A.D.

1897   *Herzl calls the first World Zionist Congress in Basel, Switzerland*

1898   von Zeppelin invents the airship

         The Spanish-American war breaks out, which ends Spanish control in Latin America

1899   An international court of justice is set up at The Hague

1900   Movies become a popular medium of communication

1901   Ibn Saud begins the conquest of Arabia

         Oil discovered in Persia

         Theodore Roosevelt becomes President of the United States

1903   Henry Ford begins to mass-produce cars

         Fierce pogroms against Jews break out in Russia

         The British government offers land in east Africa as a possible national home for the Jews

         The Wright Brothers inaugurate the age of flight

1905   *Albert Einstein proclaims the theory of relativity*

1910   George V becomes king of England

         Japan annexes Korea

         The Union of South Africa formed

1914   The Panama Canal opened

         World War I breaks out

         Egypt becomes a British protectorate

1916   President Wilson's peace overtures ignored by the warring European powers

         Rasputin murdered

         Lawrence of Arabia leads the Arabs against the Turks

1917   The Bolshevik Revolution breaks out in Russia

         The British government signs the Balfour Declaration

         General Allenby occupies Palestine

1918   Russia makes peace with Germany

         Kaiser Wilhelm abdicates, the World War ends, and Germany adopts the Weimar Constitution

         Building of the Hebrew University on Mount Scopus in Jerusalem begins

         The Austro-Hungarian Empire ends

         Civil War breaks out in Russia between the White and Red Russians

A.D.

1919   Mussolini founds the first Fascist party in Milan
        The Treaty of Versailles is signed
        Kemal Ataturk begins moves to make Turkey a republic,
            end the Caliphate, and westernize the country
1920   *The Western powers confirm Britain's Mandate over Pal-
            estine, and Zionists hail the beginning of "The Third
            Jewish Commonwealth"*
        The League of Nations established at Geneva
        Syria and Lebanon become French-mandated territories
        *Palestine (and Jordan) become British-mandated terri-
            tories*
        Former German colonies in Africa mandated to Britain
        *Britain appoints Sir Herbert Samuel to be the Civil Ad-
            ministrator of Palestine*
1921   Economic collapse and widespread famine in Russia lead
            to the death of five million people
        The Chinese Communist Party founded
        *The Arabs revolt against increasing Jewish immigration
            into Palestine*
        The Jewish Histadrut is founded
        The Hagana (the Jewish Army) comes into being
1922   Russia becomes The Union of Soviet Socialist Republics
            and the world's first communist state
        *The League of Nations formally ratifies Britain's mandate
            over Palestine and incorporates into it the Balfour Dec-
            laration*
        *The League of Nations recognizes Hebrew as a spoken
            language*
1923   Hitler is imprisoned in Germany and writes *Mein Kampf*
        Rhodesia placed under British rule
        Wholesale slaughter of Jews in Russia
1924   *The US labor market dries up, and the government acts
            to virtually halt further immigration*
        Power struggle in Russia after Lenin's death leads to
            Stalin's dictatorship
1925   *Arabs and Jews alike reject Sir John Chancellor's pro-
            posals for joint government of Palestine*
1928   Stalin's drive to collectivize the farms of Russia and to

A.D.

industrialize the country leads to the liquidation of more than five million peasants

Chiang Kai-shek subdues the warlords of China

1929   Vatican City becomes a sovereign state

Arab terrorism increases in Palestine

Stock Market crash on Wall Street leads to the Great Depression

In the United States more than 16 million are unemployed

1930   The economic depression becomes worldwide; Socialist and extremist movements take deep root

Hitler's growing power in Germany gives impetus to the migration of European Jews to Palestine

1931   Britain establishes her Commonwealth of Nations

Japan invades Manchuria

Mao Tse-tung elected chairman of the Soviet Republic of China

1933   Hitler comes to power in Germany

Franklin D. Roosevelt becomes president of the United States

1935   *The Nuremberg Laws deprive German Jews of citizenship*

Italy invades Ethiopia

Stalin and his colleagues purge the Russian Communist Party of Trotsky, Zinoviev, and Kamenev, and Jews cease to have control and influence in Russia

The US Congress opens the door of immigration to 300,000 refugees from Nazi terror

1936   Hitler marches into the Rhineland

The Rome-Berlin axis formed

Civil war breaks out in Spain between the Communists and the Fascists

Stalin begins to systematically liquidate his foes in Russia

George VI becomes king of England

Farouk becomes king of Egypt

1938   Germany marches into Austria

The Munich Pact signed

Sir Harold MacMichael becomes Administrator of Palestine with instructions to deal with growing Arab terror

1939   Germany and Russia sign a nonaggression pact

The Stern Gang is founded in Palestine to fight British rule

Britain issues a White Paper restricting further Jewish immigration into Palestine

Pius XII becomes pope

Germany invades Poland and World War II begins

1940   France falls

Churchill becomes British prime minister

1941   Pearl Harbor bombed by Japan

1942   Germany declares war on the United States

1943   Mussolini's regime collapses

The Germans defeated at Stalingrad

1944   D-Day, Normandy invaded by the Allies

1945   World War II ends

The Nuremberg Trials bring the Nazi leaders to justice

Menachem Begin's Irgun fights British rule in Palestine

The Americans drop atom bombs on Hiroshima and Nagasaki; Japan surrenders

The Arab League formed to integrate Arab economic policy and oppose the establishment of a Jewish state in Palestine

1946   The United Nations Organization meets for the first time

Jewish terrorists blow up the King David Hotel in Jerusalem

Civil war in Greece

Bulgaria and Rumania become puppet communist states

1947   North Atlantic Treaty Organization formed

The Italian constitution incorporates the Lateran Agreement making Vatican City an independent state

Britain refers to Palestine problem in the UN; the Hagana prepares for war

The UN General Assembly votes to partition Palestine

India and Pakistan achieve independence of Britain

A.D.

1948   Truman upsets Dewey in US elections
       The Organization of American States formed
       The state of Israel born, May 14
       War breaks out between Israel and the Arab League
       Israel plans the reforrestorization of the country
1949   Russia explodes an atomic bomb
       First elections in Israel—David Ben Gurion becomes
          prime minister
       Israel admitted to the UN
       Arab-Israeli war ends with Israel's victory over the Arab
          League
       Israel moves its government to Jerusalem, ignoring the
          UN vote to internationalize the city
       Pope Pius XII announces his support for the plan to in-
          ternationalize Jerusalem
       Chiang Kai-shek evacuates China for Taiwan, and China
          becomes a communist state under Mao Tse-tung
       Jewish population of Israel reaches the one million mark
1950   The Korean War breaks out
       The Law of Return promulgated affirming the right of all
          Jews to live in Israel
1951   Libya achieves independence
1952   Mau Mau terrorism begins in Kenya
       Nasser comes to power in Egypt
       Elizabeth II becomes queen of England
       Chaim Weizmann, Israel's first president, dies
       Germany agrees to pay Israel $822 million in reparations
1953   Eisenhower becomes President of the United States
       Stalin unveils plans for the extermination of all Jews in
          Russia
       Stalin dies
       Israel enters the atomic age
       Israel discovers oil and gas near the Dead Sea
1954   The Civil Rights movement begins in the United States
1956   *The Suez Crisis; war breaks out between Israel and*
          Egypt, with Israel having support from Britain and
          France
       Israel strikes oil in the Negev

A.D.

The Warsaw Pact signed by the communist powers

1957   The Treaty of Rome signed, inaugurating the European Common Market

The Russians launch "Sputnik" and usher in the space age

1958   The US launches its first satellite

John XXIII becomes pope

1959   Castro seizes Cuba

Chinese Communists suppress an uprising in Tibet

Krushchev visits the United States

1960   Congo achieves independence

Israel activates its first atomic reactor for research and medical use

The Russians help Egypt build the Aswan Dam

1961   Kennedy becomes President of the United States

Russia orbits a man in space

The Bay of Pigs disaster

The Eichmann trial opens in Jerusalem

Israel launches its first solid-fuel rocket

1962   Pope John XXIII opens the Second Ecumenical Council, heralding changes in the Roman Catholic church

Eichmann executed in Israel

The Cuban missile crisis brings Russia and America to the brink of war

An American astronaut orbits the earth

1963   Pope John XXIII dies, and Paul VI becomes pontiff

Kennedy assassinated; Johnson becomes President of the United States

The US Supreme Court outlaws prayer and Bible reading in public schools

Kenya achieves independence

Russia and China split over communist ideology

1964   *Israel and the Common Market nations sign trade agreement*

China explodes an atomic bomb

1965   The US starts bombing North Vietnam

The pope addresses the United Nations

1966   Indonesia outlaws the Communist Party

A.D.

1967   China explodes an H-bomb
The Six Day War breaks out; Israel seizes Arab lands and unifies Jerusalem

1968   US spacemen orbit the moon
Martin Luther King assassinated

1969   Nixon becomes President of the United States
The United States lands a man on the moon
Widespread riots in the United States over the Vietnam War

1970   Millions of Americans support an antipollution rally
American forces cross into Cambodia to destroy North Vietnamese bases
The Kent State riot raises the protest movement in the US against the Vietnam War to a new pitch

1971   The United States returns Okinawa to Japan

1972   Nixon visits China
The war in Vietnam intensifies
Nixon visits Moscow
The Watergate scandal surfaces in the US

1973   The Vietnam War ends
China and the US set up liaison offices in each other's countries
The Yom Kippur War breaks out
The Arabs first use oil as weapon against the United States
Soviet leader Brezhnev visits the United States

1974   Nixon resigns over the Watergate scandal; Ford becomes President of the United States

1975   The Communists complete their takeover of South Vietnam
Russian and United States astronauts link up spacecraft 140 miles above the Atlantic
Israel signs an agreement with the Common Market allowing for free trade

1976   The United States celebrates its Bicentennial
The United States lands a spaceship on Mars
Mao Tse-tung dies

1977   Carter becomes President of the United States

A.D.

Menachem Begin becomes prime minister of Israel;
bringing the conservatives to power for the first time
Egyptian President Sadat and Israeli Prime Minister
Begin begin talking peace

1978   Pope John Paul I becomes pontiff; dies of heart attack
Pope John Paul II becomes pontiff, the first non-Italian
to be elected pope in 456 years
The United States and China establish full diplomatic
relations
Russia signs a treaty of friendship with Vietnam and puts
her weight behind Vietnam aggression in the area

1979   A new European monetary system goes into effect
Egypt and Israel sign a historic peace treaty, which in-
furiates the other Arab powers in the Middle East
The Russians allow 5,000 Jews to leave the Soviet Union
Russia invades Afghanistan
The Shah is forced to leave Iran
Greece agrees to join the Common Market, bringing
membership up to a total of ten nations
The price of gold begins to soar
Widespread communist atrocities in Cambodia reported

1980   The Israeli Knesset votes to "unify" Jerusalem, and Begin
announces his intention of setting up his office in the
occupied part of the city, reaffirming Jerusalem as
Israel's capital
The UN votes overwhelmingly to establish a Palestinian
sovereign state in Palestine and ignores Israel's right to
exist
Israel launches a new currency based on the shekel
Syria and Libya announce political merger

1981   Reagan becomes President of the United States
Assassination attempts on US President Ronald Reagan,
Pope John Paul II
Israel bombs Iraq's nuclear reactor
Menachem Begin narrowly wins re-election
Anwar Sadat assassinated

BIBLIOGRAPHY

ISRAEL AND THE JEWS

Abba Eban. *My People: The Story of the Jews.* New York: Random, 1968.

Brilliant, Moshe. *Portrait of Israel.* New York: American Heritage, 1970.

Churchill, Winston. "Zionism versus Bolshevism: A Struggle for the Soul of the Jewish People." London: *Illustrated Sunday Herald,* 8 February 1920.

Clarke, Comer. *Eichmann, The Man and His Crime.* New York: Random, Ballantine, 1960.

Collins, Larry, and LaPierre, Dominique. *O Jerusalem.* New York: Simon and Schuster, 1972.

Davis, George T. B. *Seeing Prophecy Fulfilled in Palestine.* Philadelphia: Million Testaments Campaign, 1937.

—————. *Israel Returns Home According to Prophecy.* Philadelphia: Million Testaments Campaign, 1950.

—————. *Bible Prophecies Fulfilled Today.* Philadelphia: Million Testaments Campaign, 1955.

—————. *Rebuilding Palestine According to Prophecy.* Philadelphia: Million Testaments Campaign, 1948.

Dimont, Max. *Jews, God and History.* New York: New American Library, Signet, 1962.

—————. *The Indestructible Jews.* New York: New American Library, Signet, 1971.

Edersheim, Alfred. *History of the Jewish Nation.* Grand Rapids: Baker, 1954.

Feinberg, Charles Lee. *Israel In the Spotlight.* Wheaton, Ill.: Scripture Press, 1956.

Gilbert, G. M. *Nuremberg Diary.* New York: New American Library, Signet, 1947.

Goldberg, M. Hirsh. *The Jewish Connection.* New York: Bantam, 1977.

Grayzel, Solomon. *A History of the Jews.* New York: New American Library, Mentor, 1968.

Hull, Williams. *Israel, Key to Prophecy.* Grand Rapids: Zondervan, 1957.

Kac, Arthur W. *The Rebirth of the State of Israel.* Chicago: Moody, 1958.

Lang, G. H. *Israel's National Future.* London: Paternoster, n.d.

Newton, B. W. *The Millennium and Israel's Future.* London: Lucas Collins, 1913.

Nurdock, Mordekhai. *Facts About Israel, 1970.* Israel: Keter, 1970.

Phillips, John. *A Trumpet in Zion.* Chicago: Moody Bible Institute Correspondence School, 1973.

Sachar, Abram Leon. *A History of the Jews.* New York: Knopf, 1964.

Ten Boom, Corrie, with Sherrill, John, and Sherrill, Elizabeth. *The Hiding Place.* Old Tappan, N.J.: Revell, Spire, 1971.

Van den Haag. *The Jewish Mystique.* New York: Stein and Day, 1969.

Velie, Lester. *Countdown in the Holy Land.* New York: Funk and Wagnalls, 1969.

Webb, Mrs. J. B., (Naomi). *The Last Days of Jerusalem.* Edinburgh: Nimmo, Hay and Mitchell, 1896.

Weiner, Jan G. *The Assassination of Heydrich.* New York: Pyramid, 1971.

Wolff, Richard. *Israel Today.* Wheaton, Ill.: Tyndale, 1970.

PROPHECY

Bruce, F. F. *Israel and the Nations.* Grand Rapids: Eerdmans, 1963.

Frost, F. D. *The Appointed Time.* London: Pickering and Inglis, 1953.

Gaebelein, Arno C. *The Conflict of the Ages.* New York: Our Hope, 1933.

Ironside, Harry A. *The Lamp of Prophecy.* Grand Rapids: Zondervan, 1940.

Lacey, Harry. *God and the Nations.* Kilmarnock: John Ritchie, 1942.

Lang, G. H. *World Chaos, Its Root and Remedy.* London: Paternoster, 1950.

Larkin, Clarence. *The Second Coming of Christ.* London: Pickering and Inglis, 1922.

Panton, D. M. *The Apocalypse of the Lord.* London: Chas. J. Thynne, 1922.

Pember, G. H. *The Church, the Churches and the Mysteries.* London: Hodder and Stoughton, 1901.

————. *The Great Prophecies of the Centuries Concerning the Church.* New York: Revell, n.d.

————. *The Great Prophecies Concerning the Gentiles, the Jews and the Church of God.* London: Hodder and Stoughton, 1887.

————. *The Great Prophecies of the Centuries Concerning Israel and the Gentiles.* London: Hodder and Stoughton, 1895.

Pentecost, J. Dwight. *Prophecy for Today*. Grand Rapids: Zondervan, 1969.

—————. *Things to Come*. Findlay, Ohio: Dunham, 1958.

Phillips, John. *Only God Can Prophesy*. Wheaton, Ill.: Shaw, 1975.

Rimmer, Harry. *The Shadow of Coming Events*. Grand Rapids: Eerdmans, 1950.

Sale-Harrison, L. *The Remarkable Jew*. New York: Sale-Harrison Publications, 1934.

—————. *The Coming Great Northern Confederacy*. Wheaton, Ill.: Van Kampen, 1948.

—————. *The Resurrection of the Old Roman Empire*. New York: Sale-Harrison Publications, 1934.

Scott, Walter. *At Hand*. London: Alfred Holness, 1909.

Smith, Wilbur M. *This Atomic Age and the Word of God*. Boston: W. A. Wilde, 1948.

—————. *World Crisis and the Prophetic Scriptures*. Chicago: Moody, 1951.

—————. *Egypt in Biblical Prophecy*. Boston: W. A. Wilde, 1957.

Stanton, Gerald B. *Kept from the Hour*. Grand Rapids: Zondervan, 1956.

Tatford, Frederick A. *God's Program of the Ages*. Grand Rapids: Kregel, 1967.

Wood, Leon J. *Is the Rapture Next?* Grand Rapids: Zondervan, 1956.

Wuest, Kenneth S. *Present Light in the Present Darkness*. Grand Rapids: Eerdmans, 1956.

COMMENTARIES

Anderson, Sir Robert. *The Coming Prince*. Grand Rapids: Kregel, 1954.

Boutflower, Charles. *In and Around the Book of Daniel*. London: SPCK, 1923.

Bullinger, E. W. *The Apocalypse*. London: Eyre and Spottiswoode, 1935.

Gaebelein, Arno C. *The Prophet Daniel*. Grand Rapids: Kregel, 1963.

—————. *The Revelation*. New York: Our Hope, 1915.

Govett, Robert. *The Apocalypse Expounded By Scripture*. London: Chas. J. Thynne, 1920.

Harrison, Norman B. *The End: Rethinking the Revelation*. Minneapolis: Harrison Service, 1948.

Lang, G. H. *The Histories and Prophecies of Daniel*. London: Paternoster, 1950.

—————. *The Revelation of Jesus Christ*. London: Paternoster, 1948.

Larkin, Clarence. *The Book of Revelation*. Philadelphia: Clarence Larkin Estate, 1959.

————. *The Book of Daniel*. Philadelphia: Clarence Larkin Estate, 1929.

Lincoln, William. *The Book of Revelation*. London: Pickering and Inglis, n.d.

Newberry, Thomas. *Notes on the Book of Revelation*. Kilmarnock: John Ritchie, n.d.

Newton, Benjamin Wills. *Thoughts on the Apocalypse*. London: C. M. Tucker, 1904.

Phillips, John. *Exploring Revelation*. Chicago: Moody, 1974.

Pollock, Algernon J. *Things Which Must Shortly Come to Pass*. London: Central Bible Truth Depot, n.d.

Pusey, E. B. *Daniel the Prophet*. New York: Funk and Wagnall, 1885.

Sale-Harrison, L. *The Wonder of the Great Unveiling*. Wheaton, Ill.: Van Kampen, 1930.

Scott, Walter. *Exposition of the Revelation of Jesus Christ*. 4th ed. London: Pickering and Inglis, n.d.

Seiss, J. A. *The Apocalypse*. Grand Rapids: Zondervan, 1964.

Tatford, Frederick A. *The Climax of the Ages*. London: Marshall, Morgan and Scott, 1953.

————. *Prophecy's Last Word*. London: Pickering and Inglis, 1947.

Walvoord, John F. *The Revelation of Jesus Christ*. Chicago: Moody, 1966.

HISTORY

Boyer, James L. *Chart of the Period Between the Testaments*. Winona Lake, Ind.: James L. Boyer, 1962.

————. *New Testament Chronological Chart*. Winona Lake, Ind.: James L. Boyer, 1962.

Langer, William L. *An Encyclopedia of World History*. Boston: Houghton Mifflin, 1968.

Morris, Richard B., and Irwin, Graham W., eds. *Harper Encyclopedia of the Modern World*. New York: Harper & Row, 1970.

Whitcomb, John C., Jr. *Chart of Old Testament Patriarchs and Judges*. Winona Lake, Ind.: John C. Whitcomb, 1965.

————. *Chart of Old Testament Kings and Prophets*. Winona Lake, Ind.: John C. Whitcomb, 1962.

MISCELLANEOUS

Edersheim, Alfred. *The Bible History, Old Testament*. 2 vols. Grand Rapids: Eerdmans, 1956.

Naismith, Archie, and Fraser, W. *God's People and God's Purpose.* Kilmarnock: John Ritchie, 1949.

Phillips, John. *Exploring the Scriptures.* Chicago: Moody, 1970.

Sauer, Erich. *The King of the Earth.* London. Paternoster, 1962.

————. *From Eternity to Eternity.* Grand Rapids: Eerdmans, 1954.

————. *The Dawn of World Redemption.* London: Paternoster, 1951.

————. *The Triumph of the Crucified.* London: Paternoster, 1951.

Scroggie, W. Graham. *The Unfolding Drama of Redemption.* London: Pickering and Inglis, 1953.